Published by arrangement with BBC Books,
a division of BBC Enterprises Ltd.

# CONTENTS

# FOREWORD

Between 1978 and 1985 the British Broadcasting Corporation produced for television the complete dramatic works of Shakespeare and, to coincide with the productions, a set of paperback editions of the plays was issued in thirty-seven volumes (one for each play), each containing the text used for the production, a glossary, an introduction, which included comments by the director, designer and actors, and a general critical introduction. As the Literary Consultant to the television series, I wrote all the critical introductions and these are here gathered together in a single volume.

The circumstances in which I wrote these prefaces account for the style and approach which I adopted. Although I hoped that they might be of some interest to students of Shakespeare, they were designed primarily to be read by television viewers, an audience as varied as the one for which Shakespeare originally wrote, and far more numerous. I had to assume that my readers would know little or nothing about the plays, especially the less popular ones such as *Cymbeline* and *Timon of Athens*, and I therefore had to write about them in as simple and easily intelligible a style as I could manage and to give some impression of the distinctive features of each play without summarizing the plot.

The plays were not shown on television in the order in which Shakespeare wrote them because it was felt that a seven-year project which began with the three parts of *Henry VI* was unlikely to attract a large audience. Instead, the six plays shown each year included a mixture of comedies, histories and tragedies and a combination of well-known and unfamiliar works. Among the first six were *Romeo and Juliet* and *Henry VIII*. The only plays shown in chronological order of their composition were the two sets of English history plays. Since the prefaces had to be written to coincide with the broadcasts, it was impossible for me to pay any attention to Shakespeare's development. Each preface, of necessity, was designed to be read on its own and without reference to the others.

While assembling them for this present volume, I did consider linking them. After all, a series of essays which starts with *Henry VI* and ends with

*Henry VIII* does invite some thought about the dramatist's development. Yet it is almost impossible to think about his development without assuming that he got better with practice and this is not really what happened. In its own particular way, *The Comedy of Errors* is as accomplished a work as *The Tempest*. Nor do the plays appear to evolve and grow one out of another. *Macbeth*, it is true, was built on the foundations of *Richard III* and *King Lear* on those of *Richard II*, but, in general, Shakespeare never tried to repeat his successes. Each time he wrote a new play, he set himself a different kind of challenge and each play is unique. I therefore decided to leave the prefaces more or less as they were. This is not, then, a book to be read from cover to cover but to be dipped into by non-Shakespeareans who would like to know something about a particular play. Anyone who does read the whole book will find that I have occasionally repeated myself, a weakness which I could not avoid if I was to make each preface intelligible on its own.

My emphasis throughout has been on the effect of the plays in performance. I have therefore written frequently about the ways in which they are constructed, since it is by means of dramatic construction that Shakespeare controls the responses of his audience, arousing curiosity, tension and suspense and creating irony, fear and laughter. I have looked closely at passages of dialogue only when they seemed to me to reveal something important about an entire play, as when the constant references to darkness in *Macbeth* contribute to the pervasive impression of evil. I have been less concerned with Shakespeare's ability to create lifelike characters than to show the parallels and contrasts he sets up between different characters. In other words, I have regarded the patterning of characters as part of a play's dramatic construction.

Certain kinds of information have been deliberately excluded. Dates when the plays were written – often, in any case, a matter for conjecture – are given only when they may help to make the plays more intelligible, and the sources of the plots are discussed only when Shakespeare's adaptation of them casts immediate light on the plays themselves, as when, for example, his portrayal of Henry V differs significantly from Holinshed's. Act, scene and line references are not supplied because I wanted to avoid creating the impression that this was a textbook. For the same reason there are very few allusions to works of criticism, even though, as I realize, many of the ideas put forward in the following pages have been derived from the critics whose work I have read over the past forty years. Although the title is a presumptuous one in that it invites comparison with Granville Barker's *Prefaces to Shakespeare*, I have nevertheless retained it because it was from Barker's *Prefaces* that I first learned something of Shakespeare's achievement as a writer for the theatre, and because I believe, as Barker did, that literary criticism ought to be intelligible to practically anyone.

Quotations are taken from Peter Alexander's edition of *The Complete Works of Shakespeare* (1951), the text used for the television productions.

John Wilders

# THE FIRST PART OF
# KING HENRY THE SIXTH

We do not know the precise order in which Shakespeare composed his plays and the chronology, particularly of the earliest ones, has proved impossible to establish. Some scholars believe that he began his career with *The Comedy of Errors*, others with *The Two Gentlemen of Verona*, and he may well have written sketches or even complete plays which he destroyed or which have suffered the fate of hundreds of sixteenth-century dramatic works and disappeared without trace. There is strong evidence to suggest, however, that the first of his plays to survive were the three parts of *Henry VI*. Part I was certainly performed in March 1592, when the dramatist was nearly twenty-eight, and it was presumably written shortly before then. It may well be that with the opening words of this play Shakespeare made his first impact on a theatre audience:

> *Dead March. Enter the funeral of King Henry the Fifth*

> Bedford    Hung be the heavens with black, yield day to night!
> Comets, importing change of times and states,
> Brandish your crystal tresses in the sky
> And with them scourge the bad revolting stars
> That have consented unto Henry's death!
> King Henry the Fifth, too famous to live long!
> England ne'er lost a King of so much worth.

It is an opening of great dramatic force, the work of a man who knows how to write for the theatre, and the source of its power can fairly easily be discovered. For one thing, Shakespeare chose to begin the play right in the middle of a sudden and serious political crisis, the death of the most successful and admired of all English kings, and hence the audience's attention is immediately arrested and absorbed. They are thrown into the midst of a crucial episode in English history, one which, as his first audiences knew, had prolonged and terrible consequences in the form of civil war and the armed struggle between rival contenders for power. These opening lines are also a model of rapid dramatic exposition. Once we have seen the funeral

procession and heard Bedford's seven lines, we have learned all we need to
know in order to understand the action which follows. Again it is a moment
in which the visual tableau, the coffin of the late king being carried for burial
by his peers, works together with the dialogue. The visual image of mourning is accompanied by the lamentations of the mourners, and the presence of
the Bishop and the peers of the realm, together with the cosmic references to
the heavens and the comets, informs us that we are watching a ritual of great
public significance. The style of the poetry, too, is distinctively dramatic: its
active, imperative verbs ('hung', 'yield', 'brandish') demand to be sent echoing into an auditorium like a public oration or an aria from an opera. These
lines are clearly the work of a man who understood the resources of the
theatre and knew how to use them.

Where had he learned to write like this? It is likely that before he became
a writer Shakespeare had spent some years as an actor, a member of the professional theatrical company which, under the management of James Bur-
bage, had built and occupied the first permanent theatre in England, erected
in 1576 roughly on the site of what is now Liverpool Street Station, and
known, simply, as The Theatre. It was probably from his first-hand experience of the skills required to attract, engage and sustain the attention of an
audience that Shakespeare acquired the art of writing in a specifically
theatrical way. Moreover, when he first came to London from his home in
Stratford-on-Avon in the late 1580s, the theatrical scene was already
dominated by his exact contemporary Christopher Marlowe, whose two
parts of *Tamburlaine* were first performed in 1587 and 1588 and whose *Dr
Faustus* appeared a year later. When he went to the theatre, Shakespeare's
imagination would have been stirred by such lines as these from Part II of
*Tamburlaine*:

> Weep heavens, and vanish into liquid tears,
> Fall stars that govern his nativity,
> And summon all the shining lamps of heaven
> To cast their bootless fires to the earth,
> And shed their feeble influence in the air.
> Muffle your beauties with eternal clouds,
> For hell and darkness pitch their pitchy tents,
> And Death with armies of Cimmerian spirits
> Gives battle 'gainst the heart of Tamburlaine.

The influence on the opening of *Henry VI Part I* of a passage such as this, with
its strong commanding verbs and expansive astronomical references, is
unmistakable. Shakespeare was able to write oratorical verse because Marlowe
had done so before him. His first audiences may well have sensed that the new
dramatist was, in effect, inviting them to compare his work with that of the
dominant playwright of the time. It is the work of an ambitious man.

Shakespeare displayed his ambition even more plainly, however, by embarking not on a single play but on a set of four plays. The three parts of *Henry VI* and *Richard III* are planned and constructed as one single twenty-act drama depicting the history of England from the death of Henry V in 1422 to the accession of Henry VII in 1447 and include the complex series of events which led to the loss of the empire in France which Henry V had won, and the civil wars which terminated in the defeat of Richard III at the Battle of Bosworth. That the four plays are designed to be seen as a single, continuous unit is clear from the links which Shakespeare made between the plays. Only *Richard III* has anything like a decisive conclusion: the other three plays finish in a state of irresolution in which the action is left uncompleted only to be picked up and continued in the play that follows. Hence Part I of *Henry VI* ends with rivalries between Gloucester and Winchester and between York and Somerset as yet unresolved, and with Suffolk's determination to have the King married to Margaret of Anjou and thereby, through her, to control the King. At that point the play stops and it is only in Part II that Gloucester is murdered, Winchester dies, Margaret begins to dominate the King and the quarrel between York and Somerset breaks out into full-scale war. Part I is fully intelligible only if we follow the action through into Part II, and the latter makes sense only if we know Part I. There are similar links between Parts II and III and between all three and *Richard III*. Although the last of the four plays is quite often performed on its own, it is nevertheless clear that, at an early stage of composition, Shakespeare set out to write the largest, most ambitious drama that had yet been seen on the professional stage.

It is interesting to speculate why he chose to launch his career as a playwright by writing a set of historical plays. In view of the predominantly classical education he had received as a schoolboy, we should expect him to have written a comedy of situation in the manner of the Latin dramatists Plautus and Terence, as some of his predecessors (in Italy as well as England) had done, but which in fact he did not attempt until a few years later when he composed *The Comedy of Errors*. There were plenty of widely known comedies and tragedies in Latin and Italian as well as in English on which he could model his own first experiments in the theatre, but, although a few plays on English historical subjects had been written earlier in the sixteenth century, the history play as Shakespeare designed it was more or less his own invention. The question is really unanswerable but we can make a few guesses.

With the accession of Queen Elizabeth in 1558, the English began to develop a sense of their own national identity and a patriotism derived from the belief that God had bestowed on them his special blessing. This new awareness was brought about partly by the influence of a book which was almost as widely known as the Bible, the *Acts and Monuments* of John Foxe, better known as 'Foxe's Book of Martyrs', published in 1563, a copy of which was kept in all churches. The work was violently anti-Catholic and entirely fulfilled the promise given on its title-page to describe 'the great persecutions that have been wrought and practised by the Romish Prelates'. It contained graphic accounts, accompanied by vivid engravings, of the martyrdoms suffered by the protestants during the reign of Elizabeth's predecessor, her half-sister Queen Mary. A recurring theme of the book was of thanksgiving to God for liberating the English people from the tyranny of Mary and of celebration of God's instrument, Queen Elizabeth, who had restored the true church. The effect of Foxe's argument was to give the English the sense that they were God's chosen people who had been led back into the promised land of the protestant church and this, in turn, aroused their interest in their own distinctive characteristics and history. The English history plays which Shakespeare wrote between about 1592 and 1599 (and, apart from *Henry VIII*, he wrote no English histories after that) are, among other things, an expression of the sense of nationhood which characterized that period. We owe to it such nationalistic speeches as John of Gaunt's 'This royal throne of kings' and Henry V's St Crispin's day oration.

Almost all of Shakespeare's history plays deal with civil war and none more starkly and unrelievedly than the three parts of *Henry VI*, in which battles are regularly portrayed on the stage in such episodes as the deaths of Talbot and his son and the taunting of York with the napkin soaked in the blood of his own child. They are plays about internal dissension and violence written during a time of relative unity and peace and to that extent may have been, indirectly, tributes to the Queen who had brought to the country more than thirty years of stability. Perhaps the subjects of Elizabeth I, looking back from the security of their own time, felt a fascination for the hazards and violence of battle comparable to that now shown by the subjects of Elizabeth II, and indeed the plays have been produced with great success in the 1960s and 1970s, having been absent from the theatrical repertory for almost four centuries.

They can also be seen as a revelation of the national and domestic agonies which internal disruption brings about, though they are far too complex to convey that simple message alone. In these early plays Shakespeare shows an analytical interest in politics, in the processes whereby political changes are brought about, and in the causes which lie behind the events of military and political history. One feature which distinguishes them from the historical plays written by his predecessors, such as John Bale's *King John*, composed during the reign of Henry VIII, or the anonymous *Troublesome Reign of King John*, is that whereas theirs tend towards political propaganda, Shakespeare's tend towards political analysis. He continued to pursue this interest throughout his professional career, not only in his later history plays such as the two parts of *Henry IV*, but in the tragedies, especially *Julius Caesar* and *Macbeth*.

As the opening scene of *Henry VI Part I* unfolds, we discover that the characters are themselves interested in the causes behind this specific event, the early death of Henry V. Bedford, who speaks first, believes that it was brought about by astrological influence, the effect of the 'bad revolting stars' which 'consented unto Henry's death'. Exeter accuses the 'subtle-witted French' whose sorcerers have, he believes, destroyed the King by spells and incantations, and Gloucester, who has a private animosity against the Bishop of Winchester, accuses the church of praying for Henry's death. The debate is never resolved and the audience is left with the impression that this national calamity was what is now loosely called an act of God.

Shakespeare himself, to judge from the evidence of the play, did not believe that all events were acts of God. Much more often they are brought about by the personalities, and the consequent actions, of individual men. Hence the victories over the French are shown to have been won largely because of the bravery and leadership of the English general Talbot, and his defeat and death are the direct result of a shortage of men and supplies. The failure of the English to provide Talbot with the reinforcements he needs is, in turn, the result of envy and bickering between the staff officers, York and Somerset, each of whom attempts to discredit the other, using the troops as pawns in a personal squabble. The hostility between York and Somerset itself arises from what was at first no more than an argument over a legal nicety, but the argument is enflamed by Somerset's contemptuous accusation that York was the son of a traitor who was executed for treason. Hence the execution of York's father years earlier (and all the unfathomable motives which lay behind that event and which are discussed in the play) is indirectly a cause of the defeat and death of Talbot and the loss of France. Shakespeare shows that the course of history is determined largely by men and that their deeds have long-term consequences which they could never have intended or, indeed, foreseen. Now and again a perceptive observer has a hazy intimation of what may happen, as when Warwick predicts the result of the quarrel between York and Somerset:

> This brawl today,
> Grown to this faction in the Temple Garden,
> Shall send between the Red Rose and the White
> A thousand souls to death and deadly night.

Warwick senses that disaster of some kind is imminent though he cannot foresee what precise form it will take, but Shakespeare, who knows exactly what it will be, is indicating to us through Warwick that national calamities can spring from trivial human origins.

The blame for the loss of France cannot, however, be placed exclusively on Somerset and York. It also rests on the King for failing to keep his peers in order. Indeed the whole play depicts the kind of personal and political rivalries which break out as soon as a powerful ruler is removed. Henry V's death immediately results in a struggle for power between his peers whose wrangling starts even before his body is decently buried. His death leaves a power vacuum which his son, still a child on his accession and helplessly naive even in his maturity, is temperamentally unable to fill, and hence a succession of political adventurers – Winchester, Suffolk, York and, finally in Part III, Richard of Gloucester – attempt to control the King and thereby command the nation. At regular intervals Shakespeare places before us a character in the moment of making a resolution to outwit his rivals and, in the absence of a King of any real authority, to take control of the kingdom. Winchester makes such a decision at the end of the first scene:

> Each hath his place and function to attend:
> I am left out; for me nothing remains.
> But long I will not be Jack out of office.
> The King from Eltham I intend to steal,
> And sit at chiefest stern of public weal.

We hear a similar resolution at the end of the last scene, this time from Suffolk:

> Margaret shall now be Queen, and rule the King;
> But I will rule both her, the King, and realm.

Saddled with the task of controlling such cunningly ambitious subjects, the young King is incapable of doing anything more than wring his hands and deliver pious reprimands:

> Good Lord, what madness rules in brainsick men,
> When for so slight and frivolous a cause
> Such factious emulations shall arise!
> Good cousins both, of York and Somerset,
> Quiet yourselves, I pray, and be at peace.

The King's complaint is, of course, entirely justified, and he is one of the few characters who is thoroughly honest, has a deep sense of right and wrong and tries to act for the good of the country. The desire to do good is, however, not enough. Henry lacks the authority, the strength of character and the insight into the devious personalities of his subjects to enforce his will. It is as though he expects everybody to be as pious and dutiful as he is himself, and hence, although he is pathetically ineffectual, he also arouses our sympathy.

The only character in this play who has at the same time a sense of public responsibility and the shrewdness and the courage to put it into effect is Talbot. Whereas the other peers are mostly concerned with satisfying their own lust for power, Talbot prides himself on his 'duty to his sovereign',

> In sign whereof, this arm that hath reclaim'd
> To your obedience fifty fortresses,
> Twelve cities, and seven walled towns of strength,
> Beside five hundred prisoners of esteem,
> Lets fall his sword before your Higness' feet,
> And with submissive loyalty of heart,
> Ascribes the glory of his conquest got
> First to my God, and next unto your Grace.

Talbot, however, is a kind of relic who has survived from the age of Henry V. In his military virtues, his religious piety and his patriotism, he is made to seem typical of that lost era towards which, from time to time, the characters look back with regret as they contemplate the self-interest and incompetence of their own time. It is significant that Talbot, so much the embodiment of the ideals which characterized the previous reign, should be destroyed by the petty jealousies which characterize the present.

Although Shakespeare dramatizes events on the assumption that they are determined, for the most part, by the aspirations of the people who are caught up in them, he also recognizes that not everything can be accounted for in this way. Sometimes things happen by mere fluke, or what the characters call Fortune. Hence it is mere chance that brings Talbot, Salisbury and Gargrave into the turret outside Orleans at the very moment when the gunner's boy has his cannon aimed at it, and it is apparently chance that brings first victory and then defeat for Joan of Arc. Indeed, a characteristic dramatic effect of *Henry VI Part I* is the irony which results when, by a sudden turn of Fortune, events turn out in a way quite different from that expected by the characters. For example, Talbot and his fellow-officers climb up the tower under the impression that they run no risk:

> Now is it supper-time in Orleans:
> Here, through this grate, I count each one
> And view the Frenchmen how they fortify.
> Let us look in; the sight will much delight thee.

Little do they realize that the gunner's boy has already trained his cannon on the spot they are entering, and when he fires the gun and Salisbury and Gargrave fall down, the effect is absurd. We sense how limited is the extent of their knowledge of the situation. Again, when Joan has won her first victory, she is treated to the rapturous praises of the Dauphin:

> Divinest creature, Astraea's daughter,
> How shall I honour thee for this success?

His confidence in her is, however, short-lived and, in the next scene, the French are defeated and are shown shamefully leaping from the walls of the city 'in their shirts'.

*Henry VI Part I* is a play full of ironies. The monarch, who knows what is right, is incapable of enforcing his convictions; Joan of Arc, at first greeted as the saviour of France, is ultimately captured and burned at the stake; Talbot is defeated not by his enemies but by the small-mindedness of those who should support him:

> The fraud of England, not the force of France,
> Hath now entrapp'd the noble-minded Talbot;
> Never to England shall he bear his life,
> But dies betray'd to fortune by your strife.

The larger processes of history contain a number of individual tragedies such as the fall and death of Joan and the death of Talbot and his son. There are, moreover, long-term ironies which become apparent only when we follow the careers of individuals as they are depicted during the course of all three plays: Suffolk resolves, at the end of Part I, to command the realm, but dies obscurely in Part II, murdered by an insignificant sea captain; York, whose aspiration for the crown begins to kindle in this play, is actually presented, mockingly, with a paper crown in Part III; the beautiful bride to whose arrival Henry looks forward turns out to be his ruin. If we follow the course of all three plays, we can see that Shakespeare not only was fascinated by the causes which change history but saw their effects largely as a series of ironies. For him history was a record of human inadequacy.

# THE SECOND PART OF
# KING HENRY THE SIXTH

*Henry VI Part II* cannot be understood fully in isolation from the two other parts. Looked at on its own, the plot is perfectly intelligible but the motives and the relationships between the characters are not. When we see the first, formal meeting between Henry and his bride at the start of the play, for example, we need to know that their marriage has been arranged by Suffolk not for the good of England or the benefit of the King but because Suffolk loves Margaret and intends to control the kingdom by controlling her. We need to recall his words at the conclusion of Part I:

> Margaret shall now be Queen, and rule the King;
> But I will rule both her, the King, and realm.

There is thus, behind Henry's prayer of thanksgiving, an irony of which only those audiences acquainted with Part I can be aware:

> O Lord, that lends me life,
> Lend me a heart replete with thankfulness!
> For thou hast given me in this beauteous face
> A world of earthly blessings to my soul,
> If sympathy of love unite our thoughts.

In his naive trust and piety, Henry is shown to be deceived, easily duped by the ambitious peers by whom he is surrounded. Again, when at the end of the scene York bewails the transfer of Anjou and Maine to Margaret's father, his regret can be better understood if we can recall the episode in Part I where he was told that he was the rightful heir to the throne. York is here speaking not simply as a patriot like Gloucester or Warwick, but as a man who believes, with good reason, that his own inheritance has been squandered. *Henry VI Part II* therefore begins in the middle of a continuous action. It ends even more abruptly with York's resolution, elated by his victory at St Albans, to pursue to London the king whose forces he has just defeated. The consequences of his decision – York's own defeat and his ignominious and bloody death – are not revealed before we come to Part III. Part II, then, does not have 'a beginning, a middle and an end' but in its abrupt opening and conclusion resembles several of Shakespeare's other history plays and, indeed, the experience of history itself, which is not shapely and well organized like a work of art and which can never be said to have begun or ended except in the Garden of Eden and at the Last Judgement. At the beginning of Part II we observe the characters as they try to deal, mostly unsuccessfully, with the problems they have inherited from the past: the King's ineffectiveness, the jealousy between Gloucester and Winchester, the ambitions of Suffolk. At the end we are allowed to foresee the problems they have created for their successors: Young Clifford's responsibility to avenge his father's death and the King's need to protect himself against York. We can see what these problems will be and how they have been created but, like the characters, we do not know how – or, indeed, whether – they will be solved. The experience of watching a Shakespearean history play is not unlike the experience of living through history itself. Each day the newspapers try to explain how our present troubles have come about and predict new threats over the horizon, but we have to wait until the next day, the next scene, to discover how they will develop. The history plays, like history itself, reveal that no problem can ever be said to have been finally settled, and that the resolution of one crisis more often than not creates a different kind of crisis: the King's marriage to Margaret arouses discontent among his peers, the murder of Gloucester provokes an uprising among the citizens of London, and York's victory at St Albans incites Margaret to retaliate against him. The play has no real ending because Shakespeare recognized that history never really ends.

*Henry VI Part II* is not, however, simply shapeless and chaotic. Shakespeare has so arranged its historically disordered events that they form the kind of pattern we expect from a work of art while at the same time preserving the sense of confusion we feel when we actually participate in history.

He created the pattern by a variety of means. In the first place, Part II does portray one single movement or process of which each episode is a part. This becomes apparent if we compare the first scene of the play with the last. At the opening we are shown King Henry and Queen Margaret on their first, ostensibly harmonious meeting, each attended by a group of seemingly loyal peers. By the end of Act V, Henry and Margaret have been defeated, and are forced to take flight. The intervening scenes demonstrate in analytical detail how this change has been brought about. The play is thus both a historical drama and a piece of historical analysis. To be a little more precise, it shows how, as a result of Henry's lack of will, dissension grows unchecked first among the nobility, and then among the common people until it finally erupts into civil war. *Henry VI Part I* demonstrates how the empire in France which had been won by Henry V came to be lost by his son. *Henry VI Part II* explains how an apparently stable, peaceful country was allowed to disintegrate into civil war.

The process, as Shakespeare displays it, falls into three parts: the murder of Duke Humphrey and the events which led up to it, the uprising of Jack Cade and the motives behind it, and the full-scale insurrection of York. The first of these episodes, the plot against Duke Humphrey, is a strictly internal, domestic affair in that it is conducted within the confines of the court; only the peers and their hired assassins are involved in it and the crime itself is committed in secret. The discovery of Gloucester's murder does, however, provoke the citizens of London to rise up in revenge against his murderers, Suffolk and Winchester, and hence Suffolk's crime leads directly to his banishment and death. Cade's insurrection is a far more serious affair. It is not contained within the limited world of the court but involves the working men of southern England who, like Suffolk and Winchester, are, as Cade himself says, 'inspired with the spirit of putting down kings and princes', and who succeed in entering London itself and occupying the heart of the city. The third episode, York's rebellion, is even more catastrophic. Like the peasant's leader, York proclaims himself 'descended from the Duke of Clarence' house', and, also like Cade, he 'resolves to crown himself in Westminster'. York, moreover, has some of the most powerful members of the nobility on his side, including Salisbury and Warwick, and a large army mustered in Ireland to support him. The King is now faced not with a local mutiny but with a full-scale civil war which, as we discover in Part III, does not end before both Henry and York are dead and York's son Edward has seized the crown. Shakespeare has so constructed the play that each uprising is more violent than the previous one and involves an increasingly greater part of the population. At the end of the first episode one man has been secretly smothered in his bed but at the end of the last England itself has become a battlefield.

The three sections also have a good deal in common. The first depicts the fall of Gloucester, the second the rise and fall of Cade and the third the rise of York, whose fall does not occur until the middle of Part III. In fact the entire play, as well as portraying the spread of civil insurrection, depicts the ascent of York, for York both foresees and connives at the removal of Gloucester, from which, as he tells us, he has everything to gain:

> Then, York, be still awhile, till time do serve;
> Watch thou and wake, when others be asleep,
> To pry into the secrets of the state;
> Till Henry, surfeiting in joys of love
> With his new bride and England's dear-bought queen,
> And Humphrey with the peers be fall'n at jars;
> Then will I raise aloft the milk-white rose,
> With whose sweet smell the air shall be perfum'd,
> And in my standard bear the arms of York,
> To grapple with the house of Lancaster;

And force perforce I'll make him yield the crown,
Whose bookish rule hath pull'd fair England down.

Cade's apparently popular mutiny is, moreover, deliberately engineered by
York, who has known him since their campaigning days together in Ireland,
and is designed to test public opinion before York himself embarks on what
will be the real rebellion. He is thus the figure who links the three sections,
each one of which brings him closer to the crown.

Even the earliest of his historical plays show that Shakespeare was deeply
interested in the causes and effects of political change, the forces which
compel a nation's history to change its course, and in this he was not at all
like the chronicle writers from whose bare records of events he took his
material. Yet, although he was in some ways our first modern political
analyst, he was still the product of his own time, a man whose way of thinking was shaped by the middle ages and the renaissance. This is apparent in his
conception of history as a series of rises and falls of great men, a way of thinking which had been disseminated by a collection of narratives written by the
fourteenth-century Italian prose writer Boccaccio and several popular
English works derived from it. The title of Boccaccio's collection is *De
Casibus Virorum Illustrium*, 'Of the Falls of Celebrated Men', and it deals, one
by one, with a series of individuals who rose to great power, wealth or fame,
only to die or be thrust into obscurity at the very height of their success.
Boccaccio's first example is Adam, who was cast out of Paradise, and he goes
on to describe the falls of various biblical and mythological characters such
as Samson and Hercules. The fifteenth-century English poet John Lydgate
not only freely translated Boccaccio's gloomy narratives into English in his
*Fall of Princes* but added to them to include more recent historical figures,
and this process was extended further by the authors of a book which we
know Shakespeare to have read, *A Mirror for Magistrates*, first published in
1559 and many times reprinted and enlarged. By this stage the stories had
been brought sufficiently up to date to include those of Richard II, Henry
Bolingbroke, Duke Humphrey of Gloucester and his wife Eleanor. The
underlying theme of all these narratives is the same: the fickleness and
instability of Fortune and the consequent necessity to put our trust not in
earthly power but in God, who is unchanging. These works and the many
others which were written in what has come to be known as the 'de casibus'
tradition were typical of the middle ages in that they tended to attribute all
earthly events either to Fortune or to God's providence. Individual men are
assumed to be the helpless victims of supernatural forces beyond their
knowledge or control. This way of thinking and the works that expressed it
were highly influential. One of Chaucer's *Canterbury Tales*, 'The Monk's
Tale', is made up of a series of similar narratives and nearly all the plays of
Christopher Marlowe are constructed on similar patterns: Marlowe's Tam-

burlaine falls sick and dies while he is still ruler over a vast empire; his Jew of Malta, having amassed a great treasury of wealth, falls into a cauldron of boiling oil; and Dr Faustus, having enjoyed supernatural powers by selling his soul to the devil, is finally dragged off to hell. It is scarcely surprising, therefore, that Shakespeare, who was born in the same year as Marlowe, should portray the history of England in terms of the rises and falls of the Duke and Duchess of Gloucester, Suffolk, Cade, Somerset and York. He did so because his education had induced him to think along these lines.

Shakespeare's treatment of the rises and falls of his historical characters differs significantly, however, from that of the earlier authors of the 'de casibus' stories. The latter, in the words of Machiavelli, 'hold the opinion that human affairs are so governed by Fortune and by God, that men cannot alter them by any prudence of theirs, and indeed have no remedy against them, and for this reason have come to think that it is not worth while to labour much about anything'. Shakespeare, on the other hand, believed that men themselves had the power, if they chose to use it, to determine the course of their own lives and thereby to shape the course of history. The descent of England into civil war at the end of *Henry VI Part II* is brought about not by God or Fortune but by the fatal passivity of the King, the hostility to the Lord Protector, and the ambitions of York, who is left free by Duke Humphrey's death to carve out his own future. As well as being exciting, well-constructed plays, the three parts of *Henry VI* are extremely interesting documents in the history of ideas. They reveal the shift which took place from a providential or religious interpretation of history characteristic of the middle ages to a humanistic view of history characteristic of the renaissance. This latter way of explaining events has, incidentally, now given way to yet another, the economic or sociological view of history, an attitude not conducive to the writing of great drama.

Shakespeare therefore shaped the historical material into a traditional pattern (the 'de casibus' pattern) but gave the pattern a new and different meaning. His emphasis on the power of the individual to shape and alter political affairs becomes obvious if we pick out from the play those speeches (often, for obvious reasons, soliloquies) in which the characters express their determination to do so. Here, for example, is York deciding how he will use his rivals to his own advantage:

> A day will come when York shall claim his own;
> And therefore I will take the Nevils' parts,
> And make a show of love to proud Duke Humphrey,
> And when I spy advantage, claim the crown,
> For that's the golden mark I seek to hit.

The rest of the play demonstrates how he puts his plan into action and the fact that it succeeds, at least up until the end of Part II, is proof that he, and not God or Fortune, has the power to shape his own destiny. York's soliloquy is, moreover, not the only 'aspiring' speech of this kind. Duke Humphrey's wife expresses a similar determination at the opening of the second scene, significantly just after York has revealed his intentions to us. 'Why are thine eyes fix'd to the sullen earth,' she asks her husband,

> Gazing on that which seems to dim thy sight?
> What see'st thou there? King Henry's diadem,
> Enchas'd with all the honours of the world?
> If so, gaze on, and grovel on thy face
> Until thy head be circled with the same.
> Put forth thy hand, reach at the glorious gold.
> What, is't too short? I'll lengthen it with mine.

Such ambitions are, moreover, not cherished only by the powerful, major characters. Even the hired informer, Hume, intends to rise in the world by earning cash from his employers, Suffolk and the Cardinal:

> Hume's knavery will be the Duchess' wreck,
> And her attainture will be Humphrey's fall.
> Sort how it will, I shall have gold for all.

All these restless opportunists have confided in us before the end of the second scene and Shakespeare creates a lively impression of a country sliding towards anarchy. The ambitions of few of these characters are ultimately realized, however. Though Hume no doubt retires from political intrigue once he has pocketed his gold, the Duchess if forced to parade in the streets, jeered at by the common people who formerly followed her 'proud chariot wheels', and the crown which York is given in Part III is a paper one mockingly thrust on his head at the point of his death. They may appear to be the victims of Fortune or Providence but, as Shakespeare shows us, they are actually the victims of more cunning politicians than themselves. The ultimate victor when Part III is over is Richard of Gloucester, the most quick-witted and brutal of them all.

That Shakespeare did not believe that history was guided by God's providence is evident from the way in which he portrays Henry VI himself. His disastrous refusal or inability to act springs not simply from his inherent weakness of will but from his belief in divine providence, his conviction that all things are controlled by the power of God. His reaction to the news of the loss of France is not just helpless but devoutly Christian:

> Cold news, Lord Somerset: but God's will be done.

Henry attempts to live according to Christian principles in what is essentially a secular world and his speeches repeatedly echo or paraphrase the Bible. 'Blessed are the peacemakers upon earth,' he says, reprimanding his contentious queen and, bewailing the violence of the Kentish rebels, 'O graceless men! they know not what they do.' However piously motivated, Henry's Christian quietism is the chief cause of the anarchy which overwhelms the country during the course of the play. His trust in God's providence is shown to be misplaced. Those people like Suffolk, Winchester, Eleanor and York who trust only in their own will power are, however, also shown to have, at best, a limited success. They ultimately become the victims of other adventurers determined to shape the world to their own advantage. It is a world in which nobody is the winner.

# THE THIRD PART OF
# KING HENRY THE SIXTH

We can get a clear idea of the way in which the action of the three parts of
*Henry VI* develops if we compare the first scene of Part III with the
opening scenes of the two earlier parts. Part I begins with a ceremonial
procession in which the peers – Gloucester, Bedford and the rest – accom-
pany the coffin of Henry V to its place of burial. In retrospect this formal
grouping of the characters may be seen to have represented, visually, the
last manifestation of the authority which Henry V held over his subjects.
The orderly group into which the characters arrange themselves around his
coffin bears witness to the King's capacity, even in death, to organize and
control his subjects. The first scene of Part II also consists of a public ritual,
the first meeting between Henry VI and his bride. This later ceremony,
however, is less harmonious than it appears, for we know that the marriage
has been contrived by Suffolk in order that he may control the country by
controlling the King through Margaret. The ritual does not actually represent the harmoniousness it appears to display. Part III, in strong contrast,
opens in confusion. The country is temporarily in the hands of the Yorkist
rebels, the King has taken flight and, as the scene rapidly unfolds, York
seats himself on the throne and Warwick threatens to establish York's
authority by force:

> Do right unto this princely Duke of York;
> Or I will fill the house with armed men,
> And over the chair of state, where now he sits,
> Write up his title with usurping blood.

At this point York's soldiers break into the Parliament house and prepare to
make an assault on the King himself. All consideration for ceremony and the
hierarchy of rank and mutual respect of which ceremonies are the manifestation have long since been abandoned in the open and unrestrained struggle
for power. The confusion of the action in this first scene, the rapid ascents to
and descents from the throne (on which first York sits and then Henry), the
peers' sudden changes of allegiance and the violence of the language with

which both sides threaten each other, all express the anarchy into which the country has degenerated.

The confusion increases as the play develops, though it is a confusion which Shakespeare plots with some care. As the first act concludes, the Lancastrians are, for the time being, in the ascendant as their troops defeat York's army and their leader, Queen Margaret, kills York and has his head stuck on the city gates. By the end of Act II, however, York's sons have risen to power and, having beaten the Lancastrians at the Battle of Towton, they remove York's head from the battlements and replace it with Clifford's. The King's description of the battle could equally well apply to the action of the play:

> Now sways it this way, like a mighty sea
> Forc'd by the tide to combat with the wind;
> Now sways it that way, like the selfsame sea
> Forc'd to retire by fury of the wind.

During the course of the three remaining acts, the leaders of the two opposing factions are established on or unseated from the throne with increasing and ever more confusing rapidity, depending on which of them happens to have won the last battle. Shakespeare could scarcely have devised a simpler or more vivid way of portraying political chaos and instability.

As this descent into chaos takes place, the characters simultaneously begin to lose touch with any sense of right or wrong. When in Part I York was content to remain in the wings, divulging his ambitions only to a small circle of sympathizers, he did at least justify his aspiration to the crown by a sincerely held conviction that it was his by right of his descent from Edward III. By the end of Part II, however, York has risen up in defence of his claim and very soon after the beginning of Part III he confronts Henry face to face and we are compelled to recognize that the problem is morally, politically and legally insoluble:

| | |
|---|---|
| *Henry* | My title's good, and better far than his. |
| *Warwick* | Prove it, Henry, and thou shalt be King. |
| *Henry* | Henry the Fourth by conquest got the crown. |
| *York* | 'Twas by rebellion against his king. |
| *Henry* | I know not what to say; my title's weak. |

The truth is, however, that by this stage no one is much concerned with legalities and each justifies his ascendancy by nothing other than his military success:

> We are those which chas'd you from the field,
> And slew your fathers, and with colours spread
> March'd through the city to the palace gates.

It is not, however, only the people at the heart of the conflict who have lost all sense of morality and the law. The abandonment of principle in favour of mere practical self-interest extends to the common people and across the sea to the court of France. Hunted down in rural Scotland and taken prisoner by the gamekeepers, King Henry asks them why they can allow themselves to take hold of the monarch to whom they have sworn allegiance. They reply that they were bound to obey him while they were his subjects but that they are now 'true subjects to the King, King Edward'. They feel no moral qualms nor do they regard themselves as guilty of perjury, but unhesitatingly resolve the question by obeying whoever happens, for the moment, to be in power.

An equally practical, and far more cynical decision is taken by King Lewis of France, who is asked, on the one hand, by Margaret to send forces to defend her husband's cause and, on the other hand, by Warwick to consent to the marriage of his sister to the currently reigning monarch, Edward IV. He is caught in the conflict of loyalties by which England is already split. By the middle of the scene he has decided, in view of Edward's 'good success', to reject Margaret's pleas and agree to the marriage. When, however, the news arrives that Edward has already married the Lady Grey, both Lewis and Warwick do a complete about-turn and, incensed by this affront to their dignity, join forces together with Margaret against the man they had formerly supported. Lewis's decision first to assist and then to attack King Edward is determined by no legal or moral principle. He follows the course which best serves his own interest. In France as in England right and wrong are of little or no consequence.

There is, however, one cause for which several of the characters are prepared to make sacrifices, even of their lives if necessary, and that is revenge, a word which is spoken with increasing frequency as the play develops:

> Earl of Northumberland, he slew thy father;
> And thine, Lord Clifford; and you both have vow'd revenge
> On him, his sons, his favourites, and his friends.

'Thy father slew my father,' cries Clifford to the young Rutland, son of the Duke of York, 'therefore die.' The reasons why men like these come to be driven by the desire for vengeance are not hard to find. With the supreme authority divided between rival claimants, and in the absence of a king of any permanence or legal or personal authority, the English nobility feel no over-riding obligations to which their own inclinations should take second place. Family loyalties take precedence over public responsibility and, moreover, as Shakespeare repeatedly shows us during the action of the play, violence provokes violence. Hence, since Clifford's father has been slain by York, Clifford himself kills York's son Rutland and is himself destroyed in battle by the Yorkists. Again, since York has risen up against Henry, Queen Margaret stabs him in revenge for his attempted usurpation. The chain of murders and revenges does not, however, stop here, for the sons of York thereupon take it upon themselves to avenge their father's death and, in due course, York's eldest son kills the young Prince Edward, and Richard of Gloucester murders the King himself. There appears to be no way in which the continuous and bloody series of actions and reactions can be stopped, nor, indeed, do they cease at the end of the play. Long before it concludes, Richard of Gloucester has vowed to 'hew his way' to the crown 'with a bloody axe' and the murders continue into the play which follows. The vendettas stop only when all the major protagonists have been wiped out.

The events depicted in *Henry VI Part III* become not only increasingly vindictive and anarchic but also more brutally inhuman. The victims of murder in the earlier plays, such as Duke Humphrey and Suffolk, were at least mature men who, in exercising power, had created enemies, but the victims in this later play, Rutland and Prince Edward, are scarcely more than boys whose only fault is to have been their father's sons. Moreover, as they become increasingly obsessed and dominated by the desire for retribution, the characters become more violent in their language and behaviour:

> I cannot rest
> Until the white rose that I wear be dy'd
> Even in the lukewarm blood of Henry's heart.
>
> Had I thy brethren here, their lives and thine
> Were not revenge sufficient for me;
> No, if I digg'd up thy forefathers' graves
> And hung their rotten coffins up in chains,
> It could not slake mine ire nor ease my heart.
>
> Butchers and villains! bloody cannibals!
> How sweet a plant have you untimely cropp'd!
> You have no children, butchers; if you had,
> The thought of them would have stirr'd up remorse.
> But if you ever chance to have a child,
> Look in his youth to have him so cut off
> As, deathsmen, you have rid this sweet young prince.

The inhumanity into which the country has descended is portrayed in two symbolic scenes. In the first, Queen Margaret orders her prisoner, the Duke of York, to be placed on a molehill and tied to a stake where she first taunts him by referring mockingly to his former aspirations to the throne and then holds up a napkin soaked in the blood of his dead son:

> Look, York: I stain'd this napkin with the blood
> That valiant Clifford with his rapier's point
> Made issue from the bosom of the boy;
> And if thine eyes can water for his death,
> I give thee this to dry thy cheeks withal.

She is not satisfied simply to murder her enemy but takes delight in inflicting a prolonged psychological torture on him as well. She is no longer concerned with the rights or wrongs of the cause for which she is fighting but has become possessed by the desire to inflict pain.

Shakespeare was very sensitive to the feelings which bind together the family, the natural and instinctive tenderness which links husband to wife, parents to their children. Later in his career he was to invoke them in the reunion between Leontes, his wife and his daughter at the end of *The Winter's Tale* and it is the violation of these bonds which causes Lear the greatest grief as he is spurned by his own daughters. Shakespeare expresses these feelings in several of the most moving scenes of the *Henry VI* plays: the death of Talbot beside the body of his dead child in Part I; the outrage of Young Clifford at his father's death in Part II, and the taunting of York by Queen Margaret in the episode mentioned above. The scene in which these emotions are invoked most tenderly, however, is in the second act where, as the Battle of Towton rages off stage, a son enters who has unknowingly killed his father and a father who had killed his son. With its formally balanced construction and muted style it is not at all a realistic scene and, in this exceptionally bloody play, it stands out by its lack of physical violence. The sense of bereavement, helplessness and futility which the two characters express conveys to us more than any other episode in the trilogy the inhumanity of civil war and the tragic waste of obscure, innocent people. We are not told who they are. They have no names and they appear only in this scene, but in their anonymity they represent all the common people whose lives have been ruined by the ineptitude and irresponsibility of those in power:

> O, pity, God, this miserable age!
> What stratagems, how fell, how butcherly,
> Erroneous, mutinous, and unnatural,
> This deadly quarrel daily doth beget!
> O boy, thy father gave thee life too soon,
> And hath bereft thee of thy life too late!
>
> These arms of mine shall be thy winding-sheet;
> My heart, sweet boy, shall be thy sepulchre,
> For from my heart thine image ne'er shall go;
> My sighing breast shall be thy funeral bell;
> And so obsequious shall thy father be,
> Even for the loss of thee, having no more,
> As Priam was for all his valiant sons.

For all its tragic qualities, it is one of the few scenes in which normal, natural human feelings are expressed. Most of the major characters feel only ambition, resentment or vengefulness towards others. These two nameless figures are among the few to express love.

The reasons why the country has fallen into this pitiful and barbaric state are clear enough. Shakespeare has taken care to trace the causes of the civil war back to their furthest origins during the course of the three plays. That is what they are about. He has also taken care to show that men have brought these troubles on themselves. They are destroying one another as a consequence of their own choices: the deliberate decision of York to pursue his claim to the throne by force, for example; the choice of Margaret to override her husband's mildness and give way to her own brutality; the determination of York's sons to avenge their father's death and take over from him the conquest of the throne. As the wearisome processes of slaughter and retribution continue, however, violence appears to acquire a momentum of its own. Individuals seem to be dragged along helplessly by the force of the war itself. They no longer feel free to make choices but behave as though their actions have been thrust upon them. Once in this predicament, they come increasingly to ascribe their success or failure not to their own efforts but to the unpredictable and over-riding power of Fortune:

> Yet thus far fortune maketh us amends,
> And says that once more I shall interchange
> My waned state for Henry's regal crown.

> Thus far our fortune keeps an upward course,
> And we are grac'd with wreaths of victory.

Indeed, as the fortunes of war shift rapidly from one side to the other, the characters do seem to have lost control over their destinies. In fact, however, by attributing their success or failure to Fortune, they are actually denying the capacity which they always have to change their lives and, thereby, to alter the course of history.

One character, however, still recognizes that his future lies in his own hands. Richard of Gloucester makes his first appearance towards the end of Part II and he immediately stands out from the others by his exceptional brutality and cynicism and his physical deformity, 'a foul indigested lump', 'as crooked in his manners as his shape'. It is he who in Part III revives his father's ambitions:

> And, father, do but think
> How sweet a thing it is to wear a crown,
> Within whose circuit is Elysium
> And all that poets feign of bliss and joy.
> Why do we linger thus? I cannot rest
> Until the white rose that I wear be dy'd
> Even in the lukewarm blood of Henry's heart.

We have heard speeches like this before, from Richard's father in an earlier play, but Richard is not simply lustful after power; he has an appetite for blood which is altogether new. He is very recognizably his father's son but is a more cruel, callous version of him. His lack of compassion and his delight in causing pain are, perhaps, the result of his having grown up during a time when violence is customary. As in Part I Talbot, in his patriotism, courage and uprightness, appeared to be a relic of a former age, so in Part III Richard, in his brutality and ruthlessness, foreshadows the times to come.

He is also the most fully developed and complex of the characters psychologically. His self-reliance, opportunism, his wise-cracking cynicism and his confident determination to carve out a future for himself make him an exhilarating character, but his ambition has the quality of an obsession, an insane determination to get to the top at no matter what cost to others or himself:

> I'll make my heaven to dream upon the crown,
> And whiles I live t'account this world but hell,
> Until my misshap'd trunk that bears this head
> Be round impaled with a glorious crown.
> And yet I know not how to get the crown,
> For many lives stand between me and home;
> And I – like one lost in a thorny wood
> That rents the thorns and is rent with the thorns,
> Seeking a way and straying from the air,
> But toiling desperately to find it out –
> Torment myself to catch the English crown;
> And from that torment I will free myself
> Or hew my way out with a bloody axe.

This is the last of those 'aspiring' speeches characteristic of the three parts of *Henry VI* and it is the most violent.

As I pointed out in my Introduction to Part II, Shakespeare saw the course of history in terms of the rises and falls of great men. Part I depicts the ascents into power of Winchester and Suffolk and gives us the first informations of York's ambition; Part II shows the falls of Winchester and of Duke Humphrey and his wife and the initial victory of York in the civil war; in Part III York is killed and Richard of Gloucester steps forward as the last of the aspirants for the crown. As each of these men attempts to satisfy his thirst for supremacy, however, and is in turn brought low by more eager adventurers, such sentiments acquire a steadily accumulating irony. For power, when achieved, is both burdensome and short-lived; it is won at the cost of others' lives and it exposes the possessor to the envy of those who are crushed in the process by which it is achieved. These truths are, however, learned only when it is too late, often at the point of death when earthly success is seen to be trivial and futile, as Warwick discovers in his last moments:

> Lo now my glory smear'd in dust and blood!
> My parks, my walks, my manors, that I had,

Even now forsake me; and of all my lands
Is nothing left me but my body's length.
Why, what is pomp, rule, reign, but earth and dust?
And live we how we can, yet die we must.

In tracing, over a long period of history, the lives of several generations – that of Duke Humphrey of Gloucester, the surviving brother of Henry V, of York and his contemporaries Warwick and Suffolk, and finally the generation of York's sons – Shakespeare is able to depict not only the anguish and bloodshed caused by the unrestrained struggle for power, but its triviality in the context of national history. This is a lesson which, unfortunately, each generation has to learn afresh and as this play comes to its conclusion, Richard of Gloucester still has a long way to go.

# King Richard III

Richard of Gloucester makes his first appearance towards the end of *Henry VI Part II*, where he immediately distinguishes himself from the other characters by his exceptional brutality, cynicism and physical deformity. It is he who in *Henry VI Part III* persuades his father, York, to break the oath of allegiance he has taken to the King, he who comments scathingly to the audience on the lustfulness of his brother Edward as the latter embarks on his courtship of the Lady Grey and he who, on his own initiative, steals away to the tower and murders Henry VI. He is the most striking and fully developed character to appear in the three parts of *Henry VI* and it seems likely that at least by the time he was composing Part III, Shakespeare was planning in his mind the play he was going to write next and which would be dominated by Richard. This would explain why he wrote the long, powerful soliloquy in the third act of *Henry VI Part III* in which Richard sets out in great detail his ambition for the crown, the impulses which draw him towards it, the obstacles which stand in his way and the methods by which he proposes to overcome them. In this soliloquy he sets out his intentions and in *Richard III* he puts them into effect.

Richard's soliloquy is one of a number of 'aspiring' speeches characteristic of the three parts of *Henry VI* in which a character expresses his desire for power and his determination to achieve it. Similar ambitions have been voiced by Cardinal Beaufort and Suffolk in Part I and by Eleanor of Gloucester and Richard's father, York, in Part II. But whereas the motivation of these other characters is fairly simple – they simply enjoy the prospect of lording it over other people or, in York's case, believe that the crown is theirs by right – Richard's ambition is shown to be connected with his physical deformity. His arm is twisted, as he says, 'like a wither'd shrub', there is 'an envious mountain' on his back and he looks like 'a chaos, or an unlick'd bear-whelp'. Disfigured as he is, he has no hope of success with women and he therefore proposes to get his revenge on those who are better endowed than himself by overpowering and dominating them.

Richard's thirst for power is thus an attempt to compensate for his physical shortcomings. He is driven by the desire to prove his supremacy over those to whom he is physically inferior and whom he envies. His ambition is therefore more passionately fierce than that of the earlier political adventurers to the extent that it is an obsession which drives him forward in spite of the pain he may inflict on others or himself:

> I'll make my heaven to dream upon the crown,
> And whiles I live t'account this world but hell,
> Until my misshap'd trunk that bears this head
> Be round impaled with a glorious crown.
> And yet I know not how to get the crown,
> For many lives stand between me and home;
> And I – like one lost in a thorny wood
> That rents the thorns and is rent with the thorns,
> Seeking a way and straying from the way;
> Not knowing how to find the open air,
> But toiling desperately to find it out –
> Torment myself to catch the English crown;
> And from that torment I will free myself
> Or hew my way out with a bloody axe.

Richard is not just another ambitious politician; he is a psychopath.

The Richard of Gloucester about whom Shakespeare read in the chronicles was scarcely a credible character, but a monster deliberately created by the Tudor historians for the purpose of enhancing the reputation of Henry VII. According to More, Hall and Holinshed, Richard was a madman from whose savage dictatorship England had been saved by the intervention of Henry Tudor, the father of Henry VIII, and if Shakespeare was to remain faithful to what, for lack of any alternative evidence, he must have believed to be historical fact, he had to portray him as a psychopath. Nevertheless he went out of his way to make him a credible one and to provide him with sufficient reasons for behaving as he did.

In the soliloquy with which *Richard III* opens, he more or less repeats what he has said in the previous play, but he also reveals that he has a further reason for exerting himself. He had been in his element in the wars which occupied much of the earlier plays, reviving his father's ambitions, rousing his brothers' spirits after their father's death, and enjoying the thrill of violent physical action. In this 'weak piping time of peace', however, he can find no outlet for his energy. He is disqualified by his ugliness from taking part in the 'sportive tricks' which his lascivious elder brother enjoys and therefore, as he says,

> since I cannot prove a lover
> To entertain these fair well-spoken days,
> I am determined to prove a villain.

Shakespeare again shows that his lust for power is a reaction against his physical deformity.

In providing Richard with a motive Shakespeare was, in psychological insight, much in advance of his time. In his conception of history, however, he was still a product of the renaissance and, like the authors of the collection of moral tales *A Mirror for Magistrates*, and like Marlowe when he wrote *Tamburlaine* and *Dr Faustus*, he thought of history in terms of the rises and falls of great men. We can see this not only in his earliest history plays which are constructed round the ascents and declines of men like Suffolk, York and Warwick, but in later plays such as *Julius Caesar* where a succession of individuals – Caesar himself, Brutus and Cassius, Antony – enjoy a short period of supremacy before giving way to sharper and more determined politicians than themselves. *Richard III*, the hero of which climbs to power over the bodies of Clarence, Hastings and the sons of Edward IV before falling himself at the hands of Richmond, is obviously constructed in this way and the point at which Richard reaches his peak can be identified precisely. It occurs at the beginning of Act IV Scene ii and is indicated both by what he says and what we see him do:

> *Sound a sennet. Enter* Richard, *in pomp, as King*; Buckingham, Catesby, Ratcliff, Lovel, a Page, *and* Others.
>
> Richard      Stand all apart. Cousin of Buckingham!
> Buckingham   My gracious sovereign?
> Richard                              Give me thy hand.
> [*Here he ascendeth the throne. Sound.*]
>                Thus high, by thy advice
> And thy assistance is King Richard seated.

By making Richard literally walk up the steps, sit on the throne and, having seated himself, point out that he has done so, Shakespeare draws our attention to the significance of this moment both in Richard's career and in the construction of the play. He has arrived at what he had earlier called 'home'.

Equally significant are Richard's next words:

> But shall we wear these glories for a day;
> Or shall they last, and we rejoice in them?

They are an expression of anxiety that, having reached 'home', he may not manage to stay there. Insecurity is not an emotion he has hitherto expressed at all but during the rest of the play he is to feel it more and more. That is further evidence that this moment marks the turning point of *Richard III*. The play falls clearly into two parts, the first of which depicts the means by which Richard acquires the crown and the second the process whereby he loses it. The moment at which he actually ascends the throne, incidentally, falls almost precisely two-thirds of the way through the play, the place at which you would expect to find the turning point of a well-constructed tragedy.

In the soliloquy in *Henry VI Part III* discussed earlier, Richard points out that 'many lives stand between me and home' and during the first part of *Richard III* we are shown how he clears them out of his way and reinforces his own position. This part of the play is constructed like a flight of steps which lead to the throne itself. On the first step Richard disposes of his brother Clarence whose right is obviously stronger than his own. Then, in order to strengthen his own claim, he woos the Lady Anne, the widow of a previous heir, Prince Edward, the son of Henry VI, and, in spite of the fact that he has murdered both her husband and her father-in-law, he induces her to marry him. That constitutes the second step. To reach the third step, the elimination of the reigning monarch, Richard is required to make no effort at all, for Edward conveniently dies of his own accord, but Richard still has to dispose of his opponents, the Queen's family and her supporter, Hastings. The executions first of Rivers, Grey and Vaughan and then of Hastings thus form the fourth and fifth steps. On the death of Edward IV, however, the right to the throne passes to the King's sons, Edward Prince of Wales and Richard Duke of York. Richard clears away this impediment by persuading the citizens of London that the two children are illegitimate and inducing them to offer him the crown by popular acclaim. That is the sixth and final step which brings him, at last, to the throne itself.

The part of *Richard III* which leads up to Richard's enthronement is also distinguished by its dramatic irony, an effect created when the audience has a fuller knowledge or sharper understanding of the play than the characters who are engaged in it. For example, in the second scene the Lady Anne enters on her way to bury the body of Henry VI, her father-in-law, whom Richard has murdered – or, at least, that is what she believes she is about to do. The audience, however, knows that she is about to be wooed by Henry's assassin, and Shakespeare has created this irony by the simple expedient of making Richard tell us what he intends to do before Anne appears:

> For then I'll marry Warwick's youngest daughter,
> What though I kill'd her husband and her father?
> The readiest way to make the wench amends
> Is to become her husband and her father.

Hence we observe her expressions of loathing for Richard with some scepticism because we have a fair idea that she is reviling the man she will shortly agree to marry. Again, when Clarence finds himself face to face with the men who have been hired to kill him, he pleads with them to go for rescue to his brother Richard, not knowing, as we do, that it is Richard who has hired the murderers. Then, when Richard is discovered by the Lord Mayor and citizens of London reading from a prayer book and accompanied by two bishops, he appears to be a model of piety. Only we can share with him the knowledge that his show of meekness is a sham and can appreciate his ability to deceive.

There is also a profusion of verbal ironies in this part of the play. Indeed it is chiefly these which make the brutal actions at the same time so richly entertaining and they are ironies which we can share only with Richard, who creates them. For example, when he meets his brother Clarence on his way to the tower, he comforts him with the assurance,

> Well, your imprisonment shall not be long

– meaning, of course, that Clarence will soon be dead, a double meaning of which the prisoner is unaware. Again, when Hastings, who is, as Richard has forewarned us, shortly to be executed, hears of the deaths of the Queen's relations, he remarks that others, too, who little expect it, will shortly meet their dooms:

> And so 'twill do
> With some men else that think themselves as safe
> As thou and I, who, as thou knowest, are dear
> To princely Richard and to Buckingham.

We know that these words are truer than Hastings realizes and that he is the next victim on Richard's list.

The effect of these ironies is, paradoxically, to increase the suspense we feel as we watch the play. Unlike Richard's victims – Anne, Clarence, Hastings and the rest – we know well in advance of the fates he has prepared for them and we wait tensely for them to drop into his net, powerless to save them. The ironies which Shakespeare has created also make Richard himself congenial and engaging to us because they are all of his making. It is he who, unknown to anyone but ourselves, actually directs and controls the action. The other characters are merely his passive, helpless, trusting dupes. In other words the ironies work in Richard's favour and at their expense and hence we are compelled to become his fellow-conspirators, pitying their ignorance and admiring his manipulative genius. He is, moreover, eager to share with us the delight he feels at his own ingenuity:

> Was ever woman in this humour woo'd?
> Was ever woman in this humour won?
> I'll have her; but I will not keep her long.

No other character in the play talks to us like that. He assumes that we are on his side, flatters us by sharing with us his confidences, and we are compelled, whatever moral objections we may have towards him, to respond sympathetically. It is a further irony that, though Richard deceives practically everyone on the stage, he seems absolutely frank and straight with us. We feel that we, at least, can trust him. The monster created by the Tudor historians has been made not simply credible but perversely attractive.

Although he commits acts of extreme brutality, Richard feels neither compassion towards his victims nor guilt for his crimes. That is the reason for his success. If you wish to be an efficient man of action, particularly criminal action, then a sense of conscience can only be an impediment. 'Conscience,' as one of Clarence's murderers says,

makes a man a coward: a man cannot steal, but it accuseth him; a man cannot swear, but it checks him; a man cannot lie with his neighbour's wife, but it detects him . . . It fills a man full of obstacles.

Richard, however, labours under no such obstacles. As he himself tersely declares,

Tear-falling pity dwells not in this eye.

What he does not realize, however, is that although he himself feels no remorse for his crimes, they do create a powerful sense of guilt among those whom he employs, such as the murderers of Clarence and of the little princes, and hence each successive act of violence he commits arouses an increasing sense of outrage in his subjects. The killers he has hired to dispose of the young princes, although they are 'flesh'd villains', 'bloody dogs',

Melted with tenderness and mild compassion,
Wept like two children in their deaths' sad story.

Instead of claiming their reward, they take flight, overcome with 'conscience' and 'remorse'. This instinctive capacity for human feeling, for compassion and moral outrage, is the one obstacle for which Richard is unprepared. He overlooks the possibility that others may be incensed at his crimes because he is incapable of such feelings himself. As a result, every step which he takes towards the crown strengthens the hostility towards him. Unknowingly it is he himself who provokes the opposition which finally beings him down. He is responsible both for his short-lived success and his own downfall.

The downward movement actually begins precisely at the moment when he has seated himself on the throne. His triumph lasts no more than a few seconds. For the first time the man who has hitherto spoken with a brutal directness finds himself hesitant, unable perhaps to name the crime which must now be committed, the murder of the two children, Richard Duke of York and Prince Edward. For the first time, too, his henchman Buckingham fails to obey him at once. A split has occurred between the King and his most loyal supporter. It is a split which widens rapidly. Then there enters the first of a series of messengers, a new phenomenon in this play, bringing unexpectedly bad news, and all these events contribute to the impression that Richard is no longer firmly in control of his affairs. It is also now that we hear almost for the first time the name of the man who will overcome him:

> The Marquis Dorset, as we hear, is fled
> To Richmond, in the parts where he abides.

and the name 'Richmond' continues to chime intermittently throughout the rest of the scene like a bell warning Richard of his doom. It is at the climax of this series of setbacks that Queen Margaret enters and announces that the last of her prophecies is about to be fulfilled:

> So now prosperity begins to mellow
> And drop into the rotten mouth of death.

Since every one of her earlier prophecies – the deaths of Edward IV, Prince Edward, Rivers, Hastings and the rest – has already been fulfilled, we feel that Richard's defeat is a foregone conclusion. He has now to contend with his destiny. The play's final irony is therefore created at Richard's own expense. The very crimes he performed in order to secure his safety have ensured his defeat. As so often happens in Shakespeare's history plays, his actions have produced the opposite effect from that he had intended.

# THE COMEDY OF ERRORS

It is practically certain that Shakespeare was educated at the Grammar School which still stands in Church Street, Stratford-on-Avon. The curriculum there, as at scores of similar institutions throughout the country, was a classical one (though with a great deal more Latin than Greek) and, once the young Shakespeare had mastered the rudiments of Latin grammar, he would have proceeded to read fairly simple works, such as the *Fables* of Aesop, before progressing to Ovid's *Metamorphoses*, Vergil's *Aeneid*, the orations and *De Officiis* of Cicero, the tragedies of Seneca and the comedies of Terence and Plautus. The plays of these last two authors, Terence and Plautus, occupied a substantial place in the syllabus and the boys would have become thoroughly well acquainted with them, partly because their language was considered to be unusually pure, and partly because from them the boys could gain experience in conversational Latin. Moreover it was customary for the schoolboys not simply to study and translate those comedies in the classroom but to take part in performances both among themselves and for the entertainment of the local public.

The study of the Latin dramatists in sixteenth-century schools had a considerable effect on the development of English drama. We know that several schoolmasters of the time wrote their own original plays in Latin in imitation of these Roman models, and the first surviving comedy in English, *Ralph Roister Doister*, composed in about 1553 by a schoolmaster, Nicholas Udall, was written under the influence of Terence, on whom he had published a scholarly work. It is therefore entirely understandable that when the young Shakespeare embarked on what may have been his very first comedy, *The Comedy of Errors*, he should write it in the manner of Plautus.

In fact the greater part of the play is based on two of Plautus's comedies. The first, *The Menaechmi* (or *The Brothers Menaechmus*) is about the misunderstandings which arise when two identical twin brothers find themselves, unknown to each other, in the same town and are repeatedly mistaken for each other. In the second of Plautus's comedies, the *Amphitruo*, the god Jupiter, infatuated by a beautiful woman, transforms himself into the shape of her husband and is entertained by her while the true husband is shut out of his own house. This episode, slightly modified, occurs in the third act of *The Comedy of Errors* when Antipholus of Ephesus arrives home for dinner but is kept outside while his wife dines inside with his twin brother.

Shakespeare did not simply fit together parts of the two Latin plays, however, but made to the *Menaechmi* an ingenious addition. Whereas the misunderstandings of Plautus's comedy arose from the confusion between two twin brothers, Shakespeare took the boldly inventive step of giving to each of them an identical twin servant and thereby increased the opportunities for mistaken identity. It was the brainwave of an ambitious young dramatist who was, in effect, announcing himself to the Elizabethan playgoers as an English Plautus who could, moreover, outdo his master in comic inventiveness. Indeed, one of the chief pleasures of *The Comedy of Errors* arises from our recognition of Shakespeare's ingenuity, his ability to keep the plot moving from one situation to another, developing the mistaken identities with steadily increasing complexity until, with the final encounter between both sets of twins, the dramatic tensions are resolved. A similar kind of dramatic construction was used by Shakespeare's younger contemporary Ben Jonson in his *Volpone* and *The Alchemist*, comedies written under the influence of the same Latin dramatists.

Although the ingenuity of its construction has always been appreciated by Shakespeare's critics, *The Comedy of Errors* has often been regarded as an inferior play, at least in comparison with the later, romantic comedies such as *As You Like It* and *Twelfth Night*. William Hazlitt, for example, complained that Shakespeare appeared 'to have bestowed no great pains on it' and that it contained 'but a few passages which bear the decided stamp of his genius'. It is not difficult to see why it was poorly thought of. *The Comedy of Errors* is essentially a farce, the effects of which arise chiefly from the absurdity of its situations. Moreover the characters are copied from the traditional, stock types of Latin comedy – the shrewish wife, the infatuated lover, the courtesan, the clever servant – and have very little psychological complexity. They must inevitably disappoint anyone who expects the subtleties of a Rosalind or a Benedick. Furthermore there are few passages of lyrical writing because this is a play designed chiefly not to move but to entertain an audience. For those reasons it has been criticized as 'merely ingenious', an improvement on Plautus but in Plautus's brittle, farcical style.

In fact a good production of the play reveals that it is much more than a cleverly constructed box of theatrical tricks. It can create a comic suspense unrivalled by any play that had hitherto been written and there are episodes which are genuinely moving, especially the conclusion in which the whole family, after their long separation, are reunited, a scene which was Shakespeare's first sketch for the great reconciliation scenes at the end of *Pericles* and *The Winter's Tale*. To achieve effects of this kind, he obviously had to do a great deal more than merely double the number of twins he found in the Latin source. We can find out more precisely what he did by comparing an episode in *The Comedy of Errors* with its Latin original.

In the *Menaechmi*, the resident brother, driven to distraction by his nagging wife, resolves to enjoy a little peace by having dinner with a prostitute and, in one of the play's early scenes, instructs the latter to prepare a good meal for him. His twin brother, arriving in the town for the first time, is mistaken for the resident brother (who, like himself, is called Menaechmus), is told by the whore that the food is ready and, at the end of the second act, accepts with some bewilderment her invitation to dine. The situation is developed no further and, once the episode is finished, Plautus scarcely mentions it again. In adapting it, however, Shakespeare made a number of very substantial changes which reveal what a thoroughly professional grasp he had, even at this early stage of his career, of the theatre and the means whereby the attention of an audience can be caught and held. For one thing, he transfers the dinner from the courtesan's house to the home of the resident brother and thereby makes the mistaken identity much more comically disturbing. To be entertained to dinner by a totally strange, passionate woman is far more surprising to the visiting twin when the woman is not a prostitute but actually claims to be his wife. Secondly, Shakespeare shifts the dinner scene to a much later point in the play (from the second act to the third) and thereby gives himself more playing time in which to build up the audience's expectations of it, an opportunity of which he makes ample use. By preparing the audience for it at considerable length, he transforms it from a minor episode into the first major climax of the play, the moment towards which the action has so far been leading.

The preparation begins very early in the play (Act I Scene ii line 44). The visiting brother (who, like his twin, has now been renamed Antipholus) has scarcely arrived in the town before a servant – apparently his own faithful Dromio – approaches him in some agitation and urges him to come home to dinner:

> The capon burns, the pig falls from the spit;
> The clock hath strucken twelve upon the bell –
> My mistress made it one upon my cheek;
> She is so hot because the meat is cold,
> The meat is cold because you come not home,
> You come not home because you have no stomach,
> You have no stomach, having broke your fast;
> But we, that know what 'tis to fast and pray,
> Are penitent for your default today.

References to the delayed meal continue all the way through the rest of this scene and form a major topic of conversation when, in the next scene, we are taken into Antipholus's house and given our first glimpse of his distraught wife, Adriana, whom her sister is attempting to console:

> Perhaps some merchant hath invited him,
> And from the mart he's somewhere gone to dinner;
> Good sister, let us dine, and never fret.
> A man is master of his liberty;
> Time is their master, and when they see time,
> They'll go or come. If so, be patient, sister.

Our interest in the apparently doomed repast is kept up when the resident Dromio returns home and reports to Adriana and her sister the extraordinary reception he was given by Antipholus:

> When I desir'd him to come home to dinner,
> He ask'd me for a thousand marks in gold.
> ''Tis dinner time' quoth I; 'My gold!' quoth he.
> 'Your meat doth burn', quoth I; 'My gold!' quoth he.
> 'Will you come home?' quoth I; 'My gold!' quoth he
> 'Where is the thousand marks I gave thee, villain?'
> 'The pig' quoth I 'is burn'd'; 'My gold!' quoth he.

As the mistakes of identity multiply and the references to the as yet uneaten dinner build up, so Adriana's impatience rises and the audience feels an increasingly urgent need for one or other of the twins to come home if only to break the emotional tension and prevent a good meal from being spoiled. But Shakespeare still does not satisfy our expectations. He gives to Antipholus and his servant a piece of punning dialogue on the subject of food, meat and basting in the scene which follows (Act II Scene ii) and it is therefore with some excitement that we reach the moment when, unable to tolerate Antipholus's absence any longer, Adriana boldly walks into the public square and accosts the man she believes to be her delinquent husband:

> Ay, ay, Antipholus, look strange and frown.
> Some other mistress hath thy sweet aspects;
> I am not Adriana, nor thy wife.
> The time was once when thou unurg'd wouldst vow
> That never words were music to thine ear,
> That never object pleasing in thine eye,
> That never touch well welcome to thy hand,
> That never meat sweet-savour'd in thy taste,
> Unless I spake, or look'd, or touch'd, or carv'd to thee.
> How comes it now, my husband, O, how comes it,
> That thou art then estranged from thyself?

Lifted out of its context in the play, this long, passionate reprimand is extremely powerful. In its context, however, it is immensely comic since the man whom Adriana is addressing is a total stranger, her husband's long-lost twin brother.

Their exit together at the end of the scene with the words 'Come, sir, to dinner' and the visiting twin's increasing bewilderment continue to sustain our curiosity. We may well wonder whether Adriana will discover that she is entertaining a stranger and, if so, what her reaction will be. The audience's expectations are therefore not allowed to diminish. On the contrary, they are considerably heightened, for it is at this point (Act III Scene i) that Shakespeare incorporates into his play the episode from the *Amphitruo* and brings in an important new character, the resident Antipholus, for the first time. There is now a strong possibility that the latter will enter his house and discover a stranger at his dinner table but once more Shakespeare delays this possible event by bringing on Antipholus in the company of the merchant Balthazar, whom, it appears, he has invited home to the ill-fated dinner. In view of the surprise which the audience knows is in store for them, their courteous talk – about the virtue of hospitality and of food as a token of welcome – has an ironical relevance:

| Antipholus | Y'are sad, Signior Balthazar; pray God our cheer |
| | May answer my good will and your good welcome here. |
| Balthazar | I hold your dainties cheap, Sir, and your welcome dear. |
| Antipholus | O, Signior Balthazar, either of flesh or fish, |
| | A table full of welcome makes scarce one dainty dish. |

They are unaware, of course, that the dinner to which they are both looking forward is at that moment being eaten inside the house. It is only at this moment that Shakespeare brings us to the climax for which he has been preparing us almost since the play began: as the stranger is entertained within, the true husband and his guest are locked out of the house and are forced to suffer the insults first of Dromio, then of the kitchen maid and, finally, of Adriana herself. Moreover, the suspense is further heightened by our knowledge that both pairs of twins are separated only by a locked door, which, if opened – and the husband does threaten to break it down – would reveal all four to each other and bring the play to an end. It is only with the departure of the husband and the merchant that the tension is broken and Shakespeare embarks on the next phase of the play.

Even a synopsis such as this, a poor substitute for performance, shows how radically Shakespeare has reshaped his material, using his knowledge of audiences and his skill in dramatic construction to create a sustained comic suspense of great technical brilliance. It is possible, moreover, to discover more precisely the kind of reaction this episode arouses in an audience. We are presented on the stage with the spectacle of a woman of some dignity and self-respect publicly denouncing a perfect stranger for his supposed sexual infidelity in the belief that the man is her husband, taking him off to dine with her almost by force and then shouting abuse at her real husband in the belief that he is an intruder. This series of events, ostensibly absurd, but for which, as always in farce, there is a perfectly logical explanation, produces in us an agreeable affront to our sense of social propriety, our collective opinion of how husbands and wives ought to behave. It may be that we enjoy the breaking of conventions by fictional characters because we are reluctant to violate them ourselves and welcome the opportunity for others to do it on our behalf. The characteristic comic situations in this play always consist of some form of social misconduct: servants are beaten for faults they never committed, strangers are welcomed as though they were intimate friends, guests are shut out from the dinner to which they have been invited, payment is denied for goods received, a young woman is wooed apparently by her sister's husband, a sane man is threatened with incarceration in a madhouse and a doctor is assaulted while trying to cure his patient. With this in mind, we may conjecture why Shakespeare added several new characters to his source, the *Menaechmi*, and discarded others. The cast of *The Comedy of Errors* forms a social microcosm: a duke and his subjects, a husband and his wife, parents and their children, brothers and sisters, masters and servants, a merchant and his customer, a doctor and his patients, a prostitute and her client. Shakespeare has created a small society and is thus able to depict a dislocation of social conduct on all its levels.

As well as tightening and complicating the plot, moreover, Shakespeare added to his sources a further element, a series of moralizing passages in the form of debates and pieces of advice on the very theme of social propriety which is at the root of the comic situations. The first of these passages is the discussion between the wife, Adriana, and her young sister on the subject of the relationship between husbands and wives. Adriana, pained by her husband's lack of affection, declares that men should have no more independence than women. It is only natural that she should feel like this because, while she has prepared dinner for her husband and is tied to her housekeeping, he is allowed to wander freely in the town. Luciana, on the other hand, as yet unmarried and untroubled by such problems, argues that the subjection of the female to the male is a law of nature:

> There's nothing situate under heaven's eye
> But hath his bound in earth, in sea, in sky.
> The beasts, the fishes and the winged fowls,
> Are their males' subjects and at their controls.
> Man, more divine, the master of all these,
> Lord of the wide world and wild wat'ry seas,
> Indu'd with intellectual sense and souls,
> Of more pre-eminence than fish and fowls,
> Are masters to their females and their lords;
> Then let your will attend on their accords.

There is no doubt that she puts forward the traditional Christian view with which the majority of Shakespeare's contemporaries would have agreed – the view expressed by Katherine at the end of *The Taming of the Shrew*, another early comedy. Nevertheless, Shakespeare does not allow the younger woman to win the argument; he also sympathizes with the wife's predicament and the debate is not resolved. Their dialogue, probably not much noticed by a modern audience, does, however, provide a brief, half-serious interlude in which one of the topics which lies behind the comic situations is made explicit and discussed openly. Comic misunderstanding and moral debate are different ways of treating the same issues. In the conversation between the two sisters Shakespeare seems to be signalling to us what *The Comedy of Errors* is about.

Instruction on how wives ought to treat their husbands is also delivered to Adriana by the Abbess, who extracts from her the confession that she has unremittingly chastised her husband for his sexual infidelities:

> In bed, he slept not for my urging it;
> At board, he fed not for my urging it;
> Alone, it was the subject of my theme;
> In company, I often glanced at it;
> Still did I tell him it was vile and bad

The Abbess's frank and practical retort to this confession is to reprimand Adriana for her lack of tact and social propriety:

> The venom clamours of a jealous woman
> Poisons more deadly than a mad dog's tooth.
> It seems his sleeps were hinder'd by thy railing,
> And thereof comes it that his head is light.
> Thou say'st his meat was sauc'd with thy upbraidings:
> Unquiet meals make ill digestions;
> Thereof the raging fire of fever bred;
> And what's a fever but a fit of madness?
> Thou say'st his sports were hinder'd by thy brawls.
> Sweet recreation barr'd, what doth ensue
> But moody and dull melancholy,
> Kinsman to grim and comfortless despair,
> And at his heels a huge infectious troop
> Of pale distemperatures and foes to life?
> In food, in sport, and life-preserving rest,
> To be disturb'd would mad or man or beast.

*The Comedy of Errors* is thus made up of a series of farcical situations interspersed with passages of moral instruction and debate, and these two elements are connected by the fact that both are, though in very different ways, concerned with social behaviour. The audience is shown the comic spectacle of a small society thrown into confusion and is also offered general observations about how societies ought to function. Even apparently trivial passages, which seem to be nothing more than clever repartee, turn out to be relevant to the play as a whole in that they are concerned with questions of social behaviour. The conversation between the resident Antipholus and his guest the merchant, for example, is about the nature of hospitality, and his brother's punning chatter with his servant Dromio is about the notion that 'there is a time for all things', a principle of decorum neglected by the constantly nagging wife. It may be because of this repeated emphasis on social propriety that Shakespeare changed the location of the play from Epidamnum, where the action of *Menaechmi* takes place, to Ephesus, for it was in his address to the people of Ephesus (the Epistle to the Ephesians 5) that Saint Paul instructed them in relationships within the family:

Wives, submit yourselves unto your own husbands . . . For the husband is the head of the wife, even as Christ is the head of the Church . . . Husbands, love your wives . . . let every one of you in particular so love his wife even as himself and let the wife see that she fear her husband.

The moralizing passages, of which there are none in the original Latin comedies, provide moments of seriousness between the prevailing farcical situations, but the most extensively sombre episodes are supplied by Shakespeare's other major addition, the story of Aegeon, the father of the Antipholus twins, which he took from a totally different source, the ancient tale of Apollonius of Tyre, which he was to use again very much later for the plot of *Pericles*. Whereas the marriage of Antipholus of Ephesus and Adriana is disrupted by his infidelities and her sense of neglect, the marriage of Aegeon and Aemilia has been broken up many years before the opening of the play by the shipwreck which divided husband from wife and son from son. Now, as the play begins, Aegeon, having searched the shores of the Mediterranean in vain for his lost wife and child, is faced with the threat of imminent death. Appearing only in the opening and closing scenes of *The Comedy of Errors*, his story provides a prologue and epilogue, a frame, to the play as a whole and serves as a dark background against which the comic scenes are accentuated by contrast. His irresistible need to find his family, moreover, reinforces the need the audience increasingly feels for the comic misunderstandings to be resolved. This double tension gives to the final reunion between husband and wife, parents and children, masters and servants, brothers and brothers, an unexpectedly moving emotional power, particularly when the Abbess reveals herself to be the wife whose loss he has mourned for so long and, for the first time, calls him by his name:

> Abbess     Speak, old Aegeon, if thou be'st the man
>                That hadst a wife once call'd Aemilia,

That bore thee at a burden two fair sons.
O, if thou be'st the same Aegeon, speak,
And speak unto the same Aemilia.

*Aegeon*   If I dream not, thou art Aemilia.

In the conclusion of the play Shakespeare expresses feelings which the Roman comic writers never attempted to convey and whic⸱ ⸱when we consider the plays he wrote later, are very distinctively his own. The power of a great many of Shakespeare's plays arises from his feeling for the instinctive and necessary bonds which unite the members of the family and which we see broken and reunited not only in the very last plays, such as *Pericles* and *The Winter's Tale*, but in *Lear* in the relationship between Cordelia and her father and in *Hamlet* and *Henry IV* in the relationship between father and son. It tells much about the dramatist's own personality that he infused into this ingeniously constructed little farce that feeling for the family and the need of its members for one another which has made his plays last.

# TITUS ANDRONICUS

When we talk about Shakespeare's 'Roman plays' we are usually thinking of his three great tragedies *Julius Caesar*, *Antony and Cleopatra* and *Coriolanus*. Very early in his career, however, Shakespeare wrote another Roman play, *Titus Andronicus*, which, though immensely popular in his own time, is nowadays seldom read and rarely performed. *Titus* has been neglected because it has been considered too crudely violent and sensational, an Elizabethan horror play written in the manner of another well-tried favourite with Shakespeare's audiences, Thomas Kyd's *The Spanish Tragedy* and, in its excessive brutality, significant only as an example of a popular taste which Shakespeare rapidly outgrew as he improved in skill, subtlety and discrimination. The man who revised the play shortly after the Restoration, Edward Ravenscroft, described it as 'a heap of rubbish' and, though subsequent critics have chosen their words more carefully, most of them have agreed with his judgement.

It has recently been realized, however, that Shakespeare took more trouble in the writing of this early tragedy than had been generally assumed. With its abundance of references to Roman history, legend and literature, it is a play designed for the learned as well as the vulgar playgoer. Moreover, as in his later Roman tragedies, Shakespeare took the trouble to give it what was, for him, a characteristically Roman flavour, to create the impression of a society very different from his own with distinctive ideals, institutions, and habits of mind and life. The historical period portrayed in *Titus Andronicus* is not the same as that depicted in *Julius Caesar* and *Antony and Cleopatra*, a period in which Rome was still a republic at the peak of its military power and about which Shakespeare read in the biographies of the historian Plutarch. The Rome in which *Titus Andronicus* is set is the imperial Rome of several centuries later, notorious for its corruption and the depravity of its emperors and assailed by its lawless enemies the Goths, the northern tribes who eventually destroyed it. The sexual excesses and physical violence which play an important part in the action of the tragedy, such as the rape and mutilation of Lavinia, the execution of Titus's sons and Tamora's infatuation with Aaron the Moor, were derived by Shakespeare not so much from earlier tragedies of blood but from such knowledge of late imperial Rome as he acquired from reading the historian Suetonius or, at any rate the sixteenth-century historians who took their material from him. 'When the Roman Empire was grown to its height,' began one such writer,

and the greatest part of the world was subjected to its imperial throne, in the time of Theodosius, a barbarous northern people out of Swedeland, Denmark and Gothland came into Italy in such numbers under the leading of Tottilius, their King, that they overran it with fire and sword, plundering churches, ripping up women with child, and deflowering virgins in so horrid and barbarous a manner that people fled before them like flocks of sheep.

These are the opening words of *The History of Titus Andronicus*, a little book which some scholars believe was the principal source of the play. It certainly creates a strong impression of the world of the tragedy itself.

There was, moreover, a dramatist with whose work Shakespeare was very familiar, the Latin playwright Seneca, whose works were studied assiduously by Elizabethan schoolboys and whose tragedies, already translated into English by 1581, depicted brutally sensational deeds similar to those in *Titus Andronicus* – adultery, incest, unnatural murder and, above all, revenge. The kind of events portrayed in them correspond quite closely to those recorded by the historians of late imperial Rome and, in writing this, his most Senecan tragedy, Shakespeare may not simply have been imitating a well-known Latin model but attempting to give what he believed to be a realistic impression of Roman life at that time. In other words he imitated Seneca in order to create an impression of historical authenticity.

This is certainly the motive behind the Latin quotations which crop up frequently in the dialogue. On discovering that it is the sons of Tamora who have deflowered his daughter, Titus exclaims,

> Magni Dominator poli,
> Tam lentus audis scelera? tam lentus vides?

('Ruler of the great heavens, dost thou so calmly hear crimes, so calmly look on them?') He is quoting from Seneca's tragedy *Hippolytus* and, in response to the news, he sends a bundle of weapons to the two rapists together with a scroll on which are written some lines of Latin verse which one of them identifies as a quotation from Horace. Elsewhere there are references to Roman heroes such as Coriolanus and Æneas and to Latin mythology and literature, particularly Ovid's *Metamorphoses*, a copy of which Lavinia points to:

> Soft! So busily she turns the leaves! Help her,
> What would she find? Lavinia, shall I read?
> This is the tragic tale of Philomel
> And treats of Tereus' treason and his rape.

'The tragic tale of Philomel' as told by Ovid (another author much studied in Elizabethan schools) was also a major source of Shakespeare's play, for Philomel was raped by her own brother-in-law, King Tereus of Thrace in 'a hut deep hidden in the ancient woods', and, in order to prevent her from revealing his guilt, Tereus cut out her tongue. As they watched the first performance of *Titus Andronicus*, Shakespeare's contemporaries, unlike our own, could scarcely have failed to recognize that they were being shown a recognizable Roman drama, full of references to a literature with which many of them were extremely familiar. At times, indeed, Shakespeare goes so far as to imitate Ovid's characteristically vivid metaphorical style, as in Marcus's description of Lavinia's bleeding mouth:

> Why dost not speak to me?
> Alas, a crimson river of warm blood,
> Like to a bubbling fountain stirr'd with wind
> Doth rise and fall between thy rosed lips,
> Coming and going with thy honey breath.

It has recently been pointed out that this passage is quite close in style to Ovid's account of the death of Pyramus (which Shakespeare was to turn to farce several years later in *A Midsummer Night's Dream*):

As he lay stretched upon the earth the spouting blood leaped high; just as when a pipe has broken at a weak spot in the lead and through the small hissing aperture sends spurting forth long streams of water, cleaving the air with its jets.

It is clear, then, that Shakespeare took particular care to give to his play a recognizably authentic Roman colouring. This is important because its major preoccupation is one which was extremely pertinent to Rome at the very point in its history with which the play deals. Rome is portrayed at a point of crisis, poised between the stability which had been supported by the patriotism, religious faith and moral principles of the past, and the anarchic violence displayed by its enemies the Goths and now, more dangerously, erupting from within Rome itself. In this struggle, Gothic brutality is shown in the ruthless, lustfull Empress Tamora, her vicious sons and her Moorish lover, and Roman integrity is centred in the opposing family, that of Titus and his children, who have devoted, and in some cases sacrificed, their lives to their country.

Titus himself is that not uncommon Shakespearean character, the surviver from an earlier and more honourable age, like Kent in *King Lear*, the Bastard in *King John* and Adam the old servant in *As You Like It*, shocked and bewildered by the cunning, self-interested deceivers with whom he is compelled to associate. He is distinguished principally by his military achievements, and is referred to from the outset as

> the good Andronicus,
> Patron of virtue, Rome's best champion,
> Successful in the battles that he fights,

who

> With honour and with fortune is return'd
> From where he circumscribed with his sword
> And brought to yoke the enemies of Rome.

The first emotion he expresses is of love for his country for which, already, twenty of his sons have given up their lives, and whose soil he greets with 'tears of true joy'. He also displays another characteristically Roman virtue, the love of his family. He addresses his daughter Lavinia as 'the cordial of mine age to glad my heart', and his first actions are to give decent burial to his most recently killed sons and, in accordance with religious custom, to sacrifice one of the captured enemy in order that their souls may rest in peace. The ceremony of burial at which he officiates in the first scene links him firmly with traditional religious beliefs and family piety:

> In peace and honour rest you here, my sons;
> Rome's readiest champions, repose you here in rest,
> Secure from worldly chances and mishaps!
> Here lurks no treason, here no envy swells,
> Here grow no damned drugs, here are no storms,
> No noise, but silence and eternal sleep.
> In peace and honour rest you here, my sons!

In the respect they are anxious to pay to their dead brothers and in the patriotism and courage they have already shown, Titus's children clearly act on convictions similar to their father's. His refusal to accede to the wishes of the people and stand as a candidate for the imperial throne is consistent with the self-denial he has already displayed in battle and, in this, he resembles one of Shakespeare's later Roman heroes, Coriolanus.

The opening scene of *Titus Andronicus*, with its public orations, funeral procession, ceremony of interment and the acclamation of Saturninus as Emperor, is extremely formal and ritualistic, creating the impression that ancient, traditional rites are being decently observed. These ceremonies, however, are seldom carried to their conclusions but are interrupted by sudden outbursts of violence, as when the new Emperor's brother carries off his prospective bride, Titus rashly kills his son Mutius and the two brothers Saturninus and Bassianus openly defy each other. These eruptions are a foretaste of the worse horrors to come and, in the threats they make to the proper performance of traditional ceremonies, are a representation of the conflict which develops as the play unfolds, a conflict between social and familial order and the anarchy which results when the loyalties which bind societies together are broken. The abduction of Lavinia and the subsequent marriage of the Emperor to the Queen of the Goths are the first steps towards the 'wilderness of tigers' into which the city degenerates. The observation of ceremony, and the mutual respect which such ceremonies as burial, marriage and coronation express, are one of the ways in which, according to the terms set up in this play, societies are restrained from following the law of the jungle.

The first offender against these obligations is the new Emperor himself, who, having publicly pledged himself to marry Lavinia, the daughter of the victorious general, is then led by his sexual appetite to choose Tamora, an enemy queen, as his bride and to marry her with indecent haste. Thus placed in a position of authority, Tamora uses her power not, as Titus had done, for the good of Rome, but in order to gratify her desire for revenge on Titus and his family, which now becomes the motivating force behind the tragedy.

> I'll find a day to massacre them all,
> And raze their faction and their family,
> The cruel father and his traitorous sons,
> To whom I sued for my dear son's life.

In the brutality which she both practises and encourages, Tamora becomes the most vicious of the 'tigers' which take over the city.

The outrages which are subsequently committed – the murder of Bassianus, the rape and dismemberment of Lavinia, the unjust execution of Titus's remaining sons – are carried out by Chiron and Demetrius, abetted by their barbaric mother, ostensibly as acts of vengeance for their defeat at the hands of Titus and the latter's sacrifice of their brother. But it is also clear that they take pleasure in causing pain and grief to others. The mutilation of Lavinia is made to seem unnatural and not simply because she is innocent and helpless but because it is carried out in a naturally beneficent setting when 'the morn is bright and grey, / The fields are fragrant, and the woods are green'. The 'wide and spacious' forest walks are seen by the lascivious brothers merely as 'unfrequented plots . . . Fitted by kind for rape and villainy'. For Tamora, too, the song of the birds and the 'green leaves quivering with the cooling wind' provide an apt setting for unnatural and adulterous lust. Unnaturalness is, throughout the play, the distinguishing feature of the Empress and her sons. It is she who encourages them to assault Lavinia while she is satisfying her appetite on the Moor. In his revenge on her, Titus induces her, unwittingly, to commit the most unnatural act of all, to eat a pie made from the flesh of her own children.

A similar delight in villainy is shown by her lover, Aaron the Moor, whom Shakespeare introduces into the play with some dramatic subtlety and power. Aaron is first brought on by the victorious Titus together with his other prisoners and, the only black figure on a stage otherwise occupied by white characters, he quickly makes a strong impression. As the long opening scene unfolds, moreover, he gradually becomes more noticeable as the only major character to remain silent. He says nothing until at the very end of the scene he is left alone, and at that point he delivers his first long soliloquy, and thereby satisfies the curiosity he has, by this time, aroused. The solitariness of Aaron suits him well, for he is an alien who, unlike the other major characters, has no family and no loyalties to prevent him from furthering his own desires, and it soon becomes clear that he intends to exploit the weaknesses of others for his own ends:

> Then Aaron, arm thy heart and fit thy thoughts
> To mount aloft with thy imperial mistress,
> And mount her pitch whom thou in triumph long
> Hast prisoner held, fett'red in amorous chains,
> And faster bound to Aaron's charming eyes
> Than is Prometheus tied to Caucasus.

Aaron is the forerunner of a number of unscrupulous adventurers who make their appearance in Shakespeare's later plays, such as Edmund in *King Lear* and Iachimo in *Cymbeline*. Like the sons of Tamora he is eager to satisfy his sexual appetites without scruple, but unlike them he is cunningly intelligent, teaching them how to enjoy Lavinia without being discovered and, later, how to conceal the child which he has himself fathered on the Empress. Like his associates, he openly delights in causing pain, but they need his perverse ingenuity to help them to carry out their misdeeds.

> Even now I curse the day – and yet, I think,
> Few come within the compass of my curse –
> Wherein I did not some notorious ill:
> As kill a man, or else devise his death;
> Ravish a maid, or plot the way to do it;
> Accuse some innocent, and forswear myself;
> Set deadly enmity between two friends;
> Make poor men's cattle break their necks
> Set fire on barns and hay-stacks in the night,
> And bid the owners quench them with their tears.
> Oft have I digg'd up dead men from their graves,
> And set them upright at their dear friends' door
> Even when their sorrows almost was forgot.

Aaron is, at any rate in this speech, so unhesitatingly villainous as to be scarcely credible. Like Richard III, he has in his frankness and vitality a certain bracing charm, but he is also an example of the kind of brutality which Tamora and her sons have brought into the gates of Rome. Unexpectedly, however, he does ultimately reveal a humanity of which his associates are incapable, in his love and concern for his bastard child.

It would, however, be a distortion of the play to see it simply as a struggle between Roman honour and Gothic savagery. A degeneration also takes place within the Romans themselves, in Saturninus by his marriage to Tamora, in Titus by his rejection of Tamora's plea for her son's life, by his impetuous killing of his son Mutius, and, most of all, in the monstrous revenge which he inflicts on his enemies as the play concludes. The tiger lurks within Rome as well as outside it. For most of the play, however, Titus arouses our sympathy as he endures one outrage after another. Though the actual events depicted in the tragedy are violently sensational, Shakespeare's expression of the feelings they arouse is not. He gives moving expression to emotions which in real life might be felt but could not be articulated and the play is full of the poetry of grief:

> For now I stand as one upon a rock,
> Environ'd with a wilderness of sea,
> Who marks the waxing tide grow wave by wave,
> Expecting ever when some envious surge
> Will in his brinish bowels swallow him.

Whereas his enemies are impervious to human feeling and, indeed, enjoy the spectacle of others' sufferings, Titus, in his desolation, gives voice to those natural sympathies and convictions which have been violated: loyalty to his country and paternal love. He especially invokes justice when, in his frenzy, he sends arrows up to the gods bearing the message (also taken from Ovid), 'Terras Astraea reliquit' ('Justice has left the earth'). In his impassioned protests against the wrongs inflicted on him, and in his desperate appeals for justice, Titus prefigures King Lear but, unlike Lear, he never matures into an acceptance of his sufferings. On the contrary, his grief converts to hatred and, in the act of vengeance with which he repays his enemies, he sinks to their level. As in the three parts of *Henry VI* which he had written only a year or two earlier, Shakespeare shows that violence provokes violence and that revenge breeds further revenges which cease only when all the perpetrators have been destroyed. Hence it is right that Titus should himself be killed and that not he but his son Lucius should take on the government of Rome. It is only then, as Titus's brother Marcus declares, that the Roman people, hitherto at war with one another, can unite:

> You sad-fac'd men, people and sons of Rome,
> By uproars sever'd, as a flight of fowl
> Scatter'd by winds and high tempestuous gusts,
> O, let me teach you how to knit again
> This scattered corn into one mutual sheaf,
> These broken limbs again into one body;
> Lest Rome herself be bane unto herself,
> And she whom mighty kingdoms curtsy to,

Like a forlorn and desperate castaway,
Do shameful execution on herself.

The play concludes, as it began, with preparations for the rites of burial, and this reference to the traditional proprieties suggests that the city has returned to its former stability.

# The Taming of the Shrew

It was only very rarely that Shakespeare invented the plots of his plays. He usually took them from existing novels, plays or history books and adapted them freely for the stage. If we compare the plays with the works from which he adapted them, it becomes plain that, in shaping them for the theatre, he made them more exciting dramatically and more convincingly human. For *The Taming of the Shrew*, which he wrote in about 1593, he combined three different plots, each one taken from a different source. The story of the poor tinker who is deceived into believing he is a noble lord, which forms the Prologue to the play, belongs to folklore; the story of the rebellious daughter who is tamed into a submissive wife had already been the subject of many tales and ballads; and the story of the nobleman who changes roles with his servant and gains access to the woman he loves was taken from an existing play, *The Supposes* by George Gascoigne, itself a translation from an Italian comedy, *I Suppositi*, by the poet Ariosto. By combining and interweaving the three stories Shakespeare created a number of striking contrasts: between the apparently meek but actually wilful Bianca and the boldly rebellious but finally submissive Katherine; between Lucentio's romantic infatuation with Bianca and Petruchio's unashamedly mercenary marriage to her sister; between the secretive, devious courtship of the younger sister by her suitors and the resolutely open seizure of Katherine by Petruchio. Moreover, as Christopher Sly is persuaded that he is 'a lord indeed' because he is treated as though he were one, so Kate is gradually induced to become 'pleasant, gamesome, passing courteous' because her husband repeatedly assures her, in the face of all the evidence, that she is so. Shakespeare thus gives to the central characters and situations a strength and vividness absent from the original versions by inviting us to compare and contrast them with one another, and, at the lowest level, the mixture of plots offers the audience the pleasure of variety.

In writing *The Taming of the Shrew*, however, he did a great deal more than cunningly interweave three hitherto separate stories. One of his most substantial additions was to place them in a solidly recognizable social context. Like nearly all his comedies, this is a family play dealing with the domestic processes of courtship and marriage, and its action (like that of *Much Ado About Nothing* and *Twelfth Night*) is placed appropriately in a domestic establishment – or, rather, two of them: the house of the father, Baptista, in which the marriages are arranged, and that of the husband, Petruchio, to which the couple move after their marriage.

Baptista belongs to a social class which had become prominent by the end of the sixteenth century. Successful, prosperous city merchants of his kind had been increasing in number and power as a result of the development of London as a port, a centre of the manufacturing industries, and as a base for the import of silks, spices and precious metals from the Indies and the export of cloth to Europe. Some Elizabethan merchants were richer than the old aristocracy, and the latter were not uncommonly in debt to them or attempted to preserve their dwindling fortunes by selling to them the estates which their families had owned through generations. Although Baptista has an Italian name and lives in Padua, his type would be immediately recognizable to an English audience.

He is identified quite early in the play as 'very rich', not a member of the aristocracy but 'an affable and courteous gentleman'. Like many fathers of his class, he is anxious that his children should make financially sound and socially acceptable marriages. Hence he needs to be assured that their suitors are well off and come from families similar to his own. This is the reason for the repeated interest by the characters of this play in names and parentage. Lucentio declares himself to be the son of 'Vincentio, come of the Bentivolii', 'a merchant of great traffic through the world'. Petruchio, introducing himself to his prospective father-in-law, identifies himself as 'Antonio's son, / A man well known throughout all Italy', and the sole heir to his father's estate. Again the disguised Tranio assumes that he will not be allowed to woo Bianca until he has supplied her father with 'knowledge of his parentage'. It is within this socially and financially exclusive world that Tranio is comically exposed as 'the son of a sailmaker in Bergamo'.

The rich fathers who appear in the background of this play take care to educate their children in a manner appropriate to their station in life. Lucentio arrives in Padua (an ancient and distinguished university town in Shakespeare's time) in order to educate himself in rhetoric, logic and the ethical works of Aristotle, the foundation of the renaissance university curriculum, and Baptista gladly admits to his house the tutors who will instruct his daughters in music and Latin poetry. It is by means of such realistic details that Shakespeare gives life and body to a series of conventional – indeed improbable – situations.

He also creates domestic biographies for Bianca's suitors. Old Gremio speaks of his 'house within the city', which suggests that he, too, is a merchant, and, indeed, he is called Baptista's 'neighbour'. This splendid mansion is

> richly furnished with plate and gold,
> Basins and ewers to lave her dainty hands;
> My hangings all of Tyrian tapestry;
> In ivory coffers I have stuff'd my crowns;
> In cypress chests my arras counterpoints,
> Costly apparel, tents and canopies,
> Fine linen, Turkey cushions, boss'd with pearl,
> Valence of Venice gold in needlework;
> Pewter and brass, and all things that belongs
> To house or housekeeping.

In strong contrast, Christopher Sly, the itinerant tinker of the Prologue, for all his boasts to be descended from the supporters of 'Richard Conqueror', has apparently no home and no clothing other than the doublet, stockings and worn-out shoes he stands up in.

Whereas Gremio's is a city establishment within the walls of Padua, Petruchio's is apparently a country estate which has to be reached on horse-back along muddy roads. Shakespeare creates an even more lifelike and convincing impression of his house but by different means, through the conversation between his servants shortly before the master's homecoming with his bride. The dramatist knows intimately the wisecracking comradeship which exists among servants, their curiosity about their new mistress, and their eagerness to provide her with a decent, formal welcome. In the instructions of the chief servant, Grumio, to his inferiors Shakespeare offers us a sudden glimpse into an Elizabethan household and the relationships between its members:

Where's the cook? Is supper ready, the house trimm'd, rushes strew'd, cobwebs swept, the serving-men in their new fustian, their white stockings, and every officer his wedding garment on? Be the jacks fair within, the jills fair without, the carpets laid, and everything in order? ... Call forth Nathaniel, Joseph, Nicholas, Philip, Walter, Sugarsop, and the rest; let their heads be sleekly comb'd, their blue coats brush'd and their garters of an indifferent knit; let them curtsy with their left legs, and not presume to touch a hair of my master's horse-tail till they kiss their hands. Are they all ready?

As well as sketching in the physical details of the house, Shakespeare suggests that Petruchio commands a well-disciplined establishment, and should, therefore, have no trouble in controlling his wife.

The action of *The Taming of the Shrew* is therefore set in a carefully documented social context, that of the Elizabethan mercantile upper middle class. Its senior member, Baptista, sets about finding husbands for his daughters in the customary manner of his class and time. It was the usual practice of aristocratic or rich parents to arrange their children's marriages for them and, in so doing, they considered money was as important – usually more important – than any feelings the young couple might have for each other. Indeed, the prospective bride and groom sometimes did not meet until the financial arrangements had been made between the parents and formally set down in a legal contract. By more or less auctioning off his younger daughter to the highest bidder (Act II Scene i), Baptista is behaving no more callously towards her than would any father of his time and rank. On the contrary, like Juliet's father when he arranges her marriage to the County Paris, he displays what Shakespeare's contemporaries would have seen as a proper concern for his daughter's welfare, a desire for her to live in the state to which she has been accustomed. In fact, by insisting that Katherine's husband should first obtain 'that special thing . . . her love', he shows more consideration for her feelings than would the average Elizabethan parent. The bad marriage in this play is made by Lucentio who, romantically infatuated with Bianca, fails to realize that beneath her show of meekness she is a wilfully independent girl.

Petruchio, since his father is dead, has the freedom to arrange his own marriage and he, too, sets about it in the manner of his time. Initially he wants to marry in order to enrich his estate and, on hearing that a wealthy bride is available, introduces himself to her father, shows that he comes from a respectable family, assures him that his finances are in good shape, accepts the offer of a dowry and proposes that the contract should be drawn up forthwith:

> Let specialties be therefore drawn between us,
> That covenants may be kept on either hand.

It is only then that he asks to meet for the first time the woman he has agreed to marry. Petruchio is unorthodox not in his procedure but in the rapidity and singlemindedness with which he carries it out.

Shakespeare goes to considerable trouble, therefore, to create for this play a solid, vivid, detailed and consistent social setting and to make the minor characters behave according to the orthodoxies of their class. This is an impressive achievement in itself, but when we look at the unorthodox characters, Petruchio and Katherine, in the setting Shakespeare has provided for them, we can see how necessary that environment is for the play's comic and psychological effects.

Why Katherine is a shrew we are not told, but her shrewishness consists of rebelling violently against the conventions by which the rest of the household live. She challenges the authority of her father, secretly torments her younger sister, breaks a lute over her music tutor's head and reviles her prospective husband at first sight. The impropriety of her conduct is the more startling, and the funnier, because of the obvious propriety of the rest of the family and the consequent social embarrassment they undergo.

Moreover we can understand her defiance of the rules as an assertion of her independence, an unwillingnes to conform to the code of bourgeois materialism and respectability observed by the other characters, and a refusal to be sold in the marriage market as though she had no character of her own. As a result she has too much character. In rebelling against her background she shows herself, in her own way, to be as much a product of it as the apparently conventional Bianca.

She presents to Petruchio two connected problems. In order to transform her from a virago into a tolerable wife, he has to induce in her a respect for and obedience to the social conventions she has hitherto been accustomed to defy, and he must also win from her 'that special thing . . . her love' on which her father has insisted. He solves the first problem by flouting social decorum even more outrageously than his wife. On the day of his marriage he keeps her waiting outside the church, arrives for the ceremony dressed like a ragamuffin, swears in front of the parson, and,

> after many ceremonies done
> He calls for wine: 'A health!' quoth he, as if
> He had been aboard, carousing to his mates
> After a storm; quaff'd off the muscadel,
> And threw the sops all in the sexton's face, . . .
> This done, he took the bride about the neck,
> And kiss'd her lips with such a clamorous smack
> That at the parting all the church did echo.

Finally, as the guests assemble for the customary wedding feast, he carries the bride off and leaves them, astonished, to celebrate without the two principal guests. The immediate effect of his behaviour is to create acute social embarrassment, not only for Baptista, who is worried about his reputation with his neighbours ('What will be said? What mockery will it be?') but for Katherine herself, who bursts into tears. Petruchio is, as they say, 'more shrew than she', and by depriving his wife of the usual formalities of marriage, he arouses in her a desire for those very social proprieties she has hitherto defied. He begins to make her realize that the rituals that society observes – the wedding garments, the solemn liturgy, the gathering of friends and neighbours – are not necessarily meaningless conventions or displays of wealth, but forms through which the significance of marriage is expressed. He sees directly through the outward forms to the truths they are designed to express. For example, when Baptista begs him to dress more suitably, his retort is,

> To me she's married, not unto my clothes.

So far Petruchio has merely denied his wife the customs proper to marriage. Once he has snatched her from her family, however, his treatment becomes more radical: he deprives her of the sheer necessities – food, clothing and sleep – on which domestic life must be based. *The Taming of the Shrew* is a play which in performance requires a great many solid household objects – boots, a basin of water, dishes of food, a hat and a lady's gown. In themselves they are not important but, for Katherine, they are made to become important because she needs them, and her husband not only denies her the use of them but flings them away. His treatment of them comes to seem like a kind of sacrilege. The woman who had shown her hostility to convention, and had broken that domestic object a lute over her teacher's head, now comes to recognize their real value. By undergoing a course of social education in Petruchio's 'taming school' she learns the value of good housekeeping.

Petruchio solves his other problem, the winning of her love, by treating her throughout her ordeal as though she were lovable:

> Say that she rail; why, then I'll tell her plain
> She sings as sweetly as a nightingale.
> Say that she frown; I'll say she looks as clear
> As morning roses newly wash'd with dew.
> Say she be mute, and will not speak a word;
> Then I'll commend her volubility,
> And say she uttereth piercing eloquence.

He starves her of food and sleep while assuring her that it is done 'in reverend care of her' and, as a result, she is not so much browbeaten forcibly into submission (and it was not uncommon for women of Katherine's temperament to be thrashed by their husbands) as induced psychologically to respect and need him. She comes to depend on him partly for the images of herself he reflects back at her. 'The mind sees not itself,' says Brutus in *Julius Caesar*, 'But by reflection, by some other things.' The reflection of herself which Katherine sees in Petruchio is a very attractive one. Of course she also finds herself dependent on him for her material needs and learns that, if she is to lead a tolerable life, she must subordinate her will to his. This is a belief with which few twentieth-century audiences would agree and, for this reason, *The Taming of the Shrew* may well appear a repellently chauvinistic play. But it was a belief held by the vast majority of Shakespeare's own audience, especially those of the bourgeois, merchant class in the portrayal of which he took such care. He includes in the play their assumptions as well as their way of life. How far he himself agreed with them we cannot know; as always, he remains true to his characters, which is not necessarily the same as being true to his own beliefs.

The comedy ends with an injunction by Katherine to all wives to obey their husbands, and her words recall those of St Paul's Epistle to the Ephesians:

Wives, submit yourselves unto your own husbands, as unto the Lord. For the husband is the head of the wife, even as Christ is the head of the church; and he is the saviour of the body. Therefore as the church is subject unto Christ, so let the wives be to their own husbands in every thing.

Her concluding homily is at the same time a celebration of the domestic security of the family which she sees as dependent on the subordination of wife to husband:

> Thy husband is thy lord, thy life, thy keeper,
> Thy head, thy sovereign; one that cares for thee,
> And for thy maintenance commits his body
> To painful labour both by sea and land,
> To watch the night in storms, the day in cold,
> Whilst thou liest warm at home, secure and safe.

Even in the composition of this closing speech Shakespeare remained true to the attitudes of his age, for there was, in the England of his time, an increasing respect for the institution of marriage, partly under the influence of Puritanism. As Lawrence Stone has pointed out in *The Family, Sex and Marriage in England 1500–1800* (a book on which much of this Introduction is based), 'the sanctification of marriage – "holy matrimony" – was a constant theme of Protestant sermons of the sixteenth century, which were directed to all classes in society, and is to be found in both Puritan and Anglican theology of the early seventeenth century.' He also notes that a new motive for marriage was introduced into the Prayer Book of 1549. It was defended not only for 'the avoidance of fornication, and the procreation of legitimate children', but for the 'mutual society, help and comfort that the one ought to have of the other, both in prosperity and in adversity'. We shall misunderstand this play if we assume that Shakespeare is always 'our contemporary'.

# THE TWO GENTLEMEN OF VERONA

*The Two Gentlemen of Verona* was Shakespeare's first romantic comedy and to that extent pointed in the direction he was to follow when, later, he composed *Much Ado About Nothing*, *As You Like It* and *Twelfth Night*. It is a 'romantic' comedy not only in the sense that it deals almost exclusively with the pains and pleasures of love, but because it is a dramatization of one of those prose works known as 'romances' of which the Elizabethans were extremely fond and which provided them with light, imaginative and gently instructive reading. The forefather of all the romances was the *Æthiopica* composed by the third-century Greek writer Heliodorus. This was circulated widely in manuscript, then in many printed editions, and was translated into all the major European languages. Under its influence, a very large number of romances were composed in renaissance Europe, including several which provided Shakespeare with the plots of his comedies, such as *Rosalynde* by Thomas Lodge, the source of *As You Like It*, *Pandosto* by Robert Greene, the source of *The Winter's Tale*, and the *Diana Enamorada* by the Portuguese writer Montemayor, from a version of which Shakespeare took the outlines of the plot of *The Two Gentlemen of Verona*.

Although the romance is a very flexible, infinitely expandable form, capable of accommodating every kind of material, all romances have some features in common. They are palpably works of fiction, abounding in unlikely coincidences and unrealistic conventions such as the disguise of women as men (and sometimes men as women) and consequently mistakes of identity. The action always takes place in no real geographical location but propels the characters into unfamiliar territory as, in this play, Julia makes her solitary pilgrimage from Verona to Milan and Valentine, wandering in a strange forest, is chosen as their captain by a band of outlaws. The romances are usually made up of several interwoven plots, each of which tends to break off at a point of suspense to be interrupted by a second plot which itself reaches a moment of crisis when it is broken by a third. Thus, in *The Two Gentlemen*, our attention is shifted between the affairs of Proteus at home and those of Valentine at the Emperor's court, and at the point when the latter is elected by the outlaws as their leader, we are brought back to the city to hear the serenade arranged by Proteus for Silvia. At the lowest level, the intertwining of different kinds of plot offers the reader the refreshment of variety and the mild excitement of suspense, and on a more sophisticated level it gives the author the opportunity to create parallels between plots and to set up contrasts, as when Proteus's infatuation with Julia is quickly followed by Valentine's for Silvia, or when Launce, the servant, reveals his love for a toothless dairymaid. The prose romances provided their readers with absorbing entertainment and, by the age of Elizabeth, with elaborate displays of literary artifice, richly ingenious metaphors, puns, quibbles and word-play which are also a feature of Shakespeare's comedies, including this one.

*The Two Gentlemen* contains several geographical inconsistencies. Valentine and Proteus both set off from Verona to Milan by sea whereas Julia visualizes making the journey by land. The Duke of Milan (who is also referred to as 'the Emperor') describes himself as living in Verona and, on his arrival in Milan, Launce is greeted by his friend Speed with the words, 'Welcome to Padua'. Such inconsistencies, probably the result of Shakespeare's oversight, can actually help the audience to feel that they are in no place which can be located on a map but in a purely fictional country where no pressing political or domestic tasks trouble the characters, who are thereby left free to devote themselves to the over-riding business of all romances, the processes of falling in and out of love, and the embarrassments, confusions and dilemmas which love then creates. Sexual infatuation not only pushes forward the plot of *The Two Gentlemen* and occupies the minds of all the characters – so that even the Duke claims to have his eye on a lady – but is also the subject of practially all the dialogue. Love in this play is, variously, 'a grievous labour', 'a canker', 'a testy babe', 'an uncertain glory', 'a chameleon', 'a mighty lord', 'the soul's food', 'a figure trenched in ice', and 'a blinded god', depending on who happens to be possessed by it and whether or not his feelings are reciprocated. The subject of the play is the various forms in which love reveals itself, such as friendship, loyalty, enslavement, infatuation, devotion, idealism, frustration and lust, and Shakespeare found in the conventions of romance, with its multiple narratives, its parallels and contrasts of plot and character, a form which was expansive enough to accommodate all these things.

In comparison with the characters of his later plays, the four main protagonists are not created with much depth or subtlety but they are the kind of people likely to be seized and perplexed by the changeable, violent emotions which are the dramatist's concern. It is important to realize that both Proteus and Valentine are young and at a stage in their emotional and biological development which much interested Shakespeare, particularly at this point in his professional career. Having hitherto found love and intimacy with each other – with members of their own sex – each experiences for the first time the sudden shock of infatuation with a member of the opposite sex. In this they are like the young Romeo who, when we first see him, has just separated himself off from the gang of youths of his own age – Mercutio, Benvolio and the rest – and turned his affections towards the unattainable Rosaline; or like Claudio in *Much Ado About Nothing*, who before the play opens has, as a soldier, known only the comradeship of his fellow-officers, but on his return from the front, falls instantly in love with Hero; or like the poet of the *Sonnets*, who is first enslaved by his adoration of a young man and later entangled by the charms of a dark lady. Proteus and Valentine are thus uncertain where their true loyalties lie, to each other or to their girlfriends, because each is caught in the process of changing from his adolescent into his mature self. To make matters more worrying, their affections seem to change as unpredictably as they do themselves, and hence Valentine, hitherto immune to sexual attraction, becomes possessed by love for Silvia, and Proteus, formerly the devoted servant of Julia, becomes dazzled by Silvia from the moment he sees her:

> Even as one heat another heat expels,
> Or as one nail by strength drives out another,
> So the remembrance of my former love
> Is by a newer object quite forgotten . . .
> She is fair; and so is Julia that I love –
> That I did love, for now my love is thaw'd;
> Which like a waxen image 'gainst a fire
> Bears no impression of the thing it was.

Proteus and Valentine, like the young men in *A Midsummer Night's Dream*, are unable to account for their sudden unforeseen changes of affection. Although they are not fully realized characters, they do behave consistently with their age, and also with their sex: it is the men who are giddy and undependable; the women, having matured earlier, remain steadily faithful to their first loves throughout. First and foremost the play portrays the attempts of two young men to discover who they are, attempts made more difficult by the fact that they are emotionally unstable. Valentine, who originally scoffs at the love-lorn Proteus, no sooner arrives in Milan than he finds himself infatuated. He has become a different kind of person, 'metamorphosed with a mistress', as his servant Speed describes him, 'that, when I look on you, I can hardly think you my master'. Valentine himself describes his transformation more eloquently:

> Ay, Proteus, but that life is alter'd now;
> I have done penance for contemning Love,
> Whose high imperious thoughts have punish'd me
> With bitter fasts, with penitential groans,

> With nightly tears, and daily heart-sore sighs;
> For in revenge of my contempt of love,
> Love hath chas'd sleep from my enthralled eyes
> And made them watchers of mine own heart's sorrow.
> O gentle Proteus, Love's a mighty lord,
> And hath so humbled me as I confess
> There is no woe to his correction,
> Nor to his service no such joy on earth.

They may not know who they are, but they do know that the strange feelings which possess them admit of no resistance.

*The Two Gentlemen of Verona* is a romance and it is also a debate – or, rather, a series of debates, on travel and education, on loyalty to friends and parents, but mostly, again, on the absorbing and paradoxical sensations of love. The first debate occurs at the very opening of the play, in which Valentine argues for the benefits of foreign travel and Proteus for the necessity of remaining at home with his mistress, and, like typical debaters, each supports his case by quoting written authorities. According to Proteus, to be in love is a sign of a refined sensibility:

> Yet writers say, as in the sweetest bud
> The eating canker dwells, so eating love
> Inhabits in the finest wits of all.

According to Valentine, on the other hand, love is a sign of premature decay:

> And writers say, as the most forward bud
> Is eaten by the canker ere it blow,
> Even so by love the young and tender wit
> Is turn'd to folly, blasting in the bud,
> Losing his verdure even in the prime,
> And all the fair effects of future hopes.

In the little soliloquy with which Proteus ends the discussion, he neatly defines their opposing points of view:

> He after honour hunts, I after love;
> He leaves his friends to dignify them more:
> I leave myself, my friends, and all for love.

As with most of the debates in this very argumentative play, their differences are not resolved, probably because Shakespeare recognized that love could be at the same time ennobling and degrading, depending on whether you happened to be in love or not. Each of the young men, the one eager for fresh experiences, the other captivated by present ones, sticks to his point of view as they take their leave. Speed, who appears at the end of the same scene, also has his point of view: he is interested not in love but in money.

The conversation between Julia and her maid Lucetta in the next scene (Act I Scene ii) also takes the form of a debate, this time on the merits of Proteus, in which Lucetta defends him and Julia, hiding her real feelings, argues against him:

> Julia   And wouldst thou have me cast my love on him?
> Luc.   Ay, if you thought your love not cast away.
> Julia   Why, he, of all the rest, hath never mov'd me.
> Luc.   Yet he, of all the rest, I think, best loves ye.
> Julia   His little speaking shows his love but small.
> Luc.   Fire that's closest kept burns most of all.
> Julia   They do not love that do not show their love.
> Luc.   O, they love least that let men know their love.

This is a kind of formal argument, made more apparent by the way in which one line chimes in with another, but the motives which lie behind it are not unsubtle: whereas the waiting maid speaks up for Proteus in order to induce her mistress to a confession of love, the mistress pretends to despise him in order to conceal her real feelings. The truth is that Julia is in some confusion, unable to resist her love for Proteus, yet anxious to keep up the appearance of self-control proper to a young lady. Hence she tears up Proteus's letter while Lucetta is with her, but pieces it together again when she is left alone. She expresses these conflicting impulses in a soliloquy which is really a little debate with herself:

> Fie, fie, how wayward is this foolish love,
> That like a testy babe will scratch the nurse,
> And presently, all humbled, kiss the rod!
> How churlishly I chid Lucetta hence,
> When willingly I would have had her here!
> How angerly I taught my brow to frown,
> When inward joy enforc'd my heart to smile!

Like Proteus and Valentine later in the play, Julia finds herself caught between two equally demanding claims or obligations, those of love and modesty, and she is unable to shake off either of them. She manages to get the best of both worlds by allowing her maid to pick the letter up for her. Proteus, in the following scene, is in an almost identical situation, trying to conceal Silvia's letter from his father. Both are going through the struggles and embarrassments of growing up, trying to work out their relationships with other people and themselves.

The really big inward debates take place, however, in the mind of Proteus, whose already divided character becomes enmeshed in further emotional complications. Having been forced by his father to abandon Julia and join Valentine in Milan, he not only finds that his friend is now head over heels in love, but, himself, becomes infatuated with Sylvia, the mistress of his closest companion. Like Julia earlier in the play, Proteus finds himself on the horns of a dilemma, divided between his vows to Julia and his loyalty to Valentine on the one hand, and his passion for Silvia on the other. He obviously cannot remain faithful to all three of them and whatever he decides must inevitably amount to a betrayal. The nature of his quandary could not be more precisely stated:

> To leave my Julia, shall I be forsworn;
> To love fair Silvia, shall I be forsworn;
> To wrong my friend I shall be much forsworn;
> And ev'n that pow'r which gave me first my oath
> Provokes me to this threefold perjury:
> Love bade me swear, and Love bids me forswear,
> O sweet-suggesting Love, if thou hast sinn'd,
> Teach me, thy tempted subject, to excuse it!
> At first I did adore a twinkling star,
> But now I worship a celestial sun . . .
> I cannot leave to love, and yet I do;
> But there I leave to love where I should love.
> Julia I lose, and Valentine I lose;
> If I keep them, I needs must lose myself;
> If I lose them, thus find I by their loss:
> For Valentine, myself; for Julia, Silvia.

The speech is composed of paradoxes and contradictions because Proteus finds that he is, himself, paradoxical, caught between contradictions, urged on by impulses which he both embraces and despises. Like Valentine, he is a changed man, but unlike Valentine he is torn between the pledges made by his former self and the desires his present self is unable to resist. The one idea to which Shakespeare keeps returning in this play is the essentially divided nature of these young men, caught between their loves and loyalties to other people and themselves. It has been pointed out that the play tends to fall into passages of duologue, soliloquies and asides and therefore does not have the variety and expansiveness of Shakespeare's later work. Once its basic form has been perceived, however, the reason behind this simple construction becomes clear. It consists of a series of discussions between opposing points of view or between opposing elements within a single character.

This kind of conflict reaches its greatest complexity in the episode in which the serenade is sung outside Silvia's window. Before the lady herself appears, four characters are present: Thurio, Proteus, the disguised Julia and the Host. Each of them interprets the performance in a different way. Thurio believes that the music has been arranged in order that Silvia may be induced to look favourably on him; Proteus, on the other hand, knows that he is using the serenade to win Silvia for himself; Julia, disguised as a boy, is desolated by her lover's unfaithfulness, and the Host, who has no personal interest at all in the affair, just listens to the music and then falls fast asleep. Each character is living within his own subjective world, and this becomes clear when Julia and the Host converse with each other:

> Host  How do you, man? The music likes you not.
> Julia  You mistake; the musician likes me not.
> Host  Why, my pretty youth?
> Julia  He plays false, father.
> Host  How, out of tune on the strings?
> Julia  Not so; but yet so false that he grieves my very heart-strings.

The threads can be unravelled only when all the characters know the truth and all the conflicting points of view have become reconciled.

The two servants, Launce and Speed, provide earthy comic relief, but Launce, the more fully developed of the two, finds himself placed in situations comparable to those of his superiors. As soon as we have seen Proteus take his leave of Julia, we are given Launce's account of the parting between his parents and himself with his dog, Crab. The two episodes have a number of details in common so that the latter serves as a kind of parody of the former. In the first of these episodes Julia is practically silent, expressing the speechlessness of true devotion, whereas Proteus is extravagantly eloquent:

> Here is my hand for my true constancy;
> And when that hour o'erslips me in the day
> Wherein I sigh not, Julia, for thy sake,
> The next ensuing hour some foul mischance
> Torment me for my love's forgetfulness!
> My father stays my coming; answer not;
> The tide is now - nay not thy tide of tears:
> That tide will stay me longer than I should.

Launce and Crab, too, have just come from a leavetaking but, although Launce's whole family have given way without inhibition to their grief, the dog naturally has, like Julia, remained silent:

My mother weeping, my father wailing, my sister crying, our maid howling, our cat wringing her hands, and all our house in a great perplexity: yet did not this cruel-hearted cur shed one tear. He is a stone, a very pebble stone, and has no more pity in him than a dog.

The moment of parting which, in the previous episode, had been full of pathos, now appears simply ridiculous and the speechlessness which, in Julia, was evidence of devotion, in Crab is a sign of heartlessness. Both dog and master, each in his different way, provide a comic contrast to the young lovers. Launce's exaggerated displays of emotion are absurd counterparts to the heightened, all-consuming passions which possess the young gentlefolk, and Crab's silent acceptance of all situations makes the eloquence of the human characters seem exaggerated. The dog's lack of concern for other people (it is he who makes water against a gentlewoman's farthingale) is a necessarily silent but none the less pointed criticism of the tendency of all the other characters to become entangled in one another. Crab's self-love, as Launce interprets it, adds another colour to the spectrum of love which Shakespeare creates in the play as a whole. Even he has his unique point of view.

The tension between conflicting attitudes becomes most acute, as we might expect, in the final scene, the moment which has provoked the strongest protests from Shakespeare's critics. By now Shakespeare has written himself into a situation which admits of no really satisfactory outcome. Valentine, in his banishment, has been forcibly separated from Silvia; Silvia has taken flight, pursued by the loathsome Proteus; Julia, devotedly following him, witnesses her lover's attempt to commit a rape on Silvia and, when Valentine intervenes, the characters begin to see the true state of things for the first time. At last perceiving his friend's treachery, Valentine is immediately thrust into an impossible dilemma of a kind which, by now, has become typical of the play. He is divided between his love for Silvia which requires that he should avenge himself on Proteus and his friendship for Proteus which demands that he should refrain. Like his friend, at an earlier point in the play, he is forced to choose between the claims of love and those of friendship. Unlike Proteus, however, he decides in favour of friendship, but only when the former has shown his contrition:

> Then I am paid;
> And once again I do receive thee honest.
> Who by repentance is not satisfied
> Is nor of heaven nor of earth, for these are pleas'd;
> By penitence th' Eternal's wrath's appeas'd.

His reference to Christian doctrine ('forgive us our trespasses as we should forgive them that tresspass against us') suggests that Shakespeare intends us to take his decision seriously, and, though he is nobly denying himself the woman he adores, we might be able to approve his choice were it not that he goes on to demonstrate his loyalty by spontaneously handing Silvia over to his rival:

> And, that my love may appear plain and free,
> All that was mine in Silvia I give thee.

Such unhesitating altruism is consistent with what we have seen of Valentine. He has, throughout, been the trusting innocent, remaining loyal to one woman, unaware of the treachery practised on him by his friend. But such high-mindedness, hard to accept even from a simple idealist like Valentine, shows no concern either for poor Silvia, who finds herself thrown into the arms of a man she despises, or (did he only know it) for Julia, who sees the man she loves handed over to another woman. 'There are by this time,' as Quiller-Couch tartly commented, 'no gentlemen in Verona.' In resolving one problem, Valentine has created two others and it is a situation which, in real life, would be intolerable. Fortunately, however, we are not in real life but in an imaginary forest outside a non-existent Milan or Padua or Verona, and in this romance setting Julia performs the conventional romance gesture: she reveals her true identity, instantly regains her lover's affection and releases Silvia (who, understandably, says not a word throughout these proceedings) to rejoin Valentine. Shakespeare has solved his impossible problem but at the expense of credibility. It is the kind of satisfactory ending which makes us realize the improbability of such resolutions in the world we actually live in.

The Two Gentlement of Verona shows Shakespeare making experiments with situations he was to develop more subtly later in his career. The disguised Julia is the prototype of the disguised Portia, Rosalind and Viola; the friendship of the young men is a sketch for the similar relationship between Antonio and Bassanio; the shifts of affection were to develop into the more complicated cross-wooings of A Midsummer Night's Dream; the move from the court to the country, already a feature of the prose romances well before this play was written, reappears in The Dream, As You Like It, Cymbeline, The Winter's Tale and even in King Lear; the use of the comic sub-plot to parallel and cast light on the main plot becomes a feature of all Shakespeare's comedies which, like this one, display the delights and absurdities of love in all its manifestations. It is because these features were later developed in dramatically more accomplished plays that The Two Gentlemen has been neglected or regarded condescendingly by both critics and theatre audiences. Yet the sketchbook of a great artist is of interest not simply as a series of trials for more major works. It has its own inherent value. Shakespeare plots the developing complexities of his narrative with great skill; the verse, often scarcely distinguishable from that of a dozen Elizabethan love poets, can take on an astonishing lyrical intensity and, in spite of the conventional mode in which the play was conceived, it does deal, at the same time ironically and with sympathy, with a perennial experience, the search of necessarily unstable individuals for some lasting, stable identity.

# Love's Labour's Lost

Shakespeare arranged the characters of *Love's Labour's Lost* in a very orderly, symmetrical way. The King and his three courtiers are balanced by the Princess and her three gentlewomen; the aristocrats at the top of the social scale are balanced by the professional men in the middle – the parson, the schoolmaster and the Spanish tutor – and they in turn are paralleled by the rustics, Costard and Jaquenetta, and Constable Dull, who stand at the bottom. Together they form a small, self-sufficient community. This pattern of contrasts and parallels also extends to the arrangement of the various plots. As each lord falls in love with a lady, so Armado becomes infatuated by Jaquenetta; as Berowne's love-letter is delivered to the wrong recipient, so is Armado's; as the aristocrats display their skill in punning and word-play, so does the schoolmaster; and as the Masque of Muscovites is ridiculed by the ladies, so the Pageant of the Nine Worthies is ruined by the lords. The men's vow to withdraw from the world in the first scene is contrasted with their promise to enter it in the last, and the play ends with two songs, one in praise of spring and the other in praise of winter. The contrasts can even be seen in the location of the play: on one side stands the court to which the men have resolved to confine themselves, and on the other the world of politics from which the Princess has come as an ambassador; the action takes place in the territory between them as the men are persuaded to relinquish the contemplative for the active life on which they embark at the play's conclusion.

The careful symmetry with which Shakespeare organized his material is one source of its pleasure. We find satisfaction in the order which the dramatist imposes on the naturally formless, loose-ended material of life. It also allows him to set up opposing and conflicting ideas and points of view so that the dialogue between characters frequently resolves itself into a series of arguments or debates. In the first scene the King and Berowne argue about the virtues and limitations of the reclusive, scholarly life; the parson takes pride in his poem about the deer-hunt which is stubbornly criticized by the constable, and Berowne's sonnet in praise of Rosaline is soundly attacked by the schoolmaster. Berowne's two soliloquies are really debates within himself about the joys and absurdities of love. Much of the play, like the earlier comedy, *The Two Gentlemen of Verona*, and the later one, *As You Like It*, is made up of disputations on subjects of topical interest, an art in which Shakespeare had been trained as a schoolboy at Stratford.

The topic about which the characters argue most frequently, however, is language and rhetoric, the use and abuse of words. To understand why, in about 1593, Shakespeare wrote a play on the subject of language, we need to know something about the attitudes towards it held by his contemporaries, for it was a subject in which many of them were extremely interested. The period into which Shakespeare was born was one of rapidly expanding knowledge, not only of foreign literatures but of science, theology and, as a result of the voyages undertaken by renaissance seamen, the life and customs of other peoples. This increasing knowledge required a growing vocabulary in which it could be discussed and recorded, and the authors of the mid-sixteenth century often found themselves, literally, at a loss for words. One early Elizabethan complained that there were 'more things than there are words to express things by'. It was above all the translators who felt themselves frustrated by the limitations of the English language; they often found that no English equivalents existed for the foreign words they were struggling to translate and they became sharply aware of the dismal contrast between the subtlety and expressiveness of foreign works and the rough simplicity of their own versions of them. For this reason, the men of letters – poets, scholars, philosophers and translators – deliberately embarked on a programme of linguistic expansion. They set out to enrich their language. They revived words which had fallen out of use, adapted others from foreign languages, invented words where none could be found to serve their needs, formed new verbs from old nouns, new adjectives out of old verbs and created compound words by joining two or more existing ones together, as in Berowne's memorable expression, 'a world-without-end bargain'. It is partly because the writers of the middle and late sixteenth century created this extraordinary language explosion that it became one of the greatest periods in our literature. The poets Spenser, Sidney and Donne, the prose writers Nashe, Greene and Dekker, and the playwrights Lyly, Marlowe and Shakespeare, were able to write expressively because they had a language in which they could do so.

They were also excited by the sensation of actually using this new language, by the discovery of how gratifyingly expressive it could be. It was an achievement comparable to the discovery, a century earlier, of the art of perspective in painting, and we can sense this excitement in the early plays of Shakespeare (himself a prolific inventor of words) such as *A Midsummer Night's Dream*, *Romeo and Juliet* and especially *Love's Labour's Lost*, where his own linguistic enthusiasm is transferred to his characters:

His humour is lofty, his discourse peremptory, his tongue filed, his eye ambitious, his gait majestical, and his general behaviour vain, ridiculous and thrasonical. He is too picked, too spruce, too affected, too odd, as it were too peregrinate, as I may call it ... He draweth out the thread of his verbosity finer than the staple of his argument. I abhor such fanatical phantasimes, such insociable and point-devise companions, such rackers of orthography.

These are the words of Holofernes, the schoolmaster, and, as befits a man of his profession, they are predominantly Latin in origin. But he is by no means the only character who is intoxicated by the power of language. Costard, the labourer, prefers to say 'remuneration' instead of 'three farthings', Don Armado, the Spaniard, refers to the afternoon as 'the posteriors of the day', Moth, the page, swaps Latin phrases with his master and both the lords and the ladies constantly make puns on one another's words. Moreover they do not simply carry out experiments with language but also discuss its use. Language itself is one of the topics they talk about. The parson praises the schoolmaster for being 'sharp and sententious; pleasant without scurrility, witty without affectation, audacious without impudency, learned without opinion and strange without heresy', a speech which itself reveals the character's relish for words. Again, the schoolmaster criticizes Don Armado for what he believes to be his affected pronunciation and finds fault with the love-poem written by Berowne; the Princess objects to Boyet's excessive praise of her beauty and, in his declaration of love to Rosaline, Berowne promises to give up the use of 'taffeta phrases, silken terms precise'. The only character who is immune to this linguistic fever is Constable Dull, who says little and understands less.

Love's Labour's Lost is thus, in part, a play about the Elizabethan enthusiasm for language. It also contains several debates about its use and function. The purpose of words is, basically and obviously, to act as a means of communication between people. This is a fact which we now take for granted. But some of Shakespeare's contemporaries, such as Thomas Wilson, the author of a textbook on language, The Art of Rhetoric, pointed out emphatically the benefits which mankind had gained from it. For him the capacity to use language was something which distinguished civilized people from mere animals or inarticulate savages, and which had enabled them to form societies, establish law and government, engage in education and trade and thereby improve their condition generally. The renaissance improvers of language were, likewise, motivated by the desire to improve communication, not simply of elementary facts but of complex feelings, psychological conflict, subtleties of perception, the material out of which literature is made. The excitement created by the rapid development of the English language, however, encouraged some authors to use novel, eccentric words not in order to communicate but to display their own inventiveness and virtuosity. Complex language can be a means of communication but it can also be a barrier to it, depending on the motives of the speaker and the receptiveness of the listener.

In *Love's Labour's Lost* it is largely the women who criticize the men for the ostentatiousness of their words, as when the Princess reprimands her counsellor Boyet for flattering her:

> Good Lord Boyet, my beauty, though but mean,
> Needs not the painted flourish of your praise.
> Beauty is bought by judgement of the eye,
> Not utter'd by base sale of chapmen's tongues;
> I am less proud to hear you tell my worth
> Than you much willing to be counted wise
> In spending of your wit in the praise of mine.

Later in the same scene (Act II Scene i), the ladies describe each of the four men in turn, mentioning in particular Berowne's ability to jest in 'apt and gracious words', an indulgence of which they disapprove and of which they subsequently resolve to cure him. In the scenes involving the schoolmaster and his friends, it is the former who shows the most ingenious talent with words, especially in the 'extemporal epitaph' he composes on the death of the deer:

> The preyful Princess pierc'd and prick'd
>     a pretty pleasing pricket.
> Some say a sore; but not a sore
>     till now made sore by shooting.
> The dogs did yell; put el to sore,
>     then sorel jumps from thicket –
> Or pricket sore, or else sorel;
>     the people fall a-hooting.

A 'pricket', incidentally, is a two-year-old deer, a 'sore' is a four-year-old, and a 'sorel' a three-year-old – it's that kind of play. The parson, Sir Nathaniel, is moved to admiration at his colleague's brilliance but the constable listens in silent incomprehension. For all his talents, Holofernes has said little more than Dull has stated in a simple sentence: that the Princess has killed a pricket. Constable Dull's silence is an eloquent contribution to the debate.

A contrast between the ostentatious and the plain style is continually being made in this play. In the final speech we are told that the words of Mercury, the messenger, are harsher than the songs of Apollo, the god of music and poetry, and we may wonder which of these two opposing positions Shakespeare himself adopted. As always he does not speak directly to us and no single character conveys the author's own point of view. If we want to discover his opinion we have to look at the play as a whole, from which it appears that he appreciated both the delights and the dangers of language and rhetoric. The ingenuity with which the noblemen, the schoolmaster and the Spaniard use words is shown to be exciting in itself and satisfying for the characters who are capable of it, but it is also shown to impede rather than assist communication. The poems which the lords address to the ladies fail to achieve their purpose, which is to convince the latter of their love. The play is not, however, an argument in favour of plain speaking. If it were, then Shakespeare would want everyone to talk like Constable Dull. Moreover, *Love's Labour's Lost* is itself created out of 'taffeta phrases, silken terms precise', and these are a principal source of its delight. For Shakespeare, language is at the same time an asset and a liability.

The debate about language is, however, only one of several arguments out of which this comedy is constructed. It actually starts with a discussion about the relative merits of the contemplative as opposed to the active life, a topic about which philosophers had argued since Roman times and which was familiar to at least some members of Shakespeare's audience. In the first speech of the play, the King reveals that he has established a community in which he and his companions will eat and sleep sparingly and shun all association with women in order to devote themselves to the cultivation of their minds, and he exhorts them to 'war against their own affections' in order that they may achieve fame for their learning in time to come. The opposite point of view is expressed by Berowne, who declares that book-learning is merely a cumbersome method of discovering what is obvious to common sense: you don't need to be an astronomer to appreciate the beauty of the stars. This discussion, like all the debates in the play, comes to no conclusion, for the men quickly discover that, whatever the merits and deficiencies of their proposed academy, they will have no chance to establish it, for the Princess of France is about to arrive on a diplomatic mission and, in receiving her and her retinue, they must necessarily break their oath of abstinence. As Berowne says, 'Necessity must make us all forsworn.' Hence they are compelled to make a choice. They can either keep the vows they have made and exclude the ladies from their company, or they can obey the rules of duty and hospitality and receive them, thereby breaking their oaths. To refuse them access would be discourteous, but to admit them would amount to perjury. As the Princess points out,

> 'Tis deadly sin to keep that oath, my lord,
> And sin to break it.

The debate is resolved in the sense that the men abandon their learned academy, but whether or not they are right to do so is another matter. Their predicament, as Shakespeare makes clear, is one in which no course of action would be wholly right. Shakespeare's view of the contemplative life is similar to his view of language: it is both an asset and a liability. It may open up the world of learning but, at the same time, it shuts out the active world of human relationships.

This discussion is now replaced by a different one, for no sooner have the ladies arrived than the men fall in love with them, and the dialogue turns to a consideration of love. Each of the courtiers writes a poem in praise of his mistress and, if these verses were taken out of their context, they would look like typical examples of the love-poetry written at this time – indeed, two of them were reprinted shortly afterwards in popular anthologies. Yet, though each of the poems is well-intentioned and essentially serious, the effect they create is absurd. By mistake, Berowne's is handed not to Rosaline, as he intends, but to the parson, who recites it in stumbling embarrassment. The other three are read not in solitude, as their authors believe, but to Berowne who, unknown to them, is eavesdropping and is delighted to discover that his companions are as weak and susceptible as himself:

> O, what a scene of fool'ry have I seen,
> Of sighs, of groans, of sorrow, and of teen!
> O me, with what strict patience have I sat,
> To see a King transformed to a gnat!
> To see great Hercules whipping a gig,
> And profound Solomon to tune a jig,
> And Nestor play at push-pin with the boys,
> And critic Timon laugh at idle toys.

Since all four men are thus made to look ridiculous, it is tempting to conclude that Berowne expresses Shakespeare's own opinion, that they have disgraced themselves by brushing aside their former vows of celibacy and giving way to the most basic of all human impulses. But although, collectively, they have made fools of themselves, each one individually feels elated and, indeed, inspired, and within moments of delivering his attack on love, Berowne is praising it as the highest source of wisdom, superior even to the book-knowledge to which he and his companions had formerly dedicated themselves:

> Love, first learned in a lady's eyes,
> Lives not alone immured in the brain,
> But with the motion of all elements
> Courses as swift as thought in every power,
> And gives to every power a double power,
> Above their functions and their offices.

Within the same scene, love is shown to be both debasing and elevating, an enemy to learning and a source of the highest knowledge, a snare and a liberation. Shakespeare again writes both for the prosecution and the defence.

The more closely we look into this play, the more elaborate its system of oppositions and contrasts turns out to be. The idealism of the men is set off against the practicality of the women, the verbosity of the men of learning against the simple language of the rustics, Berowne's initial belief that love is degrading against his later affirmation that it is the highest kind of wisdom. The contrasts tend to be created by attributing different opinions to different groups of characters, but they are also created by the means of anti-climax, the distinctive dramatic effect of this play. Hence the King's plan for a school of learning collapses on the arrival of the women, Berowne's poem in praise of Rosaline is actually read by the parson, and the Masque of Muscovites designed by the noblemen for the entertainment of the guests is a failure when they try to perform it. In every case, actions which were seriously intended become the object of laughter or ridicule.

Nowhere is this effect so obvious as in the performance of the Pageant of the Nine Worthies, which Shakespeare allows us to observe both through the eyes of the inept amateur actors who put it on and of the arrogant young noblemen (still smarting from the failure of their own masque) who form its audience. To some extent the men are justified in making fun of it. Not only is it impossible for five actors to play nine parts, but it is far beyond the powers of these provincial amateurs to rise to the challenge of the roles they have undertaken. Moreover, the script does not exactly support them:

> I Pompey am, Pompey surnamed the Great,
> That oft in field, with targe and shield, did make my foe to sweat.
> And travelling along this coast, I here am come by chance,
> To lay my arms before the legs of this sweet lass of France.

Such liabilities, together with the nervousness of the actors, aggravated by the interruptions of the audience, ensure that the performance is a fiasco and deserves the ridicule it receives. On the other hand, inept though the performers may be, their motives are kindly and generous. The pageant is put on, at the King's request, as an expression of welcome, a means of 'congratulating' the Princess and her fellow-guests, and the unruly aristocrats well deserve the rebuke delivered to them by the schoolmaster: 'This is not generous, not gentle, not humble.' The noblemen see only the incompetence of the performers; they fail to appreciate the motives for which they perform. Like their own love-poems and the masque they themselves have performed, the Pageant of the Nine Worthies falls on deaf, or unappreciative, ears.

Time and again in this play, the characters fail to communicate with one another. The King and his companions fail to perceive the good will of the actors, the women regard the men's love-poems as elegant but empty compliments and not as genuine declarations of their feelings. As the Princess declares shortly before she leaves,

We have receiv'd your letters, full of love;
Your favours, the ambassadors of love;
And, in our maiden council, rated them
At courtship, pleasant jest, and courtesy,
As bombast and as lining to the time;
But more devout than this in our respects
Have we not been; and therefore met your loves
In their own fashion, like a merriment.

Berowne, however, corrects her: 'Our letters, madam, show'd much more than jest.' Words having once again proved fallible, the women therefore need more certain proof of the men's intentions and they ask that it should be given in deeds. The King is told to spend a year in solitude in some 'forlorn and naked hermitage', and Berowne to visit the 'speechless sick' and to apply his wit to 'enforce the pained impotent to smile'. If they can endure this penance as a proof of their devotion, the ladies will, at the end of the year, accept the men's love as genuine.

Unlike any other Shakespearean comedy, *Love's Labour's Lost* does not conclude with a marriage, but with the possibility of marriage, and we may feel inclined to think that Shakespeare supports the women in their demand that their suitors should leave the safe, enclosed world of the palace in order to expose themselves to the pains of the world outside. Yet the effect he creates is more ambiguous than that. No doubt in a year's time the men will be wiser for their experience, yet the little community of Navarre, for all its narrowness and self-satisfaction, is a high-spirited, intelligent, hopeful place and, with the departure of the leading characters, we realize that it has come to an end. Like every other event in this play, the conclusion shows both a gain and a loss.

# KING JOHN

No historian can ever manage to make a wholly accurate and complete record of past events. We only need to read a newspaper report of an event which we ourselves have witnessed to realize that one man's view of it can be radically different from another's. The historian, moreover, cannot attempt to record every single episode in the life of a country. He must select and his selection must depend not simply on the number and nature of the documents which have survived but on his assumptions as to which events are significant and which are merely trivial. He sees what he is looking for.

This truth is clearly illustrated by the case of King John. His reign had already been described by the chroniclers and had been the subject of at least two plays before Shakespeare embarked on his own version and, needless to say, it has been treated by countless historians since Shakespeare's play was written. John's reign, as we should expect, has been interpreted in a variety of conflicting ways. The King has been portrayed as a fearless, patriotic opponent of the catholic church and thus as a precursor of Henry VIII and Queen Elizabeth; as a corrupt heretic who defied the authority of the Pope and attempted to have his own brother, Richard the Lionheart, murdered; and as a ruler who, in signing Magna Carta, took the first step along the road from monarchical to parliamentary government.

It is the last of these three impressions which is now strongest in the popular imagination, influenced by historians like G. M. Trevelyan, who in his *History of England* declared that with the signing of Magna Carta, 'a process began which was to end in putting the power of the crown into the hands of community at large'. Historians like Trevelyan, enjoying the privilege of living in a democracy, fix on the granting of Magna Carta as the most significant occurrence of John's reign because it helps to account for the political circumstances in which they themselves are living, since a major function of history is to explain how we have come to be as we are. Shakespeare and his predecessors, however, did not see John's reign in this light at all. Magna Carta was of such slight interest to Shakespeare that he chose not even to mention it, nor is it alluded to in *The Troublesome Reign of King John*, an anonymous play printed in 1591, nor in an even earlier play, *King Iohan*, which was composed in the reign of Henry VIII by Bishop John Bale. Knowing nothing of democratic government, they saw no significance in it. Both these early playwrights were, however, living in a country ruled over by monarchs – Henry VIII and Queen Elizabeth – who had challenged the authority of the Pope and had, as a consequence, been excommunicated, and it was John's defiance of the catholic church that most interested them. Bale's King John, unlike Shakespeare's, is a heroic figure who seizes the wealth of the corrupt and degenerate abbeys in order to finance his wars in defence of the British territories in France; and for the author of *The Troublesome Reign*, the King was

> This noble John who, as a faithful Moses,
> Withstood proud Pharoah, for his poor Israel,
> Minding to bring it out of the land of darkness.

– that is, out of the darkness of papistry and into the sunshine of protestantism which radiated from Henry VIII. In the later of these two plays, we actually see the treachery of the catholic church at work when we are taken to Swinstead Abbey and shown an evil monk poisoning the King. Shakespeare's only allusion to this murderer is brief and tentative: 'The King, I fear, is poisoned by a monk.' For him, the significance of John's reign lay elsewhere.

At the time *King John* was written, England was again under the threat of invasion by a catholic monarch, Philip of Spain, and the parallel between him and John's adversary, Philip of France, could not have passed unnoticed by Shakespeare's audiences. It is probably these circumstances which account for the occasional passages of patriotic writing in this play, such as the Duke of Anjou's eulogy of England as

> that white-fac'd shore,
> Whose foot spurns back the ocean's roaring tides
> And coops from other lands her islanders
> ... that England, hedg'd in with the main,
> That water-walled bulwark, still secure
> And confident from foreign purposes.

Such sentiments are very like those expressed by John of Gaunt in *Richard II*, which was also composed during the Armada period. There is also a brief reference to John's pillaging of the monasteries when he instructs the Bastard to

> shake the bags
> Of hoarding abbots; imprisoned angels
> Set at liberty; the fat ribs of peace
> Must by the hungry now be fed upon.

Considering the timeliness of the subject, however, it is surprising how little dramatic capital Shakespeare makes out of John's exploitation of the church's wealth. Moreover the King, portrayed as headstrong and querulous by turns, could in no way have been designed to appear a forerunner of Queen Elizabeth. Such topical matters, as always, were of little interest to Shakespeare. What may have interested him was the political and human consequences which result when two rival candidates lay claim to the throne. This had been the major emphasis in *Henry VI Part III* in which the crown passes several times between Henry and Edward Duke of York, depending on whose armies happen to have won the latest victory. It had been a timely subject when, only a few years previously, Mary Queen of Scots had still been alive, a constant threat to the authority of Elizabeth, and a plot had been uncovered to murder the Queen and replace her with her catholic rival.

Such contemporary political issues, however, though they may help to explain why Shakespeare chose to dramatize this particular period of history, do little to account for his treatment of it. His emphasis is much more generally and universally human. What above all interests him is the effect of power politics on the individuals who find themselves caught up in it, both those in command such as John and the Bastard and, especially, its victims such as Arthur, Hubert and Constance. The most memorable episodes are of two contrasting kinds: formal, public, official scenes in which the politicians bargain with one another for supremacy, and intimate, private scenes in which vulnerable individuals suffer the consequences of political decisions for which they have no responsibility and over which they have no control. In this it is like *War and Peace*, the action of which shifts between the headquarters of the military leaders and the private homes of the Russian people. It is a play which, though seldom performed nowadays, can speak to our time.

The fullest example of the first kind of scene is in the third act (Act III Scene i) where, outside the walls of Angiers, John bargains with Philip for possession of the city and its occupants, and then Cardinal Pandulph bargains with both of them. The most memorable example of the second kind is the moving interchange between Hubert and Arthur in the prison, where Hubert attempts, with the greatest reluctance, to carry out his mission and put out the Prince's eyes. Each scene has its own distinctive kind of style, the one elaborate, tortuous, with a logic so refined that it seems scarcely logical, the other simple, spontaneous and deeply felt. The first scene is created by Shakespeare with a sardonic irony which is one of the play's distinctive achievements, the other with a directness which, in its context, is full of pathos. The political style is adopted by Pandulph when he attempts to persuade King Philip that his most commendable action would be to break the oath he has sworn to John:

What since thou swor'st is sworn against thyself
And may not be performed by thyself,
For that which thou hast sworn to do amiss
Is not amiss when it is truly done;
And being not done, where doing tends to ill,
The truth is then most done not doing it;
The better act of purposes mistook
Is to mistake again; though indirect,
Yet indirection thereby grows direct,
And falsehood falsehood cures.

The cardinal's subtlety and intelligence are obvious enough, but the very deviousness with which he recommends this course of action throws its morality into doubt. It is an argument, moreover, which is conducted on a purely abstract level and which therefore appears to have no relevance to the people whose lives may be affected by it. Human beings are, however, very deeply affected by the political manoeuvrings which occupy so much of this play and, when they find themselves enmeshed in the web of politics, they speak in a very different style:

Arthur    Must you with hot irons burn out both mine eyes?
Hubert    Young boy, I must.
Arthur                      And will you?
Hubert                      And I will.

This is, of course, not the only way in which the victims in this play react to crisis. Constance, deprived of the hope of her son's succession, goes distracted, and the Bastard, seeing the body of the dead Prince, is thrown into confusion.

Shakespeare's emphasis is thus not on the topical significance of John's reign but on the intimate effects on powerless people of political decisions. It is for this reason that, unlike the previous interpreters of this period, he places the most intensely private episode, the attempt by Hubert to put out Arthur's eyes, at the turning point of the play. It is this, and Arthur's subsequent death, which transforms the personalities and fortunes of the major characters and, indeed, alters the course of English history. It is Arthur and not John who is entitled by right of succession to be on the throne. In order to make Arthur's helplessness more apparent and pitiful, Shakespeare altered his age and portrayed him not as the enterprising young soldier of whom he had read in Holinshed's *Chronicles* but as a child, innocent of political strategy, the victim first of his mother's ambitions and then of John's. The centrality of the prison scene between Arthur and Hubert becomes apparent if we examine what happens before and after it.

Although a usurper who rules, as his mother says, 'by strong possession much more than his right', John at first acts with vigour and initiative.

Possessed of the throne of England, he defends it resolutely, defying the French ambassadors in full confidence that he can carry out his threats:

> Be thou as lightning in the eyes of France;
> For ere thou canst report I will be there,
> The thunder of my cannon shall be heard.
> So hence! Be thou the trumpet of our wrath
> And sullen presage of your own decay.

The energetic, imperative tone of these words suggests that John is in the ascendant and this impression is confirmed when Chatillon, the ambassador, announces to King Philip the swift arrival of John before the walls of Angiers. This is an exhilarating speech and it leads up to John's entrance, riding on the crest of fortune:

> All th' unsettled humours of the land –
> Rash, inconsiderate, fiery voluntaries,
> With ladies' faces and fierce dragons' spleens –
> Have sold their fortunes at their native homes,
> Bearing their birthrights proudly on their backs,
> To make a hazard of new fortunes here.
> In brief, a braver choice of dauntless spirits
> Than now the English bottoms have waft o'er
> Did never float upon the swelling tide
> To do offence and scathe in Christendom.

This confident start to John's encounter with the enemy, however, declines into a squalid bargaining during which his resolution is dissipated. John's bravado is short-lived and he turns out not to be a hero but a blusterer. This underlying weakness and insecurity of character is further emphasized by his dependence on his mother, Queen Eleanor, for this is a play in which dominating women play a considerable role. As John is ruled by Eleanor, so Arthur is controlled by his mother, Constance, and both women exploit the power they hold over their sons in order to satisfy their own ambitions, as, in a later play, Volumnia attempts to fulfil herself through Coriolanus.

Visually, Act IV Scene ii, which follows after the attempted blinding of Arthur, resembles the opening scene of the play. In both we are shown the King seated on his throne, surrounded by his peers. In the opening scene we may imagine that he has just recently been crowned and in the second he has just been crowned for a second time. He himself draws attention to the similarity:

> Here once again we sit, once again crown'd,
> And look'd upon, I hope, with cheerful eyes.

The significant words, 'I hope', give a hint of the King's insecurity and this becomes much more apparent when the peers, Pembroke and Salisbury, start to protest against this second coronation, which, they argue, raises suspicions among his subjects about the right to the crown of a man who has ostentatiously received it a second time. Hence an act designed to confirm his authority more securely actually undermines it. The effects of his usurpation, in the form of his own fearfulness, are not confined to him alone. Unease spreads among the nobility and, we are told, among the people generally, and this is consistent with Shakespeare's emphasis in a play in which the actions of men of power are shown to impinge on those who depend on them. The peers, however, have a further complaint and that is that Arthur is still kept captive, a situation which is also arousing discontent among the people. Arthur's imprisonment, says Pembroke,

> Doth move the murmuring lips of discontent
> To break into this dangerous argument:
> If what in rest you have in right you hold,
> Why then your fears – which, as they say, attend
> The steps of wrong – should move you to mew up
> Your tender kinsman, and to choke his days
> With barbarous ignorance, and deny his youth
> The rich advantage of good exercise?

Ironically, it is at the end of Pembroke's plea for Arthur's release that Hubert makes his entrance – ironically because John believes he is about to hear of Arthur's suffering at the very moment when he most wishes him unharmed. By a double irony, of course, we know that the Prince has in fact been unharmed, but when shortly afterwards he is actually killed by accident, the peers, with good reason, conclude that John is guilty of his death and it is this misconception which provides them with their chief motive for joining the enemy. In short, the insecurity of John's position, and thus his ostensible guilt, provokes a civil war. By a characteristically Shakespearean irony, the death of Arthur, which John had contemplated as a means of securing his position, turns out to create precisely the opposite result.

This is, however, only the first of a series of disasters which now fall thick and fast upon the King. He immediately hears of the arrival of the French army off his coast with a speed and suddenness which recalls John's own former initiative when he invaded France. As the messenger points out, 'The copy of your speed is learned by them.' Moreover the same messenger delivers a further blow when he reveals that the source of John's former dynamism, his mother, is dead. Finally we are told how the news of Arthur's death has been received by the common people, whom we never actually see, but who are described in such perceptive detail that we can easily visualize them:

> Young Arthur's death is common in their mouths;
> And when they talk of him they shake their heads,

And whisper one another in the ear;
And he that speaks doth gripe the hearer's wrist,
Whilst he that hears makes fearful action
With wrinkled brows, with nods, with rolling eyes.
I saw a smith stand with his hammer,thus,
The whilst his iron did on the anvil cool,
With open mouth swallowing a tailor's news;
Who, with his shears and measure in his hand,
Standing on slippers, which his nimble haste
Had falsely thrust upon contrary feet,
Told of a many thousand warlike French
That were embattailed and rank'd in Kent.
Another lean unwash'd artificer
Cuts off his tale, and talks of Athur's death.

This extraordinarily animated, detailed account of the way in which fear and panic spread among the citizens shows vividly the effect of kingly policy on the lives and behaviour of ordinary individual people. Shakespeare could scarcely have portrayed John's rapid decline more clearly and, coming as it does immediately after the attempt to blind the young Prince, the implication is that the decline takes place as the consequence of this act of barbarity. The assault on Arthur corresponds in this play to the murder of the Princes in *Richard III*. Both acts of violence turn the sympathies of the subjects against the monarch and both lead without a break into the process of his downfall. The basic structure of *King John* is the classic structure of an arch, a rise followed by a fall, the keystone of which is the prison scene. Shortly afterwards, burning with a fever, John hands over to the Bastard the responsibility of running the country.

To reinforce the impression that John's downfall is caused principally by the assault on Arthur, Shakespeare allows the shrewdest character in the play, Pandulph, to foresee this course of events before it takes place, so that when it actually occurs it appears inevitable, the fulfilment of a prophecy, and an illustration of the Cardinal's maxim that 'He that steeps his safety in true blood / Shall find but bloody safety and untrue.' In fact this observation is confirmed by everything that happens in the second half of the play, and it is more or less repeated by John himself when he begins to suffer the consequences of his intended crime:

There is no sure foundation set in blood,
No certain life achieved by others' ends.

Like Richard III and Macbeth, John suffers for his crimes not, according to Shakespeare, because he is the victim of some divine or supernatural retribution, some providential force which exacts penalties for crimes, but because there is within his subjects an inherent sense of right which compels them instinctively to rise up against injustice.

That the attempted violation of Arthur is the crucial episode in the play can also be seen from the nature of its distinctive language and imagery which is of consuming fire and violent assaults against the body. John's orders to the French ambassador to be 'as lightning in the eyes of France' is the first of a series of similes of this kind. As the French army stands ready to attack the town of Angiers, King Philip exhorts his troops into action:

> Well then, to work, our cannon shall be bent
> Against the brows of this resisting town

–words which conjure up a picture of a large, mechanical weapon exploding in the face of its defenceless victim, and similar impressions are created by John's declaration,

> We from the west will send destruction
> Into this city's bosom,

and the Bastard's cry,

> Let France and England mount
> Their battering canon, charged to the mouths,
> Till their soul-fearing clamours have brawl'd down
> The flinty ribs of this contemptuous city.

By the repeated use of such violent language, Shakespeare, consciously or otherwise, prepares the audience for the scene in which an assult of this kind is actually depicted. When we finally come to the prison scene and see the ropes ready to bind the boy and the irons being heated to put out his eyes, we feel that an act of unusual savagery, of which the language has already made us dimly apprehensive, is now about to take place. Significantly, after this episode such images become fewer and are replaced with references to burning fever and disease, the bodily disorders which bring about John's death.

The death of Arthur is a turning point in the life of the Bastard Faulconbridge. He is undoubtedly the most congenial person in a play whose characters are mostly preoccupied with furthering their own ambitions and are prepared to commit any crime in order to do so. Not that the Bastard is averse to promoting his own career. On the contrary, this is the first lesson he learns when he observes the practices of the two monarchs. What makes him attractive is the ironic, humorous detachment with which he watches the self-interested deviousness of his superiors, his recognition that behind the public protestations of honour and rectitude lies the real motive for political action, which is material self-interest or what he calls 'commodity', 'the bias of the world'. He is, apart from the largely silent Arthur, the only consistently honest character in the play and he is honest not only to himself and his

associates but to the audience. He is the only character who is given prolonged soliloquies and these are in the form of extended asides to the
audience, a dramatic device which induces us to feel that he is one of us,
especially since he talks to us in such an easy, unpretentious way:

> Our ears are cudgell'd; not a word of his
> But buffets better than a fist of France.
> Zounds! I was never so bethump'd with words
> Since I first call'd my brother's father dad.

During the first part of *King John*, the Bastard enjoys his position as a
detached spectator, amused at the hypocrisy of the politicians and making
his way in the world whenever an opportunity arises. He changes radically,
however, when he discovers the body of Arthur, whose death he immediately attributes to Hubert and the King. His vigorous opportunism
vanishes and he is transformed into a more deeply serious man, drawn
irresistibly into the web of politics. This is a situation which he is unable to
look at objectively:

> I am amaz'd, methinks, and lose my way
> Among the thorns and dangers of this world.
> How easy dost thou take all England up!
> From forth this morsel of dead royalty
> The life, the right, and truth of all this realm
> Is fled to heaven; and England now is left
> To tug and scamble, and to part by th' teeth
> The unowed interest of proud-swelling state.

In a sense he already knows the truth he discovers here. From the beginning
he had seen through the 'thorns and dangers of this world' and had perceived
in the shady bargainings between rulers that 'right and truth' are 'fled to
heaven'. Faced with the actual human consequences of power politics in the
form of the dead boy, he can only be stunned and sickened. His desire is now
no longer to 'tug and scamble' for his own advancement but to rescue the
kingdom from the chaos which John's ineptitude has brought about. The
deed which causes John's ruin arouses the Bastard's sense of social responsibility and although, during the King's decline, it is he who increasingly takes
on the task of government, he does not use his power for his own advancement but, on the accession of Henry III, leads the peers in a ceremonial
pledge of loyalty to the new King. The words he speaks at the play's conclusion are an exhortation to the assembled company to serve their country and
not themselves.

# King Richard the Second

Shakespeare was profoundly conscious of the effects on the personal lives of Englishmen of the fall, deposition and death of Richard II. He not only devoted a whole play to this subject but he referred to it repeatedly and at length in six other plays, the two parts of *Henry IV*, *Henry V* and the three parts of *Henry VI*, in which he portrayed the reigns of Richard's successors. The consequences of the King's dethronement, as Shakespeare saw them, were prolonged and terrible, for it removed from the seat of power a monarch who had ruled the country by a hereditary right which had been unbroken since the twelfth century and, as a result, left the throne open to be fought over by rival claimants in the Wars of the Roses, a series of civil struggles which ended only with the accession of Henry VII more than eighty years after Richard's death. The moment at which the King removes the crown from his own head and hands it to Bolingbroke is, therefore, one which, in Shakespeare's eyes, radically altered the course of English history.

It was, presumably, for this reason that Shakespeare chose to make the transfer of power – the deposition – into the central, pivotal scene of his play. Everything that occurs before this episode leads up to it and everything that happens afterwards follows as a consequence of it. Shakespeare uses the first three acts of *Richard II* as a preparation for this event and, just before it arrives, he warns us, through the words of the Bishop of Carlisle, of the bloody effects of the act we are about to witness:

> Let me prophesy –
> The blood of English shall manure the ground,
> And future ages groan for this foul act;
> Peace shall go sleep with Turks and infidels,
> And in this seat of peace tumultuous wars
> Shall kin with kin and kind with kind confound;
> Disorder, horror, fear, and mutiny,
> Shall here inhabit, and this land be call'd
> The field of Golgotha and dead men's skulls.

Then, as Richard hands over the symbols of his power to the usurper, he enumerates them in order that we may linger on this moment and grasp the weighty meaning of the process we are witnessing:

> I give this heavy weight from off my head,
> And this unwieldy sceptre from my hand,
> The pride of kingly sway from out my heart;
> With mine own tears I wash away my balm,
> With mine own hands I give away my crown,
> With mine own tongue deny my sacred state,
> With mine own breath release all duteous oaths;
> All pomp and majesty I do forswear.

Like several other episodes in this play, the deposition has the measured, deliberate quality of a ritual.

*Richard II* is, however, more than a very moving, solemn portrayal of a king's downfall: it is also an analysis of the reasons why this downfall occurred. The causes of great political crises are usually complex and originate from the pressure of circumstances which have accumulated over a period of years. Modern historians repeatedly try afresh to trace to their ultimate roots the causes of the Civil War or of the First World War and Shakespeare is in this play acting in part as a historian, tracing the deposition back to its origins, which are shown to be various and at times obscure. We know that he undertook what was, for him, considerable research before he wrote this play and that he took the trouble to read the accounts given by earlier historians, poets and dramatists of Richard's reign. Some of these accounts were biased against the King, portraying him as a degenerate, incompetent spendthrift from whose government the country was providentially saved by Bolingbroke. Other accounts were hostile to the usurper, showing him to have murdered a saintly monarch in order to satisfy his own arrogance and ambition. Shakespeare takes a more disinterested, balanced attitude, placing the responsibility for the deposition partly on Richard's incompetence and unpopularity, partly on Bolingbroke's firmness and talent for winning support, partly on mere chance, and partly on the unique relationship between the two characters. As a result, he induces us to watch the steady succession of events in such a way that we give our entire sympathy neither to the monarch nor to the usurper. Moreover this combination of circumstances, all working in the same direction, is so powerful that the catastrophe seems inevitable: the two men seem to be engaged in a process of which neither is wholly in control.

The earliest of the events which sets the drama in motion, the murder of Thomas of Woodstock, Duke of Gloucester, has occurred before the play opens, and the responsibility for this crime is the subject of the feud between Bolingbroke and Mowbray with which the first scene begins. Under the

presiding judgement of the King, each accuses the other of plotting Gloucester's death. The man actually responsible for the murder is, however,
Richard himself, but Shakespeare does no more than hint at his guilt at this
stage, perhaps in order that the central character should not lose our sympathy immediately, and perhaps so that we should perceive the difference
between the show of secure impartiality which Richard displays in the first
scene and his inner, secret guilt which is not revealed until the second scene.
This contrast or separation between the authoritative public figure and the
fallible private individual is one which is made frequently throughout the
play.

When Bolingbroke and Mowbray insist on settling their quarrel by
formal combat, Richard first postpones their encounter and later, when it is
about to begin, suddenly intervenes and sends both men into exile. This is
the second step in the process which results in the King's downfall.

So far, though we have heard of Richard's degeneracy and guilt, we have
not actually seen him commit any objectionable or unlawful act. On the
contrary, his decision to banish Mowbray and Bolingbroke is apparently
taken for the admirable motive of preventing civil strife or, as he puts it,

> For that our kingdom's earth should not be soil'd
> With that dear blood which it hath fostered.

Ironically, his decision produces the very calamity it is designed to avoid. The
next step he takes is, however, unlawful and politically inept: he seizes for his
own purposes the wealth and property which the absent Bolingbroke should
rightfully inherit on the death of his father, John of Gaunt. In so doing he
defies the very laws of succession and inheritance by which he himself
occupies the throne, as York protests:

> Is not Gaunt dead? and doth not Hereford live?
> Was not Gaunt just? and is not Harry true?
> Did not the one deserve to have an heir?
> Is not his heir a well-deserving son?
> Take Hereford's rights away, and take from Time
> His charters and his customary rights;
> Let not tomorrow then ensue today;
> Be not thyself - for how art thou a king
> But by fair sequence and succession?

Moreover, the King's seizure of Bolingbroke's possessions has disastrous
political consequences, for it provides the latter with a pretext for returning
from banishment and demanding his rights. It is at this point, moreover, that
we hear in fuller detail of Richard's incompetence and unpopularity: he is a
prey to irresponsible flatterers; he has lost his people's support by heavy taxa-
tion; he has wasted his wealth on personal extravagance. With Richard's

popularity thus low in the eyes both of his subjects and the audience, Bolingbroke takes the momentous step of defying his king and returning to
England.

What precisely were the motives for his return Shakespeare never openly
reveals. In contrast to Richard who pours out his most intimate feelings
spontaneously, Bolingbroke keeps his inner self concealed. There is no scene
(and Shakespeare could, obviously, have written one had he chosen to do so)
where Bolingbroke is shown in the actual process of deciding to return, no
soliloquy in which he displays his motives. When he meets first his uncle,
York, and later the King, he insists that he requires no more than is his due as
his father's heir. Yet, though he returns apparently to claim an inheritance,
he actually gains a kingdom. Shakespeare has omitted the evidence on the
strength of which we should either condemn or applaud him.

Moreover, while Richard has lost the support of his subjects, Bolingbroke
is very adept at winning it. Even as he passes into exile, we are told, he 'dives'
into the people's hearts and, on his return, he ingratiates himself with his
most powerful allies with promises of reward after he has succeeded:

> I count myself in nothing else so happy
> As in a soul rememb'ring my good friends;
> And as my fortune ripens with thy love,
> It shall be still thy true love's recompense.

Whereas Richard showed his rashness by taking Bolingbroke's inheritance
while the latter was in exile, Bolingbroke shows his shrewdness by choosing
deliberately to land at Ravenspurgh when Richard is in Ireland, for, when the
King returns he finds that virtually the whole country has defected and
that he is already a defeated man. By sheer misfortune his only remaining
loyal soldiers, the Welsh, have disbanded a day before his arrival. He now has
nothing with which to defend himself but his right to rule and the strength
of his character, but, when he faces his opponent at Flint Castle, even these
powers fail him. Bolingbroke declares that he has come only for what is his
due:

> My gracious lord, I come but for mine own.

Richard, however, crumbles before Bolingbroke's presence and at once
hands over his person and his kingdom:

> Your own is yours, and I am yours, and all.

He has himself completed the process of his own downfall. His deposition is
now inevitable and follows almost immediately.

Shakespeare allows the causes of this bloodless revolution to unfold and
accumulate gradually. As an analysis of political change *Richard II* is subtle,
lucid and even does justice to those hidden motives which must always

perplex the historian. The shift of power, however, serves only as a background to the figure of Richard himself, who dominates the play and whose personality and reactions to events are Shakespeare's chief interest. To begin with he is shown to be outwardly self-confident but inwardly corrupt and hence has the legal but not the moral right to govern. These two facets of his character are conveyed to us by Shakespeare's alternation of scenes of public ceremony, in which the monarch appears in the pomp of his authority (Act I Scenes i and iii) and private scenes where his callousness and degeneracy are either discussed in secret or exposed by his own unguarded talk with his intimates. For example, Shakespeare first shows us Richard's callous, flippant reaction to the news of Gaunt's sickness –

> Now put it, God, in the physician's mind
> To help him to his grave immediately!

– before he shows us the prophetic, dying man himself. These impressions reflect unfavourably on Richard and we soon hear Gaunt's impassioned and wistful eulogy of an England which has become corrupted from within by Richard's irresponsibility. During these first two acts Shakespeare has gradually and deliberately lowered the King in the estimation of the audience.

We see no more of him until his return from Ireland when, deprived of that power which allowed him to control the lives and property of other men at his whim, he sees himself for the first time as vulnerable, essentially no different from his subjects:

> I live with bread like you, feel want,
> Taste grief, need friends; subjected thus,
> How can you say to me I am a king?

From this scene onwards Shakespeare induces us to see him with increasing sympathy. What Richard loses in terms of power and adulation he gains in terms of insight into his own condition. Yet, having been transformed by circumstances from a king to a beggar he is, nevertheless, capable of learning only a limited amount from experience. He continually fluctuates between an illusion of himself as a person uniquely privileged whose enemies will evaporate before the wrath of God, and the spectacle of himself as a martyr whose agony deserves our compassion. He has, from the start, been swayed by moods, unstable, and now he alternates between pathetic bravado and shrinking self-pity. Deprived of the only identity he has ever possessed, that of a king, it is doubtful whether he ever reaches a stable point at which he can recognize and accept his own nature. His final, extended soliloquy in prison is an attempt to build a personality from the ruin of his former self, but he can find permanent satisfaction neither in the memory of what he was nor in the realization of what he has become, and he looks forward with relief to the peace of non-existence:

> Whate'er I be,
> Nor I, nor any man that but man is,
> With nothing shall be pleas'd till he be eas'd
> With being nothing.

Together with the decline and death of Richard, moreover, Shakespeare portrays the disintegration of a family and the end of a period of history. Nearly all the major characters are blood relations, the descendants of Edward III, the father of Gaunt and York and the grandfather of Richard and Bolingbroke. The memory of Edward's authoritative, dedicated, Christian leadership is repeatedly recalled as an ideal by which Richard's weakness and egotism are measured. As the play opens, Edward's seven sons are all either dead or ageing and, with the murder of Thomas Woodstock, only Gaunt and York remain. It is these two remaining sons who recall the lost golden age and complain that Richard has betrayed the land entrusted to him. The sense of decline is seldom absent from this play. Characters are frequently shown in the process of leavetaking: the Duchess of Gloucester says a last farewell to Gaunt, Gaunt to his son, Bolingbroke and Mowbray to their homeland as they go into exile, Richard to his queen as he goes to prison. *Richard II* is full of *la poésie du départ*, 'the poetry of farewell'. The sense of distintegration is also conveyed by descriptions of decay, fading light and the autumnal season:

> The setting sun, and music at the close,
> As the last taste of sweets, is sweetest last,
> Writ in remembrance more than things long past.

> The bay trees in our country are all wither'd
> And meteors fright the fixed stars of heaven.

These description of natural and seasonal decay are accompanied by stage pictures in which Richard is shown to be literally sinking, partly because this shows his natural tendency to capitulate when challenged by Bolingbroke, partly to convey to the audience the impression of his political and inner decline. When, for example, he learns, on his arrival from Ireland, that his people have deserted him, his spontaneous reaction is to cry

> For God's sake let us sit upon the ground
> And tell sad stories of the death of kings,

as though defeated by the very news of his opponent's strength. Again, at Flint Castle, he literally descends from the battlements to deliver himself up to Bolingbroke. Shakespeare uses the visual resources of drama as well as the resources of dialogue.

As the King and his land decline, Bolingbroke self-assuredly conducts his ascent. Yet, ironically, he discovers, as Richard has warned him, that to gain power is merely to gain care and, though Richard is defeated, we are left with the impression that Bolingbroke has not triumphed, or, rather, that he has suffered a defeat of a different kind. No sooner has he come to power than he is faced with the task of making peace between his peers in a scene (Act IV Scene i) of accusations and counter-challenges which recall Richard's predicament at the start of the play. Our last glimpse of him is of a man remorseful for Richard's murder, undertaking with little pleasure the responsibilities of government. When he appears at the beginning of Shakespeare's next historical play, *Henry IV Part I*, we recognize at once the price he has had to pay for his success:

> So shaken as we are, so wan with care.

Events are, by then, already moving towards the next crisis and it is the now weary, anxious, guilt-ridden Bolingbroke who must deal with it in a very different kind of England.

Shakespeare began his career as a dramatist by writing four plays on the subject of English history, the three parts of *Henry VI* and *Richard III*. *Richard II* was probably composed in 1595, some two years after these had been completed. It differs from them in its reduction of plot and stage action to a minimum and its concentration, instead, on the relationships and feelings of the characters, particularly those of the King, who dominates the play to such an extent that it may be regarded both as an account of the final years of his reign – a history play – and as his personal tragedy. Shakespeare's procedure dramatically is to place Richard in a series of critical situations – his return from Ireland, his meeting with Bolingbroke at Flint Castle, his deposition and his imprisonment – and to allow him fully and imaginatively to express his emotions. *Richard II*, like the plays which immediately preceded and followed it, *Love's Labour's Lost* and *Romeo and Juliet*, is written in a deliberately mannered, artificial style so that the listener is conscious of the way in which a character speaks as well as of the sense his words convey. This formal style, in which phrase is balanced against phrase within a sentence and metaphors are developed at elaborate length, is appropriate as an expression of Richard's self-consciousness, whether in his role as a king or as a common subject. Moreover, this elaborate manner of speech, combined with the formal, ritualistic construction of many of the scenes, such as the opening challenges and the deposition, may help to convey the impression of the long-established, hierarchical society of medieval England, now in its final years of decline. The much more varied style of the history plays portraying the reign of Richard's successor, Henry IV, reflects the life of a society which has become fragmented.

# Romeo and Juliet

*Romeo and Juliet* contains one of those Shakespearean lines that everyone knows, the words spoken by Juliet as she stands on her balcony, unaware of Romeo concealed in the darkness of the orchard below:

> O Romeo, Romeo! wherefore art thou Romeo?

The line has not become celebrated by accident but because Shakespeare used all his resources to ensure that it would make a deep impression on his audience. To try to discover why it creates such an effect is to learn something about Shakespeare's skill in dramatic construction and something about the tragedy itself.

Shakespeare prepares the audience for this moment from the very start of the play and, when it occurs, it breaks upon us both as a climax and as a summary of the action. By this point we are well aware of the long-continued feud between the Montagues and the Capulets and have seen it burst into open violence; we have felt the danger in which Romeo has placed himself by going disguised to the Capulets' ball; we have watched the first encounter between Romeo and Juliet and their instantaneous passion for each other, an adoration they can express only guardedly, because neither knows how the other will respond, and furtively in the threatening presence of his enemies and her family. When, therefore, the two are at last alone in the orchard, we are unusually attentive to their words. The balcony scene, moreover, stands out in contrast to the two which have preceded it, the brightly lit, animated, crowded scene at the ball (Act I Scene v) and the rowdy street scene (Act II Scene i) in which Benvolio and Mercutio shout obscenities at the hidden Romeo. The change of focus from the street to the orchard is from noise to stillness, the open streets to the enclosed garden where the darkness is illuminated by the single light from Juliet's balcony towards which Romeo directs his gaze. Moreover, though the lovers are now alone, Juliet is unaware of Romeo's presence and the suspense is heightened because, for a while, she says nothing; her first sound is an expressive 'Ay me!' It is at this carefully prepared moment, as though in reply to Romeo's unheard plea, 'O, speak

again, bright angel', that she delivers the lines which Shakespeare's skill has
made memorable:

> O Romeo, Romeo! wherefore art thou Romeo?
> Deny thy father and refuse thy name;
> Or, if thou wilt not, be but sworn my love,
> And I'll no longer be a Capulet.

Juliet's actual words, moreover, have a significance for the tragedy as a
whole. Her first line is a question about names, and names have a particular
importance in this play. For example, when Juliet has first met Romeo at the
ball, she sends the nurse with the instruction, 'Go ask his name'. Again, when
the newly married Romeo encounters Tybalt, he addresses him as 'good
Capulet',

> which name I tender
> As dearly as mine own.

And his sense of his own name is expressed most violently when, after he has
killed Tybalt and lies concealed in the Friar's cell, Romeo treats it as though
it had an independent existence:

> That name's cursed hand
> Murder'd her kinsman. O, tell me, friar, tell me,
> In what vile part of this anatomy
> Doth my name lodge? Tell me that I may sack
> The hateful mansion.

His impulse is to destroy himself and thereby to eradicate his own, guilty
name.

Each of the lovers has a family name, Montague and Capulet, and this
represents the unbreakable chains which bind them to their respective, war-
ring households; it represents the enmity into which they have been born.
And each has a unique name, Romeo and Juliet, which signifies his and her
individuality, those qualities which distinguish and separate each of them
from all the other Montagues and Capulets. 'Romeo' signifies the particular
'face, leg, hand, foot and body' to which the nurse refers admiringly and with
which Juliet falls in love. One way of understanding the play is to see it as the
attempt and the tragic failure of the two young people to 'deny their names'
and thereby to become exclusively themselves. They are, needless to say,
attempting the impossible.

Juliet's 'Wherefore?' (or, 'For what cause?') is one of the lovers' many
uncomprehending protests against a hidden and malevolent power in the
heavens which has decreed that the one person most dear to them should
also have been born into that family which most hates their own: 'My only
love sprung from my only hate!', as Juliet succinctly declares. It is against

these same powers that Romeo cries out in the most bitterly searching lines
of the play:

> Heaven is here
> Where Juliet lives, and every cat and dog,
> And little mouse, every unworthy thing,
> Live here in heaven, and may look on her;
> But Romeo may not.

This is an anguished complaint against the injustice of the supernatural
powers which seem to govern the world. Shakespeare, incidentally, was to
recall and revise these words of Romeo's in the most tragically bleak moment
in his entire works, the moment when King Lear stands, holding in his arms
the body of his dearest child:

> No, no, no life!
> Why should a dog, a horse, a rat have life,
> And thou no breath at all?

As well as being, at this relatively early stage in his career, a brilliantly skilled
writer for the theatre, Shakespeare was also able to look beyond the immediate, specific predicament of his characters to the greater metaphysical
powers which seem to have placed them in it.

Shakespeare shows us very vividly what it means to be a Capulet and a
Montague. His quick, lively sketches of the domestic life of the Capulets are
among the small triumphs of *Romeo and Juliet*. The family belongs to the
wealthy Italian upper middle class which he had already portrayed in *The
Taming of the Shrew*, written about a year earlier. It is dominated by the father,
a fussy, impatient, easily flustered little dictator, generously hospitable to his
guests but determined to impose his will over the younger generation, such
as Tybalt (when the latter struggles to attack Romeo during the ball) and particularly Juliet when she defiantly refuses to marry Paris. Shakespeare rapidly
sketches into the background of the play the agitation and concern for
material comfort in the Capulet family by inserting a short dialogue between
the servants at the opening of the scene at the ball:

Away with the joint-stools, remove the court-cubbert, look to the plate. Good thou,
save me a piece of marchpane; and as thou loves me let the porter let in Susan Grind-
stone and Nell, Antony and Potpan!

We can size up the Capulets on the evidence of these two hurriedly spoken
sentences: the sense of confusion (also conveyed by Capulet himself during
the ball) suggests that they do not put on their social entertainments with
quite the ease and confidence of the aristocracy, yet they are wealthy enough
to possess silver plate, to serve marchpane (marzipan) to their guests, and to
employ a number of servants. (Since they have to be 'let in', Susan, Nell,

Antony and Potpan may be extra, hired help.) A similar impression is created as the family prepare through the night for the wedding reception with such haste that Juliet's parents themselves appear to be giving a hand with the cooking:

| | |
|---|---|
| *Lady Capulet* | Hold, take these keys, and fetch more spices, nurse. |
| *Nurse* | They call for dates and quinces in the pastry. |
| *Capulet* | Come, stir, stir, stir! The second cock has crow'd |
| | The curfew bell hath rung, 'tis three o'clock. |
| | Look to the bak'd meats, good Angelica; |
| | Spare not for cost. |

It is consistent with what we know of her family background that, during her first scene (Act I Scene iii), Juliet is shown to be a thoroughly conventional, polite, submissive daughter. She is, after all, only fourteen, and when she first appears she remains almost totally silent for nearly seventy lines. On being asked whether she is inclined to marriage, she modestly replies,

It is an honour that I dream not of,

and she agrees to love only a man whom her parents have chosen for her. It is easy to imagine what Juliet might have become: married to a Count, comfortably well off, producing grandchildren for her parents to dote over, and remaining passive and conventional for the rest of her life. Her love for Romeo transforms her life and personality: she acquires an independence of mind, sleeps in secret with her husband under her parents' roof, defies her father's wrath and resolutely kills herself when Romeo is dead. She ceases to be a Capulet and becomes Juliet. Yet by the process of coming to life she ensures her early death. 'So quick bright things come to confusion.'

Shakespeare shows us very little of Romeo's parents, and their relative absence is deliberate, for we see a great deal of his companions: he is at the age when young men stay out late and roam the streets in gangs. Shakespeare has identified a difference between the young Italian male and female which can still be seen today. Benvolio and Mercutio are boistrous, earthy, daring, irresponsible youths, affectionate towards one another but contemptuous of their sworn enemies, the Capulets. In their own way they are as conventional and Juliet's parents. Romeo has already, early in the play, begun to move away from the group as a result of his infatuation with his first love, Rosaline, but his passion for Juliet divorces him completely from them. This separation is shown visually in Act II Scene i where, as his friends call out for him in the street, he hides from them behind the Capulets' wall. His love, like hers, raises him above convention and yet contributes to his – and Mercutio's – death. Their love makes the hero and heroine fully themselves and also ruins them. By a similar paradox, each commits suicide as the supreme expression of love for the other.

The Montagues and the Capulets resemble each other, however, in the extreme intensity of their emotions. The first image Shakespeare gives us is of the violent enmity between the two families, a smouldering animosity which, within seconds, flares up into physical violence. Capulet is constantly in a state of fevered agitation which turns to rage when his will is crossed by Tybalt or Juliet. Moreover, the families are as unrestrained in sorrow as they are in hatred: Romeo's reaction to the news of his banishment is to collapse on the floor, 'blubbering and weeping, weeping and blubbering', and, on the apparent death of their daughter, the Capulets pour out their grief in a great torrent of complaint and lamentation. So violent are their passions that some of the characters shake, physically, under their pressure: Tybalt's 'flesh trembles' with rage, and the Nurse, taunted by the young Montagues, becomes so vexed that 'every part' about her 'quivers'. The overwhelming love which Romeo and Juliet experience is, therefore, consistent with the extreme emotions which possess almost everyone. Only the Friar remains calm, cautious and fearful of its consequences:

> These violent delights have violent ends,
> And in their triumph die; like fire and powder,
> Which, as they kiss, consume.

The impression of lives lived intensely is also created by the high speed at which the action moves. No sooner do the servants meet than they fight; no sooner have the lovers glimpsed each other than they become infatuated; no sooner does Romeo hear of Juliet's death than he resolves on suicide, demanding a poison that will work

> As violently as hasty powder fir'd
> Doth hurry from the fatal cannon's womb.

As soon as she sees her husband's body, Juliet unhesitatingly kills herself. The action of the play, as Shakespeare takes care to inform us, occupies only four days. The opening brawl takes place on a Sunday morning, the lovers meet that night, are married on the Monday afternoon, and rise from their night together the following morning. On that same Tuesday, Juliet drinks the potion and is discovered by the nurse early on Wednesday. By dawn on the Thursday, both are dead. The tragedy seems to be driven forward by the emotional ferocity of the characters.

Shakespeare interrupts the headlong rush of the action, however, with interludes where time seems to be suspended. They occur, as we might expect, when Romeo and Juliet are alone, and the motionless tranquility of their meetings is one of the qualities which isolates them from everyone else. They attempt to make for themselves a private world, cut off from the time-bound activities of ancient feuds and hasty matchmaking. Circumstances make such an achievement impossible. They are alone together only three times: in the Capulets' orchard, in Juliet's bedroom and in the tomb, a hasty, secretive courtship, marriage and death which makes their tragedy the more pitiful. The apparent immunity of their world is suggested by the fact that they meet only at night and in enclosed spaces. This is partly for practical reasons – they fear to be discovered – but it also creates the impression of an intimate, night-time world where they alone are fully awake. The darkness is illuminated for them by their own brightness. Each refers to the other as a light: to Romeo, Juliet's window is 'the east' and she 'the sun'; to Juliet, Romeo should be 'cut out in little stars' which would make all the world 'in love with night'. Shakespeare makes good dramatic use of Juliet's balcony, a secret, magical place which can be reached only with difficulty and danger: the physical height of the balcony raises them metaphorically above the rest of the world, an idea which Romeo expresses as he stands in the orchard, gazing upwards at Juliet:

> O, speak again, bright angel, for thou art
> As glorious to this night, being o'er my head,
> As is a winged messenger of heaven
> Unto the white-upturned wond'ring eyes
> Of mortals that fall back to gaze on him,
> When he bestrides the lazy-pacing clouds
> And sails upon the bosom of the air.

Their privacy is, however, always at risk and always invaded by an alien world: their courtship is interrupted by the impatient call of the nurse, and their wedding night by the fateful song of the lark which summons Romeo to his banishment.

Each of the lovers has a close companion and confidant who seems to be helpful to them but, in the event, proves fatal. Mercutio and the nurse are the most strongly and distinctively characterized people in the play. The former, like Romeo, is only partially engaged in the family feud, which he regards with a half-mocking detachment, yet, like Romeo, he becomes a victim of it. In the 'Queen Mab' speech, a kind of aria without music, Shakespeare reveals the man's witty intelligence (in contrast to Romeo's romantic passion), his sociability as an entertainer and his worldly sophistication. At the same time he establishes him as a substantial, engaging figure in order that his death may create a serious sense of loss. The nurse is the most recognizably human of all the characters: as soon as she embarks on her first, rambling, affectionate, earthy reminiscences of Juliet as a baby, she stands solidly real. Like many women of easy morals she is sentimental and is sufficiently detached from the war of the families, acting as a go-between for the lovers, that we trust her as a dependable ally. The moment when she casually reveals that she is not an ally comes, therefore, as a shock:

> Then, since the case so stands as now it doth,
> I think it best you married with the County.
> O, he's a lovely gentleman!
> Romeo's a dishclout to him.

Not only is she advising bigamy to a newly married, fourteen-year-old girl, but she shows a blindness towards Juliet's kind of love which leaves the heroine completely isolated. Thus deprived, through Mercutio's death, Romeo's banishment and the nurse's betrayal, of their only allies, the lovers are left to meet their deaths in pitiful isolation.

Shakespeare seems to have thought of *Romeo and Juliet* as a tragedy of fate, brought about by supernatural forces which the lovers are too weak to resist. They are 'star-crossed' lovers, whose 'ill-divining souls' dimly foresee 'some bitter consequence yet hanging in the stars' which will destroy them. Romeo's impulse on hearing of Juliet's death is to taunt the heavens who have contrived it:

> Is it e'en so? Then, I defy you, stars.

And he welcomes his own suicide as a positive act which will

> shake the yoke of inauspicious stars
> From this world-wearied flesh.

In fact the tragedy results from a variety of causes: the rash, impulsive actions of nearly all the protagonists, the sheer bad luck which delays Friar Lawrence's letter and Juliet's awakening from her trance, the miscarriage of the Friar's well-intentioned plans which, in the end, prove fatal. But *Romeo and Juliet* resembles Shakespeare's later tragedies, such as *Othello* and *Hamlet*, in that the catastrophe is brought about, ironically, by the very qualities in the central characters which most commend them to us. The hero and heroine possess that characteristic which A. C. Bradley recognized in Shakespeare's great tragic heroes, 'a fatal tendency to identify the whole being with one interest, object, passion or habit of mind', a tragic quality of character 'which is also his greatness', so that his virtues 'help to destroy him'. Those qualities which distinguish Romeo and Juliet from all the other Montagues and Capulets – their transcendent love, their altruistic courage, the tenderness of their affections, their impulse to be intensely and defiantly themselves – enable them to live more generously for a few hours than others accomplish in a lifetime. Their brief association is both their doom and their triumph.

# A Midsummer Night's Dream

*A Midsummer Night's Dream* was probably the fifth comedy Shakespeare wrote, and it was at the time the most theatrically accomplished and poetically brilliant play he had yet created. There is a greater variety of characters in the *Dream* than in any of his earlier comedies and they express themselves in a dazzlingly inventive range of styles: fluently supple blank verse for Theseus and his courtiers, rhyming couplets for the four young lovers, various lyric metres for the fairies and, for Bottom and his associates, an easy colloquial prose which still sounds natural and lifelike. There is also the deliberately cumbersome verse of 'Pyramus and Thisby':

> O grim-look'd night! O night with hue so black!
> O night, which ever art when day is not!
> O night, O night, alack, alack, alack,
> I fear my Thisby's promise is forgot.

Not only is such technically inept and imaginatively limited dialogue convincing as the best to which the dramatist Peter Quince can rise, it also makes us more strongly aware of the effortless vitality of the rest of *A Midsummer Night's Dream*. The language of this play is distinguished by its scarcely controlled luxuriance:

> Thou hast by moonlight at her window sung,
> With feigning voice, verses of feigning love,
> And stol'n the impression of her fantasy
> With bracelets of thy hair, rings, gawds, conceits,
> Knacks, trifles, nosegays, sweetmeats – messengers
> Of strong prevailment in unhardened youth.

> Feed him with apricocks and dewberries,
> With purple grapes, green figs, and mulberries;
> The honey bags steal from the humble-bees,
> And for night tapers crop their waxen thighs,
> And light them at the fiery glow-worm's eyes,
> To have my love to bed and to arise.

As these copious lists of words pour from the mouths of Shakespeare's
characters, we recognize him as an artist who enjoys the verbal medium in
which he works.

A great deal of this richly plentiful language is used by the dramatist in
order to evoke in the imaginations of his audience a picture of the place, the
Wood near Athens, where most of the action occurs. Throughout the play,
the characters express not simply the feelings aroused by their predicaments
but their awareness of their surroundings:

> I know a bank where the wild thyme blows,
> Where oxlips and the nodding violet grows,
> Quite over-canopied with luscious woodbine,
> With sweet musk-roses and with eglantine;
> There sleeps Titania sometime of the night,
> Lull'd in these flowers with dances and delight.
>
> Sleep thou, and I will wind thee in my arms.
> Fairies, be gone, and be all ways away.
> So doth the woodbine the sweet honeysuckle
> Gently entwist; the female ivy so
> Enrings the barky fingers of the elm.

The stage for which Shakespeare wrote had little or no scenery. It was not
much more than a bare, wooden platform thrust into the middle of the spectators, and backed by a wall which separated it from the dressing room. Such
scenery as the play required had, of necessity, to be supplied by the playwright's language operating on the imaginations of his audience. Nevertheless, the sense of place is, even by Shakespeare's standards, exceptionally
vivid. The presence of the wood is felt as strongly as that of the characters and
they are as much affected by it as by one another. It is noticeably a midsummer forest, populated by the wild creatures – snakes, reremice, owls,
hedgehogs, newts, spiders – and by the wild thyme, musk roses, honeysuckle,
grapes, figs – the flowers and fruits of the summer season. The plenitude of
Shakespeare's descriptive writing reflects the ripeness of the countryside. It is
also a landscape which is visualized as organically alive and constantly in
motion: the 'nodding' violet 'grows', the woodbine gently 'entwists' the
sweet honeysuckle, and the ivy 'enrings' the elm. Moreover the landscape at
times appears to transform itself under the effect of the changing light: the
dew, illuminated by the moon, is transformed into 'liquid pearl', and the sea
turns into 'yellow gold' in the rays of the dawning sun.

It is entirely appropriate that this richly fertile, living, fluctuating landscape should, during the greater part of the play, be watched over by two
creatures who are themselves characterized by their capacity for change. The
first of these presiding figures is the moon, whose changeableness, her

waxing and waning, is mentioned in the opening lines of the play. 'Four happy days bring in another moon,' declares Theseus,

> but, O methinks, how slow
> This old moon wanes!

Hippolyta, picking up this idea, connects it with the constantly changing light as day fades into night:

> Four days will quickly steep themselves in night;
> Four nights will quickly dream away the time;
> And then the moon, like to a silver bow
> New-bent in heaven, shall behold the night
> Of our solemnities.

The forest scenes all take place at night – not the thick, palpable darkness of the night of Duncan's murder in *Macbeth*, but the deceptive half-light of the moon in which common sights appear disturbingly unfamiliar and the characters feel uncertain of their surroundings. 'Dark night,' as Hermia says, 'from the eye his function takes' and 'doth impair the seeing sense.' The moonlight adds to an already elusive landscape a further sense of unreality.

The other genius of the forest is Puck, who announces on his first appearance that he can transform himself into any shape he chooses – a crab apple, a three-legged stool, or the Will o' the Wisp, the phosphorescent light which hovers over marshes and tempts travellers in the night to stray from their path. But Puck assumes more terrifying shapes as the play develops:

> Sometime a horse I'll be, sometime a hound,
> A hog, a headless bear, sometime a fire;
> And neigh, and bark, and grunt, and roar, and burn,
> Like horse, hound, hog, bear, fire, at every turn.

It is not surprising that the city people, wandering by moonlight in this eerily transformed forest, subjected to the tricks of Robin Goodfellow in his various shapes, should feel that they have lost their hold on reality. Their very fears, moreover, add further to their confusion, for terror creates its own illusions and, as Theseus observes, 'in the night, imagining some fear, / How easy is a bush suppos'd a bear.' This is precisely what happens to Bottom's friends when, panic stricken at his transformation into an ass, they take flight through the once familiar but now apparently enchanted wood:

> Their sense thus weak, lost with their fears thus strong,
> Made senseless things begin to do them wrong,
> For briers and thorns at their apparel snatch;
> Some sleeves, some hats, from yielders all things catch.

At this point in the play, the wood is not simply alive but seems terrifyingly hostile.

Everything in the forest – the light, the changing vegetation, the supernatural influence of Puck and the apprehensions of the characters – conspires to distort their powers of perception. Nothing, however, so radically transforms the perception as the power of love. As Hermia tells us,

> Things base and vile, holding no quantity,
> Love can transpose to form and dignity.
> Love looks not with the eyes, but with the mind;
> And therefore is wing'd Cupid painted blind.

The two pairs of lovers – Hermia and Lysander, Helena and Demetrius – are all at that stage of late adolescence when they fall suddenly and irrationally in and out of love, and transfer their affections rapidly from one to another. Before the beginning of the play, Demetrius, we learn, had been in love with Helena but is now infatuated with Hermia. Hermia, on the other hand, who her father insists should marry Demetrius, is enamoured of Lysander to the extent that she is willing to defy her father's will and the Duke's command and to elope to a clandestine marriage. The effect of the juice of 'love in idleness' (the wild pansy) which Puck pours into the eyes of the men is simply to accelerate and intensify the changeable infatuations by which they have already been possessed. As long as he is in love with Hermia, Demetrius finds Helena merely a troublesome irritation, but under the influence of the love potion she becomes, in his eyes, transformed:

> O Helen, goddess, nymph, perfect, divine!
> To what, my love, shall I compare thine eyne?

Conversely, Lysander, who had been so in love with Hermia as to defy the law of Athens and escape with her, now finds her loathsome:

> Hang off, thou cat, thou burr; vile thing, let loose,
> Or I will shake thee from me like a serpent.

Not knowing that the men's affections have been influenced by Puck's magic potion, the women attempt in vain to make sense of a situation which, by the middle of the third act, has become increasingly unpredictable and baffling. Adored by both Demetrius and Lysander, Helena mistakes their protestations of love for brutal mockery, and, rejected by both men, Hermia accuses her old school friend Helena of conspiring with them against her. Eventually all four are so perplexed by the transformations they see in each other that they begin to doubt the truth of their own identities.

> Am not I Hermia? Are not you Lysander?

The brilliantly comic effect created by this scene (Act III Scene ii), in which the confusions of the lovers become increasingly violent and bewildering, arises from their desperate but perfectly logical attempts to understand a situation which must lie beyond their comprehension. The audience, who understands fully what has happened, can only laugh in ridicule at the attempts of the characters to make sense of their predicament.

Into this world of shifting appearances and changing illusions, Shakespeare introduces the solidly prosaic figures of Bottom and his fellow-artisans. Bottom is so unimaginative, so incapable of being anything other than himself that, even though he is the only character in the play to suffer a literal, physical metamorphosis, and undergoes the most extraordinary of all the night's adventures – nothing less than an amorous encounter with the fairy queen – he remains thoroughly calm, rational and unperturbed. To Titania's passionate declaration that she has fallen instantaneously in love with him, he replies, sanely,

Methinks, mistress, you should have little reason for that. And yet, to say the truth, reason and love keep little company now-a-days.

In spite of his humble station in life, and his slow-wittedness, Bottom has a practical wisdom of which the more sophisticated, aristocratic characters are incapable. In this he resembles Shakespeare's other working-class characters, Costard in *Love's Labour's Lost* and Dogberry in *Much Ado About Nothing*.

Whereas the four lovers are the victims of the illusions created by Puck, Bottom and his fellow-actors are trying, in their literal-minded way, to create illusions. They are rehearsing a play. Indeed, so confident are they of their ability to transform themselves into the characters they represent that their only anxiety is that the audience will find their performance too convincing:

There are things in this comedy of Pyramus and Thisby that will never please. First, Pyramus must draw a sword to kill himself; which the ladies cannot abide.

To avoid terrifying their audience by the sheer authenticity of their performance, they must, they believe, constantly remind them that the play is not actually real:

Write me a prologue; and let the prologue seem to say we will do no harm with our swords, and that Pyramus is not kill'd indeed; and for the more better assurance, tell them that I Pyramus am not Pyramus but Bottom the weaver.

The comedy of the scenes in which these working-men first discuss, then rehearse and finally perform their play is all derived more or less from the same joke, but it is a good joke and one which bears repeating. It arises from the discrepancy between their belief that they can create a totally convincing theatrical illusion and the audience's knowledge that they cannot. Whereas

Peter Quince and his troupe believe they are performing a deeply moving, wholly serious tragedy, the Duke and his court can see that they are creating a ridiculously unconvincing farce. The theatre audience, observing both actors and spectators at the same time, are both touched by the mechanicals' attempt to give pleasure and amused by their ineptitude.

The very failure of the performance of 'Pyramus and Thisby' is part of the success of *A Midsummer Night's Dream*. It enables Shakespeare to bring this apparently chaotic, bewildering comedy to a conclusion by persuading us that stability has at last been reached. Throughout most of the play, the characters have undergone a series of either real or imaginary transformations which have led to quarrels, broken friendships, thwarted love, open hostility and physical violence. When, with the coming of the dawn and the arrival of Duke Theseus, the four young people prepare to return home to Athens, we have some confidence that their disturbing and apparently inexplicable changes of affection have come to an end. This is partly because their experience of inconstancy has been so disturbing that they are likely to welcome the peace of a stable marriage, and partly because Oberon, who has the power to control them, assures us that all will now be well:

> When they next wake, all this derision
> Shall seem a dream and fruitless vision;
> And back to Athens shall the lovers wend
> With league whose date till death shall never end.

But a further, reassuring sense of stability is created by the very failure of the mechanicals to perform their little play convincingly. For one thing, the story of Pyramus and Thisby is one of tragically frustrated love, not dissimilar to the tragedy of Romeo and Juliet which Shakespeare had completed in the previous year. It is an illustration of Lysander's maxim that 'the course of true love never did run smooth'. By turning this tragic tale, through their ineptitude, into a joke, by compelling the audience to mock the trials of thwarted love, the ineffectual actors create the impression that such a tragedy is too ridiculous to contemplate. One way of insuring against disaster is to make fun of it and that, unwittingly, is what Peter Quince's troupe of actors accomplish. But they also ensure that the assembled couples need no longer fear the kind of disruptions they have suffered during the course of the play. For Bottom, Flute and Snout struggle to bring about the kind of experiences which have caused the young people so much distress. They attempt to metamorphose themselves into Pyramus, Thisby and Wall, and they palpably fail:

> In this same interlude it doth befall
> That I, one Snout by name, present a wall;
> This loam, this rough-cast, and this stone doth show
> That I am that same wall; the truth is so.

The truth is that Snout and his colleagues are firmly and stubbornly themselves. The powers of illusion seem to have vanished.

Throughout *A Midsummer Night's Dream* the audience's attention is constantly held by the variety of characters, styles and situations. Shakespeare interweaves the various plots with a marvellous control over his material. We may wonder, however, why he chose to combine in the same comedy the story of the mature love of Theseus and Hippolyta, the fickle infatuations of the young courtiers, the quarrel between Oberon and Titania and the incompetent performance of a play. The answer is not exactly supplied but is at least hinted at by Duke Theseus as the play draws to a close. Theseus is convinced that the improbable nightmare which the young people claim to have been through could not actually have occurred. It must have been a delusion created by the deceptive power of love. And in his meditation on the way in which love transforms one's view of reality, he goes on to consider the effects of the imagination generally:

> The lunatic, the lover, and the poet,
> Are of imagination all compact.
> One sees more devils than vast hell can hold;
> That is the madman. The lover, all as frantic,
> Sees Helen's beauty in a brow of Egypt.
> The poet's eye, in a fine frenzy rolling,
> Doth glance from heaven to earth, from earth to heaven;
> And as imagination bodies forth
> The forms of things unknown, the poet's pen
> Turns them to shapes, and gives to airy nothing
> A local habitation and a name.

This speech, read out of the context of the play, may look like Shakespeare's own statement of his theory of the imagination, but it is not. As always, Shakespeare allows his characters to speak for themselves, and the words are spoken by Duke Theseus in response to the tale he has just been told. He has a very sceptical, pragmatic view of the imagination. Whether it is manifested in the delusions of the madman, the idealizing visions of the lover or the fictions of the poet, Theseus believes that the imagination is a kind of insanity, a force which prevents men from perceiving the plain truth. In one sense, of course, he is wrong, for the lovers actually have suffered the adventures they have described. We know because we have witnessed them. Yet in another sense he is right because the entire play (including this speech) consists wholly of illusions 'bodied forth' by Shakespeare's own imagination. The various plots of *A Midsummer Night's Dream* are held together by their common preoccupation with the nature and effects of the imagination. The play is at the same time a delightful entertainment for the audience and a contemplation by the dramatist of his own art.

# THE MERCHANT OF VENICE

Shakespeare created *The Merchant of Venice* out of two existing traditional stories: the tale of the heiress who can be won only by the choice of one of three caskets, and the tale of the malevolent usurer who tries to murder his debtor by cutting away a pound of his flesh. Both tales were already very ancient and had been told many times before Shakespeare wove them together in this one play. When combined they contain the ingredients of what could have been a thoroughly conventional romantic comedy: a rich, beautiful and intelligent heroine, a young, handsome, eligible hero and a villain whose animosity casts a temporary cloud over their marriage.

In adapting these stories for the stage, however, Shakespeare created a play which is far from simple or conventional, for he gave to the characters a complexity - even obscurity - of motivation which did not exist in the original versions. We have no doubt about how Shakespeare's characters act but we are constantly left uncertain as to why they act, and this sense of uncertainty is created by the very first scene, where we are invited to consider Antonio. Indeed in his opening speech Antonio admits that he himself is baffled by his own state of mind:

> In sooth, I know not why I am so sad.
> It wearies me; you say it wearies you;
> But how I caught it, found it, or came by it,
> What stuff 'tis made of, whereof it is born,
> I am to learn;
> And such a want-wit sadness makes of me
> That I have much ado to know myself.

The affectionate, concerned young merchants who are his friends offer various reasons for Antonio's dejection: one believes that he is anxious for the safety of his ships, another that he is in love, and a third - Gratiano - mockingly suggests that he puts on the appearance of solemnity in order to be thought wise. In view of the peril in which he later finds himself it may be that his sadness is a premonition of disaster but, since the true cause is never disclosed, we have no means of knowing.

As the scene develops, however, Shakespeare hints at another possible explanation if we choose to find it. The friendship between Antonio and Bassanio is shown to be a very intimate one. Bassanio confesses that to Antonio he owes the most 'in money and in love', and Antonio, in turn, assures Bassanio that his 'purse, person and extremest means' are all at his disposal. It also appears that Bassanio is about to desert his friend and go in quest of a wife, and, indeed, the wooing of Portia is the first subject Antonio mentions when the two men are left alone. His sadness may, therefore, arise from Bassanio's imminent departure and possible marriage. This in itself would be of no great significance did it not, in due course, reflect on the motives behind Antonio's offer to stand surety for Bassanio's loan from Shylock. To give money freely to a friend, as Antonio has evidently done in the past, or to offer to stand surety for a loan, as he now proposes to do, places an obligation – not a financial, but a less tangible moral obligation – on the recipient. Although, in wooing Portia, Bassanio is attempting to break free of the bonds of friendship and replace them with the bonds of marriage, Antonio is nevertheless keeping a hold on him by imposing on him a debt which can be repaid only by loyalty. The bond of loyalty which ties Bassanio to Antonio is not broken even when the former has crossed the sea to Belmont. In fact Bassanio is made to feel this obligation when, immediately after he has won his bride, he hears from Venice that Antonio's ships have been wrecked and that Shylock is threatening his life. No sooner has he pledged himself to Portia than he feels his moral debt to Antonio pulling him away from her:

> I have engag'd myself to a dear friend,
> Engag'd my friend to his mere enemy,
> To feed my means.

The words of Antonio's letter serve merely to tighten the bond which links Bassanio to him:

Since ... it is impossible I should live, all debts are clear'd between you and I if I might but see you at my death. Notwithstanding, use you pleasure; if your love do not persuade you to come, let not my letter.

Antonio, we are told, 'loves the world' only for the sake of Bassanio. His apparent selflessness in standing surety for his friend turns out, paradoxically, to be the means whereby he binds Bassanio to him, as Portia perceives:

> First go with me to church and call me wife,
> And then away to Venice to your friend;
> For never shall you lie by Portia's side
> With an unquiet soul.

If, at this point in the play, we reconsider the opening scene, we may question how far Antonio's apparent liberality was an indirect or unconscious form of possessiveness.

A baffling mixture of motives also seems to lie behind Bassanio's decision to try and win Portia as his wife. When asked by Antonio about the lady he intends to woo, he replies not by describing Portia but by reminding Antonio of his impoverishment and declaring his intention to recoup his losses by embarking on a new financial venture. It is in this context that he introduces the subject of Portia:

> In Belmont is a lady richly left,
> And she is fair, and fairer than that word,
> Of wondrous virtues.

Although Bassanio is not unaware of Portia's natural endowments, it is in her wealth that he is primarily interested. He will, as he explains, try to win her because his 'mind presages thrift' (that is, 'profit'), and, indeed, once he has gained her, he finds her as generous in her offer to pay off his debt to Shylock as Antonio had been to finance his expedition. In the event, of course, Shylock refuses to be bought off with money and Portia is compelled to save Antonio by exercising the 'wondrous virtue' of her intelligence. But in successfully thwarting Shylock's intentions, she also manages to bind Bassanio even more closely to herself, no longer simply as his wife but as the redeemer of his dearest friend.

Bassanio's double obligation to Portia becomes apparent at the end of the episode involving his gift to the supposed lawyer of his wife's ring. When asked by the disguised Portia, at the conclusion of the trial, to hand over the symbol of his recent marriage, Bassanio once more finds himself caught between two conflicting duties: his obligation to his wife, to whom he has sworn to keep the ring, and his gratitude to the saviour of his friend, to whom Antonio stands indebted 'in love and service evermore'. In handing over the ring he is conscious of breaking his oath to Portia, and his consequent sense of guilt is only removed when wife and lawyer turn out to be one and the same person. Whereas the play began with the cementing of Bassanio's bond of friendship with Antonio, it ends with the strengthening of his bond of marriage to Portia. 'Pardon this fault,' he begs his wife,

> and by my soul I swear
> I never more will break an oath with thee.

As though to point out the parallel between the opening and the closing of the play, Antonio then adds,

> I once did lend my body for his wealth,
> Which, but for him that had your husband's ring,

Had quite miscarried; I dare be bound again,
My soul upon the forfeit, that your lord
Will never more break faith advisedly.

As the couple finally leave the stage for their marriage bed, Antonio is left alone and, although it is difficult to decide how much Shakespeare intended us to be aware of the merchant's solitude, we can, if we wish, notice that his hold on Bossanio is now broken.

Shylock, as a usurer, deals professionally in bonds of a more literal and legal kind, and has a better understanding of their power. In making the, for him, exceptional offer of a loan free of interest, but in return for the promise of a pound of flesh should the money not be repaid, he claims to be acting out of generosity. 'I would be friends with you, and have your love,' he assures Antonio and the latter, at least, believes him, recognizing as he does so that a free loan is, indeed, a means of 'buying favour'. After the wreck of Antonio's ships, however, the 'merry bond' which Shylock had proposed ostensibly as a sign of peace becomes the means whereby he may make an attempt on the merchant's life. His initial expression of supposed friendship, like Antonio's initial gesture of love, enables him to exercise greater power over the recipient.

Shylock's true motives for proposing the bond are, of course, not generous at all, as the audience well knows, for he tells them in an aside that he hates Antonio because 'he is a Christian',

> But more for that in low simplicity
> He lends out money gratis and brings down
> The rate of usance with us here in Venice.

The Jew's animosity towards the Christian is, however, understandable because the latter has provoked it, as Shylock sharply points out:

> Signior Antonio, many a time and oft
> In the Rialto you have rated me
> About my moneys and my usances;
> Still have I born it with a patient shrug,
> For suff'rance is the badge of all our tribe;
> You call me misbeliever, cut-throat dog,
> And spit upon my Jewish gaberdine,
> And all for use of that which is mine own.

Antonio, far from denying these accusations, admits that he will go on persecuting Shylock as before:

> I am as like to call thee so again,
> To spit on thee again, to spurn thee too.

At this point in their conversation it is difficult to know which of the two is the more culpable, Antonio for his inhumanity towards Shylock or Shylock for his consequent hatred of Antonio. Hence, when the latter stands in the courtroom exposing his flesh to the edge of Shylock's knife, we again find it difficult to decide which of the two is the more guilty party, Antonio for persecuting Shylock or Shylock for trying to get his revenge. Religious persecution is perhaps preferable to attempted murder, but a firm, simple judgement cannot be made. Yet the situation takes place in a court of law where judgement one way or the other cannot be avoided.

The responsibility for deciding the case rests, as it turns out, in the hands of Portia and her first, shrewd and humane impulse is to avoid the necessity for judgement by appealing to Shylock's mercy. Had she succeeded she would have saved not only Antonio but, as we later realize, Shylock from the justice of the court. Both she and the Duke attempt repeatedly to dissuade Shylock from taking the pound of flesh to which he is legally entitled, by offering him more than the original sum, by appealing to his humanity, and by delaying the fatal moment with enquiries about the scales and the need for a surgeon, but he is adamant. What he fails to realize is that, in rejecting her pleas and persistently demanding the enforcement of justice, Shylock is unwittingly ensuring his own absolute defeat. Having turned the law against him by insisting that he shed no blood, Portia goes on to forbid not only the payment of three times the capital which Bassanio had offered him but the original sum itself and, by the time he makes his crestfallen exit from the court, Shylock finds himself deprived of half his goods and of the religious faith by which he had governed his life. The bond which the Jew had drawn up in order to avenge himself on the Christian produces the opposite result to the one he had intended. Designed to deprive Antonio of his life, it deprives Shylock of 'the means whereby he lives'.

In having to adjudicate between Shylock and Antonio, both Portia and the court are placed in a situation where no wholly satisfactory judgement can be made. Shylock has the law on his side and Portia rightly refuses to flout the law. But had she allowed Shylock to kill his victim in open court we should obviously not have found her judgement satisfactory. Nor, however, can we unreservedly approve the outcome of the trial as it stands. In spite of his mercenary preoccupations, the violence of his hatred towards Antonio and the unconstrained relish with which he holds the merchant in his power, Shylock is at the same time an often sympathetic figure and certainly the most powerfully living character in the play. His antipathy towards Antonio, as we have seen, has strong justification, especially when he associates himself with generations of Jews, his 'sacred nation', who have endured persecution by the Christians. 'Suff'rance' has, indeed, been the badge of all his tribe. The gentiles in the courtroom no doubt feel that, by requiring him to become a Christian, they are doing him a favour, compulsorily enabling him to save his soul. But for Shylock this must seem a final, cruel penalty exacted by a Christian majority which has always persecuted him. The audience are allowed to see both points of view and find them irreconcilable, not knowing where to place their sympathies.

This uncomfortable effect is sustained into the last act, in which the Christians, preoccupied as they are with their reunion in Belmont, the problem of the rings and the news that Antonio's ships are safe, give no thought at all to Shylock, whom they mention only once, and then as the enforced benefactor of Lorenzo and Jessica. It is unlikely that the audience, however, will so easily forget the ominous figure of Shylock, whose defeat they have just witnessed, and we may wonder how far Shakespeare intended their disregard of that ruined man to be a silent comment on their frivolity. The dramatist may or may not invite us to read between his lines.

To the interwoven stories of the pound of flesh and the three caskets, Shakespeare added two sub-plots, both of which again raise awkward questions about bonds and the conflict of loyalties. As Bassanio allows his friendship with Antonio to be superseded by his marriage to Portia, so Jessica deserts her father and absconds with his money in order to marry Lorenzo, an act which arouses in us those mixed feelings characteristic of this play. On the one hand we learn, from the few hints Shakespeare supplies, that Shylock is a cheeseparing housekeeper and a tyrannical father who forbids his daughter so much as to look at the antics of the irresponsible Christians. To that extent we can sympathise with her impulse to escape to freedom with her lover. On the other hand we can also see the effect of her elopement on Shylock, who feels affronted that his own 'flesh and blood' should abandon him. In the scene in which he first bewails the loss of his ducats and his daughter and then gloats over Antonio's losses, he appears by turns pathetic, vindictive and bizarre, but the impression we receive of Jessica through him is of a heartless and trivial girl who has little thought for her father's feelings or his property. Her brief, hasty reference to Shylock is scarcely a token gesture towards family loyalty:

> if my fortune be not crost,
> I have a father, you a daughter, lost.

She compares unfavourably with Portia, who obeys the instructions of her dead father to the letter even though they limit her freedom. Jessica's gain is shown to be Shylock's tangible loss and she scarcely senses the effect her elopment will have on him. Once again it is hard to judge which of the two is the more culpable.

Launcelot Gobbo, on the other hand, in his comic exposition of a similar choice is at least aware that he is in a moral dilemma. He recognizes that duty and conscience compel him to remain loyal to his master,

Shylock, yet he also believes that to remain faithful to a Jew is to serve 'a kind of devil':

> Certainly the Jew is the very devil incarnation; and, in my conscience, my conscience is but a kind of hard conscience to counsel me to stay with the Jew.

In his inward struggle between domestic and religious scruples, he decides to offer his services to Bassanio not because this is clearly the right course of action, for in doing so he obeys what he calls the voice of 'the fiend', but because that is where his own best interests lie: Shylock is a frugal house-keeper but Bassanio 'offers rare liveries'. As Shylock is abandoned first by his servant, then by his daughter, he consoles himself with his one hope, which is the defeat of Antonio. When that fails he appears to have neither means nor motive to survive and his last words, 'I am not well' sound chillingly ominous.

By combining these several plots into a single play, Shakespeare wrote what is a romantic comedy only in the outlines of its story. Moreover, in his frequent references to the deceitfulness of outward, surface appearances, he seems to invite us to look more deeply into it:

> So may the outward shows be least themselves.

Not only do the various bonds or agreements in which the characters casu-ally engage themselves turn out to have more serious effects than they had foreseen, but the play itself raises more worrying problems than its surface leads us to expect. The characters repeatedly find themselves forced to choose between conflicting obligations: Bassanio between the ties of friend-ship and those of marriage, Portia between her duty to her father and her natural desire to choose herself a husband, Shylock between the claims of justice and those of mercy, Jessica between her obligation to Shylock and her desire for money, love and freedom, Gobbo between the voice of 'con-science' and the temptations of 'the fiend'. Indeed the central dramatic episodes all portray moments of choice, as Portia's suitors in turn assess the significance of the three caskets and she herself determines the fates of Antonio and Shylock in the courtroom. The one characteristic which all these situations share in common is that they admit of no wholly satisfactory solution: in giving Portia's ring to the lawyer, Bassanio betrays his wife's trust and in saving Antonio Portia at the same time ruins Shylock. It can be no accident that, as Lorenzo and Jessica wait idly at Belmont for Portia's return, their conversation (which could have been about all kinds of things) is about lovers whose loyalties have been betrayed: Troilus by Cressida, Dido by Aeneas, and Shylock by his faithless daughter.

So frequently is this idea repeated that Shakespeare seems to assume that insoluble dilemmas and unavoidable betrayals are an inescapable part of the human condition and this idea is underlined by the occasional comments on the frailty and corruption of human nature. 'If to do were as easy as to know what 'twere good to do,' says Portia, 'chapels had been churches, and poor men's cottages princes' palaces. It is a good divine that follows his own instructions.' And, on her return from Venice, seeing the light of home and thinking, possibly, about the drama in which she has just been engaged:

> How far that little candle throws its beams!
> So shines a good deed in a naughty world.

The one idea of perfection invoked in this play is that of the abstract, divine expression of music, especially the transcendent music of the spheres which, however, is so perfect that it cannot be heard by the mortal, corrupted senses of men. 'Such harmony,' says Lorenzo,

> is in immortal souls,
> But whilst this muddy vesture of decay
> Doth grossly close it in, we cannot hear it.

In the imperfect world Shakespeare portrayed in *The Merchant of Venice* few, if any, actions are wholly good and few, if any, choices are between the absolutes of right and wrong. Beneath the surface of this immensely popular comedy we can find, if we choose to look for them, ideas which are not comic at all.

# THE FIRST PART OF
# KING HENRY THE FOURTH

Shakespeare devoted four plays – *Richard II*, *Henry IV Part I*, *Henry IV Part II* and *Henry V* – to the history of England from the time of the rebellion of Henry Bolingbroke against Richard II to the time of Henry V's campaign against the French and his victory at Agincourt. Each play is coherent and intelligible in itself but can also be seen as part of a large-scale historical drama in twenty acts. In these plays Shakespeare does not simply portray the major political events of this period but also shows the reasons why they happened. He demonstrates why Richard was replaced on the throne by Bolingbroke; why, when he became Henry IV, Bolingbroke failed to keep his subjects at peace; how Bolingbroke's son, Prince Hal, prepared himself for his duties as King; and why, as Henry V, he created among his subjects a sense of unity and led them to victory against their traditional enemies, the French. Shakespeare is both a political dramatist and a political analyst.

He wrote *Henry IV Part I* in about 1597, when he was in his early thirties and had already completed such masterpieces as *Romeo and Juliet*, *Richard II* and *A Midsummer Night's Dream*. It is even more remarkable than these earlier plays for the variety and vividness of its characterization. Practically every character is strongly and strikingly created – not simply the major protagonists such as Falstaff, Hotspur and the King, but minor figures such as Mistress Quickly, Bardolph, Worcester and Lady Percy. Each of them displays his individuality by the uniquely personal language and style Shakespeare has created for him; the speeches of any one character could not be mistaken for those of another.

Here, for example, is Falstaff pondering on the physical evidence of his decline into old age:

Bardolph, am I not fall'n away vilely since this last action? Do I not bate? Do I not dwindle? Why, my skin hangs about me like an old lady's loose gown; I am withered like an old apple-john.

Falstaff's homely imagination not only creates a vivid impression of his own degenerating flesh but conveys his pleasure in language itself, a pleasure

which is, of course, Shakespeare's. A similarly inventive, delighted use of
language can be seen in Hotspur's explosive speeches, such as his outburst of
impatience against Glendower:

> O, he is as tedious
> As a tired horse, a failing wife;
> Worse than a smoky house. I had rather live
> With cheese and garlic in a windmill, far,
> Than feed on cates and have him talk to me
> In any summer house in Christendom.

Hotspur's tone of voice is totally different from Falstaff's, but both speeches
are expansive, voluble, filled with similes, one growing apparently spontaneously out of another. Their references, moreover, are to the intimate details
of contemporary domestic life – an old woman's ample dress, a parlour filled
with wood-smoke – with the result that we are made aware both of the
personality of the man who is speaking and of the small, telling details of the
social life to which he belongs. Shakespeare's history plays have been called
an English epic, and this is true not simply because they portray the career of
a great national hero, Henry V, but because they convey an impression of the
life of the whole country.

   This variety of character and style is not to be found in the first of the four
plays, *Richard II*, and the difference must be deliberate: the deposition of the
hereditary feudal monarch appears to have liberated a nation of individual-
ists who find themselves no longer constrained by ancient social structures
but free to assert their personal independence. It is not only the political
revolutionaries, Worcester, Northumberland and Hotspur, who are rebels.
In this play practically everyone is temperamentally a rebel, including Prince
Hal, who appears to despise his political responsibilities, Falstaff, who abuses
his authority in the war to line his own pockets, and even the King, who can
never forget that he is a usurper. Yet it is the usurper who has the job of
controlling this collection of idiosyncratic, rebellious individuals in the hope
that they may co-operate with him and one another and thereby become a
nation. Moreover the usurper, lacking the legal right to govern, has no force
to support him other than that of his own personality. The impression he
creates on his subjects is all-important.

   Henry IV fails to control his people because he suffers the consequences of
his seizure of the crown; Prince Hal succeeds partly because he inherits the
throne by right of birth and partly because he knows how to win his subjects'
loyalty. Whereas the old King provides a link with the past, with the deposition portrayed in *Richard II*, the memory of which haunts him, the young
Prince provides a link with the future, with the responsibilities he undertakes in *Henry V*, for which he skilfully prepares himself.

   Henry Bolingbroke acquired the throne through the help of the Percy family: Thomas, Earl of Worcester, Henry, Earl of Northumberland and his son Henry Hotspur. In the early days of the rebellion he took care to ingratiate himself with these men on whom his success depended. But, as *Henry IV Part I* opens, he attempts to impose his royal authority over them and thereby provokes their resentment. When, for example, Henry accuses Northumberland of disrespect, the latter retorts that the King is indebted to his family for the very power he is now trying to assert:

> Our house, my sovereign liege, little deserves
> The scourge of greatness to be us'd on it –
> And that same greatness too which our own hands
> Have holp to make so portly.

It is their resentment against the man they have themselves placed in authority that provokes the Percys to rebel. They also fear that his sense of dependence on them will prove so embarrassing that he will find a pretext to do away with them:

> For, bear ourselves as even as we can,
> The King will always think him in our debt,
> And think we think ourselves unsatisfied,
> Till he hath found a time to pay us home.

They are determined to overthrow him before he can eradicate them and, consequently, form an alliance with the Welsh and the Scots in an attempt to force their former ally from the throne. Even when, just before the opposing armies meet at Shrewsbury, Henry offers them an amnesty, Worcester persists in his conviction that the King will sooner or later want to dispose of them:

> It is not possible, it cannot be,
> The King should keep his word in loving us;
> He will suspect us still, and find a time
> To punish this offence in other faults.

On the basis of this conjecture, Worcester refuses the offered pardon and proceeds with the attack which costs Hotspur his life. Henry IV is troubled throughout his reign by the very men to whom he owes his power.

He is also troubled by his fears for the future. He regards his son as a contemptible profligate who has cheapened his reputation by consorting with the common people instead of playing his part in affairs of state. Hal, he believes, has debased himself with 'vile participation':

> Not an eye
> But is aweary of thy common sight,
> Save mine, which hath desir'd to see thee more.

For this reason Henry looks forward with dread to his son's accession to the throne and the derision with which, he believes, his subjects will treat him. Hal's accession to power is also eagerly awaited by Falstaff, not with apprehension, but in the hope that his ally in crime will give him licence to indulge his appetites without restraint. During their first scene together and in their charades at the Boar's Head Tavern, Falstaff constantly tests Hal in order to discover what his own prospects will be when his companion becomes King.

The impression the audience receives of Hal's conduct does not, however, correspond with the low opinion held of him by the King and Falstaff. Although the Prince appears to debase himself by associating with petty malefactors, he claims that he does so deliberately as an act of political policy. Unlike Richard II (to whom his father mistakenly compares him) he is not naturally dissolute but chooses to appear so in order that,when the need arises, he may appear miraculously to reform and thereby arouse the grateful admiration of his people. As he explains in his soliloquy at the end of the second scene, the association with Falstaff has been contrived in order to 'falsify men's hopes' so that his ultimate reformation may 'show more goodly and attract more eyes'. He intends to gain the loyalty of his subjects by astonishing them.

In order to rule successfully, the medieval monarch had, ideally, to display two fundamental virtues: justice in time of peace and courage in time of war. Prince Hal demonstrates his possession of the former, the civic virtue, in *Henry IV Part II* by placing his trust in the Lord Chief Justice and sending Falstaff to gaol. He reveals the latter, the military virtue, in *Part I* by the symbolic act of defeating the most distinguished soldier of his age, Henry Hotspur. Hotspur in certain superficial ways resembles Hal. They have the same name, they are about the same age (and Shakespeare altered the historical facts to make their ages similar), both are eager to acquire what they call 'honour', or fame in battle, and, indeed, the King twice compares the two men to Hal's disadvantage. For Hotspur the pursuit of honour is an obsession, an ideal which takes precedence over all others, a reward for which no risk is too great:

> By heaven, methinks it were an easy leap
> To pluck bright honour from the pale-fac'd moon;
> Or dive into the bottom of the deep,
> Where fathom-line could never touch the ground,
> And pluck up drowned by the locks;
> So he that doth redeem her thence might wear
> Without corrival all her dignities.

He is a rash, impulsive, spontaneous man, at home only on the battlefield and, like a good many English aristocrats, has as much respect for his horse as for his wife. In his element he is, as everyone agrees, unparalleled, 'the king of honour'. In challenging and defeating Hotspur in single combat, therefore, the Prince is not simply defending his father against a dangerous rebel but giving a public demonstration of his filial loyalty and his superiority in battle over the greatest soldier of his time.

Hotspur is an exciting, even an inspiring figure because of his energetic singlemindedness: he rises with enthusiasm to the challenge of war and welcomes even the desertion of his allies because, without them, he is exposed to greater danger and can thereby win greater honour. But his obsessive preoccupation with war, which is his strength, also makes him appear ridiculous. Off the battlefield, in the domestic surroundings of his home at Warkworth or in the political negotiations with Glendower, he is restless, irritable, tactless and impatient. Hal, though he respects Hotspur, has no wish to copy him. Hal has a larger mind, capable of entering into a wider variety of experiences of which war is only one and which includes his high-spirited association with Falstaff.

Falstaff has as much vitality as Hotspur, and shows a similarly whole-hearted dedication to his own way of life and a similar tendency to boast of his prowess. In all other ways the two men are total opposites. Whereas Hotspur is spontaneously truthful, Falstaff has a genius for the inspired lie; whereas Hotspur dedicates himself to honour – and, indeed, dies in the pursuit of it – Falstaff argues that honour is a delusion; whereas Hotspur embraces danger eagerly, Falstaff takes flight after the Gadshill robbery and feigns death in order to survive. He is in many ways repellent: physically grotesque, morally irresponsible, grossly self-indulgent, an ageing rake. He is also one of the most popular and enjoyable characters in the whole of literature. The reason for his popularity is, perhaps, that he represents that part of ourselves which would like to flout moral and social convention, to defy the law and to devote itself without restraint to survival and the gratification of our appetites. He expresses our secret and unattainable desire to remain irresponsible children.

The action of *Henry IV Part I* is distributed between three different places, the court, the tavern and the battlefield. Each location has what might be called a presiding character: the King, preoccupied with politics and the instability of the state; Falstaff, dedicated to pleasure and the satisfaction of his appetites; and Hotspur, obsessed with revenge on Bolingbroke and the acquisition of martial glory. The only character who moves freely between all three places is the Prince, who can be, as the occasion requires, the dutiful son, the willing foil to Falstaff and the responsible and courageous soldier. His adaptability to any society makes him destined to be a popular ruler, capable, when he becomes Henry V, of dealing firmly with the French ambassadors, chatting intimately with the common soldiers and exhorting his troops to victory. Yet this very flexibility of temperament makes him a less forceful, a more elusive and impenetrable personality than anyone else in the play. He responds so readily, so convincingly to everybody that one suspects that he may have no essential personality at all but is a mere reflection of the company he happens to keep. His first scene with Falstaff is particularly revealing – or, rather significantly, unrevealing: throughout their conversation he leaves all the initiative to the other man and either shrugs off or evades Falstaff's attempts to discover his intentions. The fact is that the man who was to become the most successful of all English monarchs, the idol of his people, is an impenetrable, enclosed person. His most intimate self, if it exists, remains hidden. To set out deliberately, as a matter of policy, to exploit his association with Falstaff for the sake of his public reputation does not commend him to us. It requires a calculated deception both of his apparent friend and of his future subjects. And, though his policy succeeds to his own advantage and that of the nation, he is guilty of assuming that the means are justified by the end.

Hal is, however, not the only character who tries to make use of others to his own advantage: just as he makes use of Falstaff for political purposes, so Falstaff hopes to profit from Hal on the latter's accession. And if Hal intends to enhance his reputation by defeating Hotspur, then he is merely playing the same game as his rival. In his dying moments Hotspur confesses that he is more deeply wounded by his loss of reputation than by his loss of life:

> I better brook the loss of brittle life
> Than those proud titles thou hast won of me:
> They wound my thoughts worse than thy sword my flesh.

In its assertive vitality, the world of *Henry IV Part I* is fiercely competitive: the King makes use of the Percys, Falstaff attempts to profit from Hal, Hotspur competes for honour against the Prince, and Hal is such a master of deception that even his own father is taken in by him. In this competitive world the victory is awarded not to the most morally deserving but to the toughest and the shrewdest. It is Hal who succeeds in the end, and in showing us how he succeeds Shakespeare makes a coldly realistic comment on the nature of politics.

# THE SECOND PART OF
# KING HENRY THE FOURTH

In certain fairly obvious ways Part II of *Henry IV* resembles Part I. In the earlier of the two plays Prince Hal separates himself from his apparently frivolous association with Falstaff, makes a pledge to the King that he will take on his public responsibilities, demonstrates his loyalty by taking part in the Battle of Shrewsbury and, in the final moments, stands victorious over the body of the rebel leader and his own rival, Hotspur. In Part II Hal is, for a second time, thought by the King to be neglecting his duty and to be likely, on his accession to the throne, to become an irresponsible ruler, incapable of winning the respect of his people. Towards the end of the play, however, the Prince again shows his good intentions by entrusting the law to the authority of the Lord Chief Justice and displays his final separation from Falstaff by banishing the latter from his company and announcing that he is no longer the profligate he once appeared to be. Whereas in Part I Hal exhibited his military virtues and loyalty in battle, so in Part II he manifests his civic virtues, his reverence for the law. And as the defeat of Hotspur forms the climax and conclusion of the earlier play, so the rejection of Falstaff completes the latter.

The action of *Henry IV Part II* is again distributed mostly between three locations: Falstaff continues to occupy the tavern, the King meditates on his own past in the isolation of the palace, and the rebels are again confronted and overcome on the battlefield, though this time without a struggle. Several of the minor characters also reappear: Mistress Quickly, Bardolph, Lady Percy, and Northumberland, whose career we can follow from his first appearance at the court of Richard II to his defeat in Yorkshire, which is reported in this play. The inclusion of these same characters conveys to us the sense of the continuing movement of history and, more importantly, makes us realize how they, and circumstances, have changed.

One striking change is the absence from *Henry IV Part II* of Hotspur. His inspired leadership and his enjoyment of the challenge of war coloured the first phase of the rebellion with an attractive vitality, an exciting recklessness. He was motivated not simply by contempt for the monarch whom his family had helped into power but by the pursuit of military glory for its own sake. With his death the rebels have no such heroic ideal to support them; they are deprived of a leader of any stature and seem uncertain of their own motives. Northumberland, maddened with grief at the death of his son, cries out for slaughter as a means of revenging himself upon the world. Archbishop Scroop, who has replaced Hotspur at the head of the rebellion, believes the nation is sick and takes upon himself the responsibility of purging it by insurrection; his ally, Lord Bardolph, appears to revolt merely in response to the earlier defeat at Shrewsbury. They are, we are told, accompanied by an army of commoners as disenchanted with Henry IV as they had been with Richard II. Such motives are not inspiring; the revolution is apparently failing for want of conviction.

The vitality has also gone out of Falstaff. In Part I, although obviously irresponsible, a liar and a cheat, he was, nevertheless, capable of transforming his weaknesses into assets by the singleminded enthusiasm with which he indulged them. In Part II, far from commanding the tavern by the largeness of his personality, he is actually dominated for a time by the bizarre, disreputable Pistol, whose misquotations from plays once fashionable but now outmoded suggest that he has lost touch with the times. Wearied by Pistol's continual ranting, Falstaff pathetically, and uncharacteristically, asks for quiet.

Another reason why Falstaff appears tarnished is the almost total absence from the tavern of Prince Hal. Among his associates Hal was his only equal in initiative, vitality and quickness of wit; the one relied upon and inspired the other. In Part II they are together only twice: once in the tavern and once during Hal's progress from his coronation, when he meets his former companion for the last time and disowns him. When the Prince, with some reluctance, pays his last visit to the Boar's Head, in a scene placed at exactly the same point (Act II Scene iv) as the great tavern scene in Part I, it is obvious that he has outgrown Falstaff. The two no longer talk to each other as equals. Hal accuses Falstaff of slandering him to the Hostess:

You whoreson candle-mine, you, how vilely did you speak of me even now before this honest, virtuous, civil gentlewoman!

But Falstaff no longer has the wit to take up this challenge. His retort is feebly ingratiating:

No, no, no; not so; I did not think thou wast within hearing . . . No abuse, Hal, o' mine honour; no abuse . . . No abuse, Ned, i' the' world; honest Ned, none. I disprais'd him before the wicked – that the wicked might not fall in love with thee; in which doing, I have done the part of a careful friend and a true subject.

He struggles ineffectually to creep into the favour of the heir apparent. Falstaff had always been a boaster but his former claims to courage, loyalty, honesty and good looks were so outrageous that they amounted to self-parody, designed to be only half believed. In Part II he is smug. His tedious, self-glorifying monologues are delivered not to the Prince but to his newly acquired page. They might as well be delivered into vacancy. Hal's absence from the tavern makes Falstaff appear shrunk and serves as a warning to the audience that the Prince has dissociated himself from the common people and is advancing towards that solitary eminence which his father is about to relinquish. It is a warning which Falstaff does not heed.

Such criticisms as Falstaff receives are not the affectionate insults he formerly suffered from Hal but the honest, disinterested truth spoken by the Lord Chief Justice. He tries to draw the latter into the game of self-deception he had confidently played with Hal:

You that are old consider not the capacities of us that are young; you do measure the heat of our livers with the bitterness of your galls; and we that are in the vaward of our youth, I must confess, are wags too.

The Lord Chief Justice is not enchanted but treats Falstaff's pretensions to youth with derision:

Do you set down your name in the scroll of youth, that are written down old with all the characters of age? Have you not a moist eye, a dry hand, a yellow cheek, a white beard, a decreasing leg, an increasing belly? Is not your voice broken, your wind short, your chin double, your wit single, and every part about you blasted with antiquity? Fie, fie, fie, Sir John!

In Part I the Prince had called him, among other things, a 'bed-presser', but the audience was denied the spectacle of Falstaff actually pressing a bed. In Part II he appears in the company of a new character, Doll Tearsheet, a whore, whom he accuses of spreading syphilis. His body is consumed with the pox as his purse is with extravagance, and both diseases are incurable. In one moment of truth he admits, 'I am old.'

Most of the time, however, he continues to behave as though neither he nor circumstances have changed, assured of his own charms, confident that the Prince will, on his accession, long to see him and will make him great. Because the audience knows otherwise and sees through his delusions they regard his optimism as pathetic. The irony with which Shakespeare induces us to view Falstaff's hopes becomes extreme when, knowing that the Prince has already entrusted the law to the Lord Chief Justice, we observe Falstaff rushing eagerly to London in the belief that the young King is sick for him:

Let us take any man's horses: the laws of England are at my commandment. Blessed are they that have been my friends; and woe to my Lord Chief Justice!

Henry V's rejection of Falstaff comes as no surprise to us. Yet Falstaff still refuses to accept the truth: he disappears from Hal's life protesting that he will be 'sent for soon at night'.

The belief that nothing has changed also afflicts another new character, Justice Shallow, and we can see why. The regular, seasonal life of his farm in Gloucestershire has repeated itself annually without alteration. We learn from his rambling conversations with his cousin Silence and his servant Davy that bullocks are still sold at Stamford Fair, that his land will again be sown with red wheat and that the smith continues to make plough irons and new links for the bucket. Shallow's neighbours have extraordinary rural names such as William Visor of Woncot and Clement Perkes o' th' Hill. Their assocation with specific places in Gloucestershire conveys the impression that their families have lived there for generations (and, indeed, the scholars have discovered that the Visors actually did live at Woodmancote, or 'Woncot', not far from Berkeley Castle, where Richard II had arrived on his return from Ireland). But as the seasonal processes of nature have recurred, Robert Shallow has grown old, and living in this rural backwater, he keeps himself alive with distorted recollections of his youth:

I was once of Clement's Inn; where I think they will talk of mad Shallow yet . . . There was I, and little John Doit of Staffordshire, and black George Barnes, and Francis Pickbone, and Will Squele a Cotsole man – you had not four such swinge-bucklers in all the Inns o' Court again. And I may say to you we knew where the bona-robas were, and had the best of them all at commandment . . . Jesu, Jesu, the mad days that I have spent!

As the ageing Falstaff lives in hopes of a spectacular future, so Shallow cheers himself with the recollection of a past which never existed: 'Lord, Lord,' says Falstaff, 'how subject we old men are to this vice of lying!'

In no other play does Shakespeare convey so fully and so intimately the effects of age. They show themselves in the dying King's anxieties for the future of his people, in Lady Percy's memories of the dead Hotspur, in Shallow's illogical, bemused conversations and the state of Falstaff's urine. Whereas the distinctive quality of Shakespeare's writing in Part I (as I suggested in my Preface to that play) is its expansive vitality, the dialogue of Part II conveys a sense of exhaustion:

| | |
|---|---|
| *King Henry* | Then you perceive the body of our kingdom |
| | How foul it is; what rank diseases grow, |
| | And with what danger, near the heart of it. |
| *Archbishop* | We are all diseas'd |
| | And with our surfeiting and wanton hours |
| | Have brought ourselves into a burning fever, |
| | And we must bleed for it. |
| *Lord Chief Justice* | [to Falstaff] You are as a candle, the better part burnt out. |

> *Shallow*    Is old Double of your town living yet?
> *Silence*    Dead, sir.

The sense of disintegration, sickness and mortality felt by so many of the characters is a manifestation of the more fundamental process of change itself which, as it propels King Henry, Falstaff and Shallow towards death and obscurity, brings Prince Hal towards power.

The world of *Henry IV Part II* is an unstable, insecure one where events turn out contrary to the expectations of the characters: the first scene opens with the arrival of three successive messengers carrying conflicting news of victory and defeat; Falstaff reaches Westminster 'stained with travel', 'sweating with desire' to see the new King, only to be brushed aside, rejected; the rebels, believing they have been offered a fair peace, disband their soldiers and are promptly escorted to the executioner's block; the Prince, thinking his father dead, takes up the crown and resolves to wear it with honour, only to discover that the King is still alive, and Henry, imagining that he will die as a pilgrim in Jerusalem, ends his life in a room in the palace of that name. The play is introduced by a Prologue spoken by the allegorical figure of Rumour, whose nature it is to spread 'surmises, jealousies [or suspicions], conjectures', and it is on false surmises that King Henry, Falstaff, Shallow and the rebels build their lives. Only the Prince foresees the future correctly and that is why he has the power and ability to control it.

A bewildered weariness with the unpredictability of life, a conviction that the only certainty is change itself, is powerfully expressed in a great speech by the King, whose own troubled experience has given him good reason to believe it:

> O God! that one might read the book of fate,
> And see the revolution of the times
> Make mountains level, and the continent,
> Weary of solid firmness, melt itself
> Into the sea; and other times to see
> The beachy girdle of the ocean
> Too wide for Neptune's hips; how chances mock,
> And changes fill the cup of alteration
> With divers liquors! O, if this were seen,
> The happiest youth, viewing his progress through,
> What perils past, what crosses to ensue,
> Would shut the book and sit him down and die.

For Henry, it seems, the only thing which makes the instability of history tolerable is our customary ignorance of it.

There is, however, a secure foundation on which a king can rest his authority and that is the man-made principles of justice and the law. If we trace the civil wars which plagued Henry IV back to their origins, we can find them in Richard II's disregard for the law in seizing the estates which belonged by right to Bolingbroke, and in Bolingbroke's consequent usurpation of the throne which was, of course, legally Richard's. To break the laws of property and inheritance is easy. They have only as much efficacy as men choose to give them. But without them nations are in danger of becoming barbarians, and that is what the King believes will happen when his apparently lawless son succeeds him:

> For the fifth Harry from curb'd license plucks
> The muzzle of restraint, and the wild dog
> Shall flesh his tooth on every innocent.

When his son actually does become king, however, the rule of justice is assured and this prospect is foreshadowed when he entrusts the guardianship of the law to the character who embodies it. The Lord Chief Justice is not an interesting man. He is not as engaging as the humanly fallible characters such as Falstaff or Shallow, and, significantly, he has no personal name, only a title. He is, however, dependably honest – not a common virtue in this play – and has a loyalty to the law which takes precedence over his obligations to any individual, including the Prince. Just before his coronation, the new King presents him with the 'unstained sword' of justice, with the injunction that he should

> use the same
> With the like bold, just, and impartial spirit
> As you have done 'gainst me.

In acknowledging the Lord Chief Justice as his father, as he calls him, Henry V implicitly disowns the 'father ruffian' Falstaff, who learns shortly afterwards that the laws of England are not at his commandment.

Of all the rulers whose lives Shakespeare dramatized, Henry V was the most successful. The seemingly frivolous, degenerate youth transformed himself into a responsible king and, out of loyalty to him, his subjects became again united. Yet his final action in this play, his dismissal of Falstaff, inevitable though it is, appears at the same time distasteful, and it confirms the uneasiness Hal has aroused in us from his first appearance in Part I. He has never actually encouraged Falstaff's false expectations. He has promised him nothing. On the contrary he has warned him that his banishment will eventually come. Falstaff's dream of power is largely self-induced, one of the fantasies indulged in by several characters in *Henry IV*. Perhaps what is offensive about Hal is his lack of spontaneity, his ability always to calculate exactly what he is doing and to carry out to the letter the plans he makes for himself. This is particularly striking when we compare him with Falstaff, a creature of instinct, even though it is an instinct to deceive or simply survive. And Falstaff never keeps his maudlin resolutions to mend his ways. When Hal relaxes in the tavern he is the heir-apparent playing at relaxation. When, in both parts, he publicly displays his reformation, he has not really reformed because he has never actually been dissolute. He plays these various roles so skilfully that he even convinces his own father. What, then, is the essential Hal, the man who performs his roles with such professionalism? Shakespeare never reveals him. This is not to say that Shakespeare disapproved of him. He believed that Hal had the qualities necessary for a ruler to be successful. He also recognized that successful kings are not the most congenial individuals.

# The Merry Wives of Windsor

*The Merry Wives of Windsor* is a different kind of play from Shakespeare's other comedies. Whereas his earlier comedies such as *The Two Gentlemen of Verona* and *A Midsummer Night's Dream* had mostly been about love, courtship and marriage, the romantic interest in this play (the wooing of Anne Page by Fenton) occupies only a small part of the action, the body of which deals with Falstaff's attempts to woo Mistress Ford for her money. Again, though the plots of the other comedies frequently depend on the disguise of women as men (as when Portia appears as a lawyer and Viola as a servant), this is the only play of Shakespeare's in which a man is disguised as a woman, and the effect is entirely different. In impersonating a man, Viola makes herself pathetically vulnerable, but Falstaff dressed up as the old woman of Brentford is simply ridiculous. The settings of this play in Ford's house and the Garter Inn are, like those of the other comedies, domestic, but *The Merry Wives* takes place not in some remote or imaginary land such as Belmont or Illyria, but in an English country town only a few miles from the theatre where the play was acted. The setting, the plot and, above all, the dialogue are more naturalistic than those of the other comedies and they developed not out of *A Midsummer Night's Dream* or *The Merchant of Venice* but out of the comic scenes in the two parts of *Henry IV* in which several of the major characters – Falstaff, Shallow, Pistol, Bardolph and Mistress Quickly – had already made an appearance.

Shakespeare's reintroduction of characters who had already proved popular in the history plays gave rise to the notion (which may or may not be based on fact) that he wrote *The Merry Wives* at the request of Queen Elizabeth who, it was said, had been so delighted by Falstaff in *Henry IV* that she wished to see him again. The idea was first put forward by the critic John Dennis, who in 1702 published his own adaptation of *The Merry Wives* under the title of *The Comical Gallant*. In the dedication he declared that Shakespeare's play had been written at the Queen's command, and that

she was so eager to see it acted that she commanded it to be finished in fourteen days; and was afterwards, as the tradition tells us, very well pleased at the representation.

Further details were added to the story by the first biographer of Shake-speare, Nicholas Rowe, who in 1709 wrote that the Queen

was so well pleased with that admirable character of Falstaff, in the two parts of *Henry IV*, that she commanded him [Shakespeare] to continue it for one play more, and to show him in love. This is said to be the occasion of his writing *The Merry Wives of Windsor*.

Whether or not the comedy was commissioned by the Queen, it does look like an attempt to capitalize on a recent popular success and the experiment worked very well: it has been a continuous favourite with theatre audiences ever since.

Its resemblance to the comic scenes of the history plays goes deeper than this, however. It also resembles them in the vitality and colloquial realism of its dialogue. *The Merry Wives* is written mostly in prose (of which there is a larger proportion than in any of Shakespeare's other plays) and it is a prose of great inventiveness and vigour. Few of the characters are content to use one word when three or four others can be brought in to emphasize and expand their meaning:

[This Falstaff] is given to fornications, and to taverns, and sack, and wine, and metheglins, and to drinkings, and swearings, and starings, pribbles and prabbles.

This is Sir Hugh Evans, the Welsh parson, and he has a characteristically Welsh eloquence, but he is not the only character who gives vent to his powers of self-expression. Here, for example, is Ford denouncing the old woman of Brentford:

A witch, a quean, an old cozening quean! . . . She works by charms, by spells, by th' figure, and such daub'ry as this is, beyond our element. We know nothing. Come down, you witch, you hag you; come down, I say.

The most verbally imaginative character, however, is Falstaff, and his inven-tiveness with language is consistent with his resourcefulness as a character, his refusal to accept that he is past his prime, his inability to be put down. 'Come,' he cries to Mistress Ford,

I cannot cog, and say thou art this and that, like a many of these lisping hawthorn-buds that come like women in men's apparel, and smell like Bucklersbury in simple time; I cannot; but I love thee, none but thee; and thou deserv'st it.

The liveliness of the dialogue expresses the animation, the vividly idio-syncratic qualities of the characters. It is the kind of excited rhetoric that Shakespeare's audiences had previously heard from the inmates of the Boar's Head tavern in *Henry IV* and its vituperative slang sounds distinctively English.

The dialogue is also full of traditional English proverbs. 'If money go before,' says Ford, 'all ways do lie open', and Page, accepting Fenton's marriage to Anne Page, declares that 'What cannot be eschew'd must be embraced.' There are also sayings which, although not strictly proverbs, have a proverbial ring about them, such as Anne Page's comment on the proposed marriage between herself and the French doctor:

> Alas, I had rather be set quick i' th' earth,
> And bowl'd to death with turnips.

Improbable though the plot of *The Merry Wives* may be, we are the more ready to believe in it because the characters sound so real.

The realistic effect of the play is also created by the profusion of domestic references which fill in the details of the characters and give us an idea of the kind of lives they lead when they are off the stage. Mistress Quickly, for example, tells us what it means to be Caius's housekeeper:

I keep his house; and I wash, wring, brew, bake, scour, dress meat and drink, make the beds, and do all myself.

Shakespeare has fully imagined the world she lives in. Similarly, we learn that at night she enjoys 'a posset' with the manservant Rugby 'at the latter end of a seacole fire', that at Hallowmass Slender lent his Book of Riddles to a certain Alice Shortcake, that Page has a greyhound which ran at the Cotswold races, and that, when he and his neighbours leave the stage, they enjoy 'a hot venison pasty to dinner' made from the venison Shallow has given him, and that there will be 'pippins and cheese' to follow. Quite apart from its success on the stage, *The Merry Wives* is a document in the social history of England. We can learn, and sense, from it how Shakespeare's contemporaries lived.

The popularity of *The Merry Wives* in the theatre has no doubt been the result not only of its eloquently realistic dialogue but of the comic suspense which it arouses in an audience, and this is derived from the skill with which it is constructed. It is worth examining how one of its most successful comic moments, Falstaff's declaration of love to Mistress Ford, is achieved. The preparation for this episode has begun in the middle of the first act, where we learn that Falstaff, down on his luck, hopes to get his hands on Ford's money by feigning love to the woman who holds the purse strings, Ford's wife. To raise our expectations, Shakespeare first tells us what is about to happen but then keeps us waiting before we see Falstaff's plan in action. As we wait, we also discover that Ford, disguised as the supposedly amorous Brook, learns of the plot from Falstaff himself and, in a fit of jealousy, resolves to 'detect' his wife and 'be revenged' on Falstaff. Finally, as the encounter between Falstaff and his paramour approaches, we watch the two wives prepare the laundry basket in which they intend the knight to make a forced exit and be thrown into the Thames. Each of the three protagonists is plotting against the other: Falstaff intends to cuckold Ford, Ford intends to expose his wife and Mistress Ford to outwit Falstaff. None of the characters, of course, is aware of the others' intentions; only the audience is in possession of all the facts, and as Falstaff's arrival at the back door of Ford's house is announced, we wait to see the three stratagems converge. The suspense is heightened, moreover, because, although all three of the characters think they know what will happen, none of them knows, as we do, what actually will happen. Falstaff's first words to Mistress Ford, 'Have I caught thee, my heavenly jewel?', are therefore brilliantly comic not simply because they are inappropriate both to him and the woman he is addressing but because they indicate that the collision of the three plots is now about to happen.

The comic effect of this episode arises from the dramatic irony Shakespeare has set up: the audience knows more than the characters. Ford's wife knows nothing of her husband's approach, Falstaff knows nothing of her plan to outwit him, and Ford knows nothing of the buck-basket. It is also a potentially violent situation in that Ford is already consumed by jealousy and his wife's practical joke is likely to degrade and discomfort Falstaff. We react to the situation as to a set of unexploded but relatively harmless bombs. When they go off we are satisfied, relieved and delighted. But, so skilful is Shakespeare's art of preparation that he has no sooner concluded this episode than he embarks on the next. The buck-basket scene ends with the two wives' resolution to play yet 'more tricks on Falstaff', and to send for him at eight o'clock the next morning. It is by this means that, as Samuel Johnson said of Shakespeare, 'The mind is carried irresistibly forward.'

By the time he wrote *The Merry Wives*, Shakespeare had already had at least ten years experience in the theatre as both actor and playwright, and his organization of his material shows that he knew exactly how to control an audience. His skill in construction can also be seen in the links and connections he has made between the various characters. The comic Frenchman Caius is a kind of twin to the comic Welshman Evans. The former, a doctor, is a curer of bodies and the other, a parson, a curer of souls; the one, as the Host says, supplies 'the potions and the motions'; the other 'the proverbs and the no-verbs'. The symmetry of the construction extends further. Fenton, the eligible suitor for the hand of Anne Page, is obviously contrasted with her two ridiculous suitors, and young Fenton's pursuit of Anne for love is contrasted with old Falstaff's pursuit of Mistress Ford for her money. It is therefore especially appropriate that these two parallel wooing plots converge and are resolved simultaneously in the final scene in Windsor Forest where Falstaff is finally and publicly exposed, the wives are shown to be faithful and Anne wins the man she loves. The assembled children with their lighted candles who come initially to torment Falstaff turn the scene into one of midnight celebration at the outwitting of folly and the triumph of virtue. Each strand in the plot gains emphasis by contrast with the others and the neatly symmetrical organization of the whole is satisfying in itself.

Although the play has been immensely successful in the theatre, it has been received unfavourably by the critics, particularly the nineteenth-century critics such as Hazlitt and Swinburne. Their primary interest in Shakespeare was in his ability to create convincing characters, and they believed that the Falstaff of *The Merry Wives* was much inferior to the Falstaff of the history plays. Indeed, they felt for the latter the kind of affection normally given to real people and not to fictional creations, and they took offence at Shakespeare for subjecting a supposedly lovable, vital man to the degradations of the cudgel and the laundry basket. The strongest objections came from A. C. Bradley, the most profound interpreter of Shakespeare's tragedies, who complained that Shakespeare depicted Falstaff

assailing for financial purposes the virtue of two matrons, and in the event baffled, duped, treated like dirty linen, beaten, burnt, mocked, insulted, and, worst of all, repentant and didactic. It is horrible.

Whether or not the Falstaff of this play is personally inferior to the one of the history plays is a question scarcely worth pursuing but he certainly has many of the same characteristics: he tries to make money out of Mistress Ford as he had previously cheated Mistress Quickly; he is outwitted in Windsor Forest as he had been outwitted at the Gadshill robbery; he has the same tendency not to admit defeat, the same confidence in his own wit and charm, the same powers of expansive eloquence. Where he differs is in his function. The two parts of *Henry IV* portray the manoeuvrings of politics and the heroism of battle. Falstaff's function in those plays is to make fun of the politicians and scoff at the heroics. In *The Merry Wives* there are no such serious topics for him to satirize. Instead it is he who becomes the object of ridicule. The former associate of Prince Hal, the Londoner taking his ease in the country, considers himself more shrewd and sophisticated than the citizens of provincial Windsor. He condescendingly agrees to instruct the supposed Brook in the art of sexual intrigue and he assumes, in his knowing, city way, that Ford's and Page's wives are of such easy virtue that they will be only too happy to be seduced. Indeed he believes that the former has already given him encouragement:

I spy entertainment in her; she discourses, she carves, she gives the leer of invitation; I can construe the action of her familiar style; and the hardest voice of her behaviour, to be English'd rightly, is 'I am Sir John Falstaff's.'

He is, of course, utterly mistaken. Mistress Ford is outraged at the assault on her reputation and she has Falstaff thrown into the Thames to cure him of his 'dissolute diseases'. What the supposedly canny Londoner has failed to realize is that he has long since lost what sexual attractiveness he might once have possessed and that the wives of Windsor are genuinely virtuous. It is true that they are warm-hearted, affectionate and outspoken but they have no doubt about their marital obligations. As one of them explains, 'Wives may be merry and yet honest too.' The play supports traditional, rural moral standards against the pseudo-sophistication of the growing city of London.

Hence, having tried to threaten the domestic stability of Windsor, Falstaff unwittingly becomes its scapegoat. Having attempted to cuckold Ford, he finds himself exposed to general derision with the horns of a cuckold on his own head. Like Shylock before him and Malvolio after him, he tries to disrupt a society in which he is really an alien but his efforts simply draw that society more closely together. Everyone unites in opposition to the intruder: Ford's suspicions of his wife are cleared, Fenton is tolerantly accepted as a son-in-law and the Pages invite everyone home to one of those neighbourly festivities to which they are so genially addicted and which are an expression of their solidarity. It is a gathering to which Falstaff is invited but not before Parson Evans has delivered his injunction, 'Sir John Falstaff, serve Got, and leave your desires.' He is welcome as a visitor but not as an intimate. He is comically rejected by the merry wives as he is pathetically rejected by Henry V. It is, apparently, his fate to try and exploit the domestic and political establishments for his own ends only to be outwitted and exploited by the members of the establishment themselves. His plans have the opposite effect from those he intends and since he is both an intriguer and a victim he is at the same time invigorating, pathetic and absurd.

# KING HENRY THE FIFTH

The two parts of *Henry IV* are devoted chiefly to two subjects: the disunity of the kingdom created by the rebellion of the Percy family against the King, and the gradual emergence of Prince Hal, the heir to the throne, as an accomplished solider and a ruler with a respect for justice. Although *Henry V* makes perfectly good sense in its own right and is usually performed by itself, it is also a continuation of the two earlier plays and a completion of them. It demonstrates how Hal, once he became King, put into effect those military and civic virtues he had gradually developed as Prince. He is shown to be a firm judge in his condemnation of the disloyal peers and a successful soldier in his conduct of the campaign against the French. Moreover, by invading France he wins the loyalty of the majority of his people and creates the national unity which had eluded his father. He thereby earns a reputation as an ideal monarch.

At first sight *Henry V* seems much simpler than either of the two earlier plays and less colourful in its characterization and style. Whereas in the two parts of *Henry IV* the centre of interest continually shifts between the King, Falstaff, Hotspur and such lively minor characters as Glendower and Shallow, Henry dominates the later play. He appears on the stage during most of the action and when he is absent he is usually being talked about. Moreover, apart from the episodes involving the Princess Katherine, the play is largely devoted to the public affairs of politics and war. And, apart from his private meditation just before the Battle of Agincourt, Henry is shown largely in his official functions as politician, judge and commander of his troops. We scarcely glimpse his inner, essential personality and may feel that, if he ever had one, he deliberately stifled it or was compelled to lose it when he received the crown. This is a play about a public figure in his public capacity, and Shakespeare adopts for this purpose a more consistently formal, often oratorical way of writing. It is, however, the hero's public surface which allows his conduct to be interpreted in various conflicting ways. Although Shakespeare amply portrays him in speech and action, he leaves his private motives concealed. To uncover them we have no choice but to read between the lines and those critics who have tried to do so have not always found the same implications. To understand *Henry V* we must understand its hero and the harder we try to do so the more elusive both he and the play turn out to be.

Shakespeare took his material for the play from the history books of his time, Edward Hall's *Union of the Two Houses of Lancaster and York* and the *Chronicles* of Raphael Holinshed. In their accounts and in other popular plays, songs and ballads, King Henry was held up as an example of all the virtues desirable in a monarch. According to Holinshed he was flawless:

This Henry was a king of life without spot, a prince whom all men loved, and of none disdained, a captain against whom fortune never frowned, nor mischance once spurned, whose people him so severe a justicer both loved and obeyed, and so human withall that he left no offence unpunished nor friendship unrewarded . . . A majesty was he that both lived and died a pattern in princehood, a lode-star in honour, and mirror of magnificence: the more highly exalted in his life, the more deeply lamented at his death, and famous to the world alway.

Shakespeare's Henry is a more credibly complex figure than Holinshed's but he does exhibit many of the virtues which the latter attributes to him.

He does not embark on the invasion of France without first consulting his religious and legal adviser, the Archbishop of Canterbury, to make certain that he has a right to do so. Indeed, so scrupulous is his apparent concern for legal propriety that he specifically warns the Archbishop not to twist the evidence to suit his case:

> And God forbid, my dear and faithful lord,
> That you should fashion, wrest, or bow your reading,
> Or nicely charge your understanding soul
> With opening titles miscreate whose right
> Suits not in native colours of the truth.

Only when he has received this assurance and the vigorous encouragement of his peers does Henry undertake the French expedition. From that point onwards he claims that he is carrying out the work of God. He confidently warns the Dauphin,

> I am coming on
> To venge me as I may and to put forth
> My rightful hand in a well-hallow'd cause.

Throughout his reign Henry IV had suffered because of his unlawful seizure of the English crown. His son is determined that his seizure of France will be supported by right and precedent.

Whereas in the first act Henry demonstrates his apparent moral scrupulousness as a politician, in the second at he shows his clemency and firmness as a judge. Before addressing himself to the disloyal peers, he decides first to leave unpunished the former rebels against his father and then to release a prisoner who has slandered him, on the grounds that the offender was drunk. His treatment of the traitors seems exemplary. He presents them with indisputable, written evidence of their guilt, the revelation of which compels them spontaneously to confess; he expresses grief that men whom he had loved and trusted should have betrayed his friendship and condemns them to death not out of personal vindictiveness but for the sake of the safety of the country. So stunned are his betrayers by this open discovery of their guilt that they welcome their execution cheerfully:

> Never did faithful subject more rejoice
> At the discovery of most dangerous treason
> Than I do at this hour joy o'er myself,
> Prevented from a damned enterprise.

And Henry dismisses them with prayers for their true repentance and for fortitude in the face of death.

His virtues as a military commander are so apparent that they need scarcely be mentioned. Whereas his father had, as he himself admitted, kept himself removed from his people in order that his rare appearances might inspire their wonder, Henry walks among his soldiers on the eve of battle and, as the Chorus tells us,

> visits all his host;
> Bids them good morrow with a modest smile,
> And calls them brothers, friends, and countrymen.

When they show signs of flagging, as at the seige of Harfleur, he exhorts them to brace themselves for the assault and stirs their confidence by appealing to their pride in their ancestors. Yet when he hears news of their victory he insists that it is God's work and not their own:

> Come, go we in procession to the village;
> And be it death proclaimed through our host
> To boast of this or take that praise from God
> Which is his only.

From the first planning of the expedition to its accomplishment he never appears in the eyes of others to be less than confident of his success and the justice of his cause. It is only once, when he is alone, that he allows his weariness and anxiety to show themselves. Behind the facade of the public man there is a care-worn, troubled individual who cannot afford to disclose his uncertainty. But his show of assurance achieves its purpose: even Pistol admits that he 'loves the lovely bully' and Fluellen compares him favourably to Alexander the Great.

There is, then, a great deal of evidence to persuade us that Shakespeare created in Henry V an exemplary ruler, concerned for those who depend on him and humble towards the God on whom he depends. Such an interpretation rests, however, on the selection of certain episodes, certain passages of dialogue, from the play and the omission of others. It can also be shown that Shakespeare regarded him as less than ideal, but the dramatist's misgivings about his hero are conveyed largely by hints and implications which are, consequently, more difficult to locate.

The King ostensibly invades France simply in order to claim that territory which is his by right. It is, presumably, for this reason that he declares the war to be holy. The text of *Henry IV Part II*, however, shows that he may have had other, more devious motives for undertaking it. In the earlier play his father, on his deathbed, advises him to divert the attention of his subjects from their own squabbles by leading them against a common, foreign enemy:

> Therefore, my Harry,
> Be it thy course to busy giddy minds
> With foreign quarrels, that action, hence borne out,
> May waste the memory of former days.

*Henry IV Part II* concludes, moreover, with Prince John's prediction that they will shortly take their 'civil swords and native fire' to France, implying that the new King intends to act on his father's advice. Henry's purpose in the expedition – though he never discloses it – may not be to seize his inheritance but deliberately to create a diversion which will induce his people to unite. If this is the case, his expressed conviction in the justice of his cause is a cover for more subtle, chauvinistic motives. But whether Shakespeare expected his audience to recall the previous play and to use their knowledge to interpret Henry's motives, it is impossible to say.

Nor are the motives of the churchmen, Canterbury and Ely, for approving the expedition as distinterested as they appear. In a private conversation at the start of the play they reveal that a bill is being considered by parliament which would deprive the church of half its wealth, and that they need the King's assistance to prevent it. They therefore have urgent personal reasons to ingratiate themselves with the monarch. It is in this context that Canterbury defends the legality of Henry's claim to France, and in an argument so long and tortuous that it casts doubt on its own validity. But whether or not the Archbishop's motives are essentially personal it is difficult to be sure. At no point does he admit to self-interest, but Shakespeare gives us more than a hint that his defence of the war is not as altruistic as it seems. Moreover, although the King ostensibly defers his declaration of war until it has been given the blessing of the scholars, his actual words to them suggest that he has already made his decision:

> For God doth know how many, now in health,
> Shall drop their blood in approbation
> Of what your reverence shall incite us to.

These sound like the words of a man who is placing on another's shoulders the responsibility for an enterprise which he feels to be dubious but to which he is already committed.

Henry's repeated declarations of the rightness of the war are thrown into doubt by hints as to his actual motives and those of others who stand to profit from it. Such criticisms, no more than implied in the opening scenes, become the central subject of the dialogue in the fourth act when the King visits his troops in disguise and attempts to restore their confidence. To the three common soldiers, Williams, Bates and Court, he declares:

Methinks I could not die anywhere so contented as in the King's company, his cause being just and his quarrel honourable.

In view of the moral uncertainty of the whole enterprise, Williams's retort is pertinent:

> That's more than we know.

His objection is not really answered. Instead, Bates argues that, as an ordinary soldier, he should not concern himself with the justice of the war:

If his cause be wrong, our obedience to the King wipes the crime of it out of us.

Nevertheless, as the shrewd and serious Williams points out, the King carries great responsibilities, for he has brought his soldiers to a point where they may die imminently and have little or no chance to prepare for death,

some swearing, some crying for a surgeon, some upon their wives left poor behind them, some upon the debts they owe, some upon their children rawly left. I am afeared there are few die well that die in a battle; for how can they charitably dispose of anything when blood is their argument?

The plight of the ordinary soldier who goes unprepared to death is, however, something with which Henry will not concern himself:

Every subject's duty is the King's; but every subject's soul is his own.

Williams and Bates seem satisfied with this answer but it is doubtful whether a spectator can so easily be convinced. Shakespeare makes us realize that, in leading his men to war, Henry risks not only the loss of their lives but the safety of their souls. Their souls may not, ultimately, be his responsibility, but it is he who has put them at risk. His visit to the troops is not the modest, smiling, comradely occasion for which the Chorus has prepared us. In fact the Chorus is not infrequently an unreliable guide to the play. Our opinion of this supposed 'mirror of all Christian kings' is further complicated when, after the victory at Agincourt, we are told in movingly specific detail by the Duke of Burgundy of the devastation it has brought on the land and people of France:

> Her vine, the merry cheerer of the heart,
> Unpruned dies; her hedges even-pleach'd,
> Like prisoners wildly overgrown with hair,
> Put forth disorder'd twigs.
>
> Even so our houses, and ourselves and children
> Have lost, or do not learn for want of time,
> The sciences that should become our country;
> But grow, like savages – as soldiers will,
> That nothing do but meditate on blood –
> To swearing and stern looks, diffus'd attire,
> And everything that seems unnatural.

In the aftermath of victory we are made to realize its terrible effect on the defeated. For every winner there must necessarily be a loser, and Shakespeare sees both points of view.

*Henry V* is neither a simple expression of militarism nor a simple plea for pacifism. It is at the same time a celebration of the excitement of war and an exposure of its brutality, a tribute to Henry's success and an estimate of the cost which it entailed. The cost is not just one of human life, both French and English. It is also a cost to Henry's personality. Whereas in *Henry IV Part I* he had joined cheerfully – even though deliberately – in the life of the tavern with Falstaff, Bardolph and the rest, in *Henry V* he stays aloof from the common people. When he does mingle with them he still acts, even in disguise, as his own official spokesman. Although some of the low-life characters – Pistol, Mistress Quickly, Bardolph – reappear in *Henry V*, they go about their business on a different social plane from that of the King, who rarely recognizes their existence. Indeed they are introduced again into this later play partly in order to indicate the gulf which separates Henry from his former companions. The extent of that gulf is revealed by his response to the news that Bardolph is about to be hanged:

> We would have all such offenders so cut off.

This of course shows a proper respect for justice, but no sign of regret, personal loss, or even recognition. Yet more significant is the way in which Shakespeare deals with the death of Falstaff. The old man's last moments, his fumbling with the sheets, his incoherent recollections of the psalms, his cries to God, are poignantly related by the hostess: 'The King,' she declares, 'has killed his heart.' Whether in fact Falstaff died of grief or of old age and self-indulgence we have no means of knowing. But Henry is not even aware that Falstaff has died. The break from his own past is absolute.

Some of the subtlety of *Henry V* arises from Shakespeare's recognition that the King's gains as a politician and a soldier required a loss of private life and spontaneity. This loss is noticeable even in the apparently light-hearted episode with which the play concludes, his courtship of the French princess. For this is to be a political marriage, one of the demands set out in the articles of peace, designed to ensure his authority over both kingdoms. And how far does his apparent awkwardness as a suitor arise from genuine embarrassment (as he says it does) and how far from a knowing attempt to win her favour?

Although King Henry became, as a result of these personal sacrifices, the most successful of all English monarchs, giving unity to his people, enjoying their admiration and winning an empire overseas, his reign was a short one, as the Chorus points out in his epilogue:

> Small time, but in that small, most greatly lived
>   This star of England.

And the Chorus also reminds us, in the concluding words of the play, that the French territories, which to Henry V had been an asset, became a liability to his son. Henry VI lost them and, under his ineffectual government, the country relapsed once more into civil war.

# Julius Caesar

*Julius Caesar* was probably written in about 1599, shortly after the English history plays, *Henry IV Parts I* and *II* and *Henry V*. It has certain similarities to these earlier works in that, like them, it is concerned with politics and civil war. Moreover, the central character, Brutus, finds himself compelled to choose between his public duty to Rome and his personal loyalty to Caesar, as Prince Hal had to choose between his political obligations as the heir to the throne and his ties with Falstaff. Yet, as a comparison between *Julius Caesar* and the English histories easily shows, the former has a recognizably Roman colouring to it. This is created not simply by references to the topographical features of the city, such as the Tiber and the Capitol, and to its political and religious institutions such as the tribunes, the senate and the augurers, but by Shakespeare's grasp of the distinctively Roman virtue of honour, an ideal which encompasses constancy, uprightness and a sense of public duty, and which appears pre-eminently in Brutus. It is a virtue on which another of Shakespeare's Roman heroes, Coriolanus, also prides himself. Like Coriolanus, Brutus shows a stoical imperviousness to pain and personal suffering, especially in his reaction to the news of his wife's death and in his suicide. In contrast to the steadfastness of the patrician Brutus, Shakespeare shows us the instability of the Roman mob who, like their counterparts in *Coriolanus*, are easily manipulated by any orator who is able to work on their emotions. The Roman plebeians are important in a way in which the common people of England are not, for the man who can control the mob can control the city. Significantly, our first impression of Rome is of the populace in a state of uneasy restlessness which can be either aggravated or quelled by the Roman art of rhetoric.

*Julius Caesar* is also a brilliantly constructed political thriller, an account of the origins, execution and consequences of a plot to assassinate the most powerful man in the western world. Throughout the first three acts Shakespeare creates a taut, steady suspense unequalled in any work he had written previously and surpassed only in the central acts of *Othello*, which he composed about five years later. The gradual, subtle process whereby Iago persuades Othello of his wife's infidelity is, indeed, a development and refinement of the process whereby Cassius persuades Brutus of Caesar's dictatorial ambitions.

Shakespeare portrays the history of Rome, as he portrays the history of England, on the assumption that its victories and failures, its wars and revolutions are determined by the personalities - or rather the relationship between the personalities - of the few men who are in a position to control it, 'the choice and master spirits of this age', as Antony calls them. The play implies that Caesar was murdered and that Antony ultimately got the better of the conspirators only because Brutus and Cassius, Caesar and Antony were the kind of men they were. Had any one of their temperaments been different, Caesar would have remained alive and Roman history would have taken a different course. Hence, the impassioned conversations between them carries, for them and for the audience, an unusual weight. We are made to realize that the fate of Rome depends on their influence on one another. There are other ways of accounting for historical change - as the effect of God's providential guidance, for example, or as the effect of social and economic conditions - but Shakespeare's way is very suitable for presentation as drama.

The conspiracy is portrayed as a delicate, complex human machine which will carry out its task only if every moving part in it, each character, performs its required function and, until the instant when the assassins' swords enter Caesar's body, we sense that the machine may very easily break down. Even though we know as a historical fact that Caesar will be murdered, nevertheless the characters and the succession of events are so convincingly depicted that we have the sensation, no matter how often we may see the play performed, that this time, in this performance, the plot may fail: Brutus may not accede to the persuasions of Cassius, Caesar may decide not to go to the Capitol this morning or may, for once, choose to pay attention to Artemidorus' warning letter. The suspense arises from Shakespeare's portrayal of all the major scenes as processes of persuasion and choice for, unlike the parts of an ordinary machine, human beings are apparently free agents who may make decisions of their own. Yet, at any rate in this play, they are not as free as they assume: their choices are determined by the nature of their personalities and their susceptibility to the persuasions of others.

The originator and motive force behind the conspiracy is Cassius, whose hostility towards Caesar arises from two motives, both of which he reveals when he attempts to enlist the support of Brutus. Cassius despises Caesar personally because he regards him as a man inferior to himself who possesses no natural right to command the lives of others:

> 'Brutus' and 'Caesar'. What should be in that 'Caesar'?
> Why should that name be sounded more than yours?

Write them together: yours is as fair a name.
Sound them: it doth become the mouth as well.
Weigh them: it is as heavy. Conjure with 'em:
'Brutus' will start a spirit as soon as 'Caesar'.
Now, in the name of all the gods at once,
Upon what meat doth this our Caesar feed,
That he is grown so great?

At the same time Cassius has – or, at least claims to have – powerful republican convictions and believes that to submit to the authority of a king is beneath the dignity of a Roman citizen:

Age, thou art sham'd!
Rome, thou has lost the breed of noble bloods!
When went there by an age since the great flood,
But it was fam'd with more than with one man?

Whether Cassius is genuinely motivated by political principles or not it is impossible to know. His republicanism may be as passionately felt as he says it is, but this honourable ideal, as he well knows, is precisely the principle to which Brutus will respond sympathetically and he needs the support of Brutus.

Whereas in Cassius envy and public interest are apparently united in driving him towards the assassination (and it is this combination of motives which gives him his fierce energy), Brutus is, throughout the period before the murder, in a state of agonized indecision. On the one hand he prides himself on a high political rectitude which will not tolerate the possibility of a dictatorship; on the other hand he is a naturally fastidious man to whom murder is distasteful, and especially the murder of Caesar, who is his intimate friend. Until the scene (Act II Scene i) when he makes a formal alliance with the conspirators he is in an intolerable dilemma, compelled to make a choice between two equally unacceptable alternatives. He can either refrain from allying himself with Cassius and thereby betray his principles, or join the faction and thereby betray his friendship with Caesar. No third course is available to him and he is allowed no opportunity to remain neutral. Even when he has committed himself to the latter course he still tries to find some means whereby he may destroy Caesar the institution without killing Caesar the man and thus remain true to both his principles:

O that we then could come by Caesar's spirit
And not dismember Caesar! But, alas,
Caesar must bleed for it!

Recognizing that the institution is inseparable from the man, Brutus then tries to make the murder palatable to himself by emphasizing the motive and the manner in which the deed should be done:

> Let's kill him boldly, but not wrathfully,
> Let's carve him as a dish fit for the gods,
> Not hew him as a carcase fit for hounds.

He is able to co-operate in the plot only because he believes himself to be doing so for the highest political motives: he sees himself as a sacrificer not a butcher. By a terrible irony, however, Caesar, as he watches Brutus advance on him with his sword, totally misunderstands Brutus's motive. In the last moment of his life, with the words 'Et tu, Brute?', he accuses Brutus of betraying a personal trust.

The tension created in these first two acts is increased by a sustained dramatic irony at the expense of Caesar. Although he makes two impressive but brief appearances on his way to and from the games, all our attention is directed on the manoeuvres of his opponents. The crucially significant ceremony in which he is offered a crown takes place off stage and our interest is placed not on the incident itself but on the effect it has in strengthening the determination of the plotters. By the time they come to escort their victim to his death (Act II Scene ii), Caesar is practically the only man in the theatre who is unaware of the imminent attempt which will be made on his life. The success of the enterprise depends, however, on the co-operation not only of the conspirators but of their victim: Caesar must be induced to come to the Capitol in order to receive the weapons his murderers have prepared for him. Here, again, Shakespeare prolongs and tightens the suspense by introducing another scene of persuasion and choice. Throughout the night before the murder there have been violent storms, unnatural portents have appeared in the sky and, moreover, Caesar's wife has had a dream that his statue is running with blood. Calphurnia's dream can be interpreted either as an omen of disaster, which is her own belief, or as a portent of good fortune, which is the interpretation offered by Decius Brutus. Caesar is compelled to choose between the former, in which case he will stay safely at home, and the latter, in which case he will go to the Capitol. He decides to believe Decius Brutus and, as a consequence, appears to the audience to submit voluntarily to his own assassination. He does so, it should be noted, not on the strength of the evidence, which allows either interpretation, but because Decius Brutus's version is flattering and Caesar is known to be as susceptible to flattery as Brutus is to the cause of honour.

Further suspense is added to these scenes by our knowledge that the plot is several times in danger of being exposed. Having been assaulted by the persuasions of Cassius, Brutus then has to receive the earnest and loving pleas of his wife that he should confess the reasons for his obvious disquiet. Once again, Brutus has to make a choice, this time between the intimate claims of marriage and those of his political allegiance. The domestic interview between them (at the end of Act II Scene i) is therefore at the same time tender and full of risk. Even in the final seconds before the murder there is a possibility that the plot will fail, for Caesar is handed a document in which all the details of the conspiracy are exposed, but which he chooses not to read. It is, then, with relief on behalf of the conspirators as well as terror on behalf of Caesar that we witness at last the deed towards which the play has so far been leading.

Shakespeare now uses his dramatic skill to revive our attention in the immediate aftermath of the murder, the point at which he is most likely to lose it. Political success in this play depends on a man's ability to foresee the future and thereby to prepare for it and, if possible, exploit the opportunities it offers. In this art Cassius is obviously more skilled than Brutus: he can predict that Brutus will respond to the call of duty and therefore enlists his support by appealing to that motive. Similarly Decius Brutus predicts that Caesar will be influenced by flattery and lures his victim into the open by flattering him. Yet none of the conspirators appears to have looked beyond the assassination to its possible consequences. They assume that by destroying a potential tyrant they have initiated a new era of 'peace, freedom and liberty' and begin to leave the Capitol as though their task was finished. They are met, however, by a messenger who unwittingly holds the power by which the murder will have results quite different from those they expect. For the messenger comes from Mark Antony who, by his skill in manipulating the emotions of the mob, will turn public opinion powerfully against the conspirators and thereby set off a civil war. The entry of the messenger is the first sign of the movement of the play, and of history, into a new phase and his speech is a transposition into it. Yet, with the arrival of a second messenger, Shakespeare hints that Antony's period of supremacy will itself be overtaken by a period in which he is controlled by the as yet unseen figure of Octavius. *Julius Caesar* shows the rise and fall of successive individuals – Pompey (whose former popularity and subsequent assassination is referred to in the opening scene), Caesar, Brutus, Cassius and Antony – in the larger context of Roman history.

Shakespeare's theatrical sense shows itself as much in his talent for concealment as in his subtlety of revelation. We see far less of Octavius Caesar, for example, than of any other significant character in this play; his first, subdued appearance comes not until the fourth act. Yet this unknown youth will eventually be the last survivor from the play and will, after it is over, become the Emperor Augustus, a leader of far greater power than Caesar. Similarly Mark Antony, whose presence dominates the middle of the action, appears very briefly at the beginning and is usually mentioned slightingly as a lightweight, a playgoer who 'revels long o'nights'. By the middle of the third act he has become transformed into a subtle and commanding orator who, for a while, is in sole charge of the political situation. His character acquires a sudden depth and seriousness of purpose. It seems that the sight of

Caesar's body and the realization that this giant has been reduced to non-existence create emotions in him which either we have not been allowed to glimpse or of which he has not hitherto been capable:

> O mighty Caesar! dost thou lie so low?
> Are all thy conquests, glories, triumphs, spoils,
> Shrunk to this little measure? Fare thee well.

When he first confronts and is encircled by the conspirators, however, he can save himself only by his wits.

Brutus, with characteristically simple trust, is content to allow Antony's request to deliver the funeral oration over Caesar's body; Cassius, sharper and more sceptical, instinctively foresees the dangerous purposes for which Antony may use his oration. Antony's fate (and Rome's) rests on a brief struggle of wills between Brutus and Cassius (Act III Scene ii, 232–44) in which Brutus, with catastrophic results, prevails. Meanwhile the audience waits to see which of their predictions will prove correct.

Each of the funeral orations – Brutus's and Antony's – reflects the character of the speaker. Brutus's speech, in prose, is sober, lucid and has the balanced sentence structure typical of a logical, thoughtful scholar:

If then that friend demand why Brutus rose against Caesar, this is my answer: Not that I lov'd Caesar less, but that I lov'd Rome more. Had you rather Caesar were living and die all slaves, than that Caesar were dead, to live all free men? As Caesar lov'd me, I weep for him; as he was fortunate, I rejoice at it; as he was valiant, I honour him; but – as he was ambitious, I slew him.

He innocently assumes that the masses are as rational as himself. Antony's oration, in verse, whips up the emotions of the mob to a state of hysteria without their realizing that they are being manipulated. Throughout, Antony claims not to be using the methods he actually practises: he claims not to praise Caesar but then proceeds to do so; he claims to applaud Brutus for his honourable nature while actually casting doubt on it; he claims not to disprove Brutus's argument yet repeatedly refutes it; he claims to be fearful of rebellion while actually inciting it; he refuses to read Caesar's will, but reveals its contents, ostensibly at the request of the people but in fact to suit his own purposes; he seems to be overcome with grief but displays it calculatedly. Hence, when the crowd are roused to mutiny, they believe they have made the decision for themselves. In a play full of scenes of persuasion and crises of choice, this is the most prolonged and powerful. The people have a choice between believing Brutus's account of Caesar as a tyrant and Antony's portrayal of him as generous and compassionate. They choose the latter version not because it is necessarily more reliable but because it is more movingly conveyed. By the time Antony's speech is finished, Brutus and Cassius have fled from Rome in panic.

Shortly after his public appearance, we are shown the supposedly impulsive Antony in private, determining with Octavius which of their potential enemies shall be eliminated. The man who wept on the death of Caesar now casually agrees to the murder of his own nephew. With this scene, the first, extended, unified and consistently tense movement of the play concludes and the action is transferred to the battlefield for the civil war which Antony's oratory and Brutus's misplaced trust have provoked.

*Julius Caesar* never regains the momentum and consistency of suspense which have so far been its most impressive achievements. This is partly because the last two acts are episodic, partly because there is insufficient playing time left for Shakespeare to give to the deaths of Cassius and Brutus the dramatic weight and length of attention they deserve. The last section of the play does, however, contain one great scene, again a clash of temperaments. During most of the so-called 'quarrel scene' (Act IV Scene iii) between Brutus and Cassius, Shakespeare does little to advance the plot, but he does expose, with wonderful psychological insight, the opposition between their two temperaments which has been detectable since their first appearance but is now brought into the open. Cassius, as always, is full of nervous energy, spontaneous, yet wary and practical; Brutus maintains his moral idealism even when it requires that he should accuse and reprimand his friend. Both realize that, in their bickering, they are violating their friendship and the principles which formerly united them, so that their outbursts of temper are interspersed with waves of remorse and embarrassment. Throughout the scene Shakespeare controls the emotional temperature in such a way as to sustain the attention of the audience while remaining faithful to the temperaments of the two characters. It is only towards the end of their encounter that Brutus confesses why he has been uncharacteristically irritable: his wife has committed suicide. This revelation gives him the moral advantage over Cassius so that the latter accedes with little protest to Brutus's plan of attack for the forthcoming battle. For purely temperamental reasons, the more astute, hard-headed Cassius gives way to the judgement of Brutus and the prophetic words of Caesar's ghost warn us that, as always, Brutus has made an error of judgement. He has 'misconstrued everything'.

Shakespeare's view of this crucial period of history is, throughout, ironical, in the sense that he, and through him the audience, has a better grasp of politics and war than the characters engaged in them. This effect is made possible because, unlike the protagonists, who peer uncertainly into the future, guessing what may happen and usually acting on false conjectures, we ourselves know what the outcome will be. The play illustrates how, in Cicero's words,

> Men may construe things after their fashion,
> Clean from the purpose of the things themselves.

But Shakespeare's ironies are also of other kinds: the fate of Rome depends not on the will of the people but on the contests between the few to influence them; the fastidious Brutus finds himself reluctantly drawn into an alliance with a 'faction' which he despises; the conspirators, in their attempt to establish peace, provoke a war; the most morally upright character, Brutus, is the most politically inept, whereas the most astute, Cassius, gives way to Brutus in those decisions which are most fatal, and Brutus is destroyed by the very qualities which, in a different context, would be admirable: his honesty and trust. For all their courage, self-confidence and strength of will, these men are shown to be pitifully limited in their freedom of choice and their understanding of the public world of which they believe themselves masters.

# Much Ado About Nothing

Whereas Shakespeare's history plays are concerned with public affairs such as government, politics and war, his comedies deal with domestic life, with love and courtship, the relationships between parents and children, masters and servants, and they always end with marriage or the prospect of marriage, the means whereby families are united and perpetuated through their children. As the sixteenth-century rhetorician George Puttenham remarked, 'Comedy meddles with no prince's matters.' The difference between the two dramatic forms is reflected in their settings. Whereas the history plays take place in courts and council chambers and on fields of battle, the comedies tend to be set in domestic establishments such as Leonato's house in *Much Ado About Nothing*, the place where all the major characters gather in the first scene and in which they are invited to stay 'at the least a month'. The impression created at the opening of *Much Ado* is of a country house party during which the characters relax after their exertions in the recent war and, lacking any pressing responsibilities, engage in the agreeable pursuits of courtship, flirtation, practical joking and witty conversation. It is the most sociable of Shakespeare's plays.

Unmistakable though the holiday atmosphere of this comedy is, however, and quite different from the world of trade and merchandise in *The Merchant of Venice* or the moonlit setting of *A Midsummer Night's Dream*, Shakespeare supplies us with practically no descriptive, physical details of the house in Messina. For this reason, the play has been successfully transplanted in recent productions from the Sicily of the renaissance in which Shakespeare placed it to a Victorian country estate or, in John Barton's 1976 production, to India at the time of British rule. It is a play with which Shakespeare's company could easily go on tour, mounting it in whatever auditorium was to hand – an inn yard or the hall of a nobleman's house – just as easily as in the Globe Theatre. The emphasis is not on the setting but on the relationships between the characters and on the pleasures and troubles they create for one another. Leonato's house is merely a convenient location in which to bring the characters together in prolonged and fairly intimate contact.

The sociability of the characters becomes quickly apparent from the good-natured, animated conversation in which they engage during the course of the first scene. This is the dialogue of people who are happy to be reunited and who express their good will in compliment, courtesy and playful insult:

| | |
|---|---|
| *Don Pedro* | Good Signior Leonato, are you come to meet your trouble? The fashion of the world is to avoid cost, and you encounter it. |
| *Leonato* | Never came trouble to my house in the likeness of your Grace; for trouble being gone comfort should remain; but when you depart from me sorrow abides, and happiness takes his leave. |

It is against this background of sociable chatter that Don Juan stands out in isolation, for he alone is silent during the greater part of the scene. When, some sixty lines after his entrance, he finally expresses himself, it is in one curt sentence:

I thank you; I am not of many words, but I thank you.

We learn no more of this uncompromising man until the third scene when he reveals a little more of his personality:

I cannot hide what I am; I must be sad when I have cause, and smile at no man's jests; eat when I have stomach, and wait for no man's leisure; sleep when I am drowsy, and tend on no man's business; laugh when I am merry, and claw no man in his humour.

He is a little more than a conventional stage villain, however, a necessary mechanism to set the plot in motion. In this pre-eminently sociable play, Don John is singlemindedly anti-social, a character who lives only to gratify his own whims, to impose his own will on others. While the other guests are gathered at the great supper, he mutters malevolently, 'Would the cook were o' my mind.' The cause of his hostility is hinted at by the fact that he is Don Pedro's bastard brother, but the more obvious reason is that it is he who has just been beaten in the war and the supper is being held to celebrate his defeat. Moreover, he has a particular cause to hate one of the returning officers, Claudio, for, as he explains, 'That young start-up hath all the glory of my overthrow.' It is therefore against Claudio that his animosity is principally directed and Shakespeare takes care to ensure that, temperamentally, Claudio is an easy victim on whom Don John's vengeance can work.

The first things we learn about Claudio are that he is very young and a good soldier. He has performed, during the recent wars, 'in the figure of a lamb, the feats of a lion'. On returning to the idleness of Messina, he does what any young soldier might be expected to do and falls in love with the first pretty woman he sees. To Don Pedro, his commanding officer, he describes his infatuation in precise terms:

O, my lord,
When you went onward on this ended action,

> I look'd upon her with a soldier's eye,
> That lik'd, but had a rougher task in hand
> Than to drive liking to the name of love;
> But now I am return'd, and that war-thoughts
> Have left their places vacant, in their rooms
> Come thronging soft and delicate desires,
> All prompting me how fair young Hero is,
> Saying I lik'd her ere I went to wars.

In other words, with nothing now to occupy his mind, Claudio begins to sense agreeably erotic emotions building up inside him and these feelings simply attach themselves to Hero. He knows nothing of her character. She is simply the object to which his emotions direct themselves. Nor does he become any better acquainted with this shy, reticent girl before their marriage is about to take place. Having made sure that she is the heir to Leonato's estate, he asks Don Pedro to act on his behalf, to woo Hero in his place and to make with her father the necessary arrangements for their betrothal. Inexperienced as he is in anything other than military affairs, and unfamiliar with the quiet girl he has persuaded himself that he loves, it is not surprising that he accepts without hesitation Don John's assurance that, far from being the innocent, chaste beauty that he took her to be, Hero is in fact a sexually promiscuous woman. To this affront to his honour and self-esteem as a soldier and a nobleman, Claudio acts, as he does throughout the play, in a thoroughly conventional manner and denounces his bride in public. What, in the context of the play as a whole, is significant, however, are the terms in which he accuses her:

> There, Leonato, take her back again;
> Give not this rotten orange to your friend;
> She's but the sign and semblance of her honour.
> Behold how like a maid she blushes here.
> O, what authority and show of truth
> Can cunning sin cover itself withal!
> Comes not that blood as modest evidence
> To witness simple virtue? Would you not swear,
> All you that see her, that she were a maid
> By these exterior shows? But she is none:
> She knows the heat of a luxurious bed;
> Her blush is guiltiness, not modesty.

In other words, conditioned as he is by the malevolent persuasiveness of Don John, Claudio interprets Hero's distraught blushes, the evidence of her genuine innocence, as evidence of her guilt. What Claudio sees is not, as he believes, the truth, but merely what, as a result of his temperament and circumstances, he is inclined to see. Having formerly, as he tells us, seen her 'with a soldier's eye', and then, later with the idealizing eyes of a lover, he now sees her with the eyes of a man who has been betrayed.

*Much Ado* is a play much concerned with the ways in which people perceive one another, with our tendency to see in other people whatever by character and experience we are predisposed to see. The scholars have pointed out that the word 'nothing' in the title is a pun connected with this process of seeing. In Shakespeare's time it was pronounced 'no thing' and in sound closely resembled the word 'noting' or 'perceiving', and the verb in its various forms crops up repeatedly in the dialogue, together with similar verbs connected with sight and observation:

*Claudio*  Benedick, didst thou note the daughter of Signior Leonato?
*Benedick*  I noted her not, but I look'd on her.

*Claudio*  In mine eye she is the sweetest lady that ever I look'd on.
*Benedick*  I can see yet without spectacles, and I see no such matter.

*Much Ado* is a play about 'noting', about the various and conflicting ways in which we respond to and judge other people. The Friar's remedy for Claudio's false accusation of Hero is to induce in him a state of mind in which he will see her as she really is:

> When he shall hear she died upon his words,
> Th' idea of her life shall sweetly creep
> Into his study of imagination,
> And every lovely organ of her life
> Shall come apparell'd in more precious habit,
> More moving, delicate, and full of life,
> Into the eye and prospect of his soul,
> Than when she liv'd indeed.

His plan (arrived at, incidentally, 'by noting of the lady') is, of course, successful. Claudio, believing Hero to be dead and that he himself is responsible, regards her in yet another light, and he describes his changed impression of her in words which are characteristic of this particular play:

> Sweet Hero, now thy image doth appear
> In the fair semmblance that I lov'd it first.

In strong contrast to the callow and easily offended Claudio, Shakespeare created the more mature, quick-witted and altogether tougher Benedick. The two men have been companions in the wars and in this play, as in *The Two Gentlemen of Verona* and *Romeo and Juliet*, Shakespeare depicts the process whereby young men of a certain age, having naturally preferred the companionship of people of their own sex, gradually separate themselves off from their peers and establish their sexual maturity and social independence by wooing and marrying people of the opposite sex. By a similar process, the young women grow out of their dependence on their parents or guardians and ally themselves to husbands, as Katherine does to Petruchio, Juliet to Romeo, Jessica to Lorenzo and Beatrice and Hero to Benedick and Claudio. The first of Benedick's soliloquies (Act II Scene iii) shows him unable to comprehend his friend Claudio's extraordinary and sudden conversion from a soldier to a lover, and apprehensive that a similar fate may lie in store for himself:

May I be so converted, and see with these eyes? I cannot tell; I think not. I will not be sworn but love may transform me to an oyster; but I'll take my oath on it, till he have made an oyster of me he shall never make me such a fool.

As he repeatedly dismisses the possibility that he may fall, like Claudio, into the matrimonial trap, he unknowingly reveals that he is ripe for marriage:

Rich she shall be, that's certain; wise, or I'll none; virtuous, or I'll never cheapen her; fair, or I'll never look on her; mild, or come not near me; noble, or not I for an angel; of good discourse, an excellent musician, and her hair shall be of what colour it please God.

At the very moment when Don Pedro and his associates are about to play their good-natured trick on him, Benedick is most likely to be deceived by it. His excited realization that he is actually in love with Beatrice comes as little surprise to the audience, who have been aware of their mutual attraction to each other almost from the moment of their first meeting. The witty insults with which they bombard each other in the first scene certainly show that they are not indifferent to each other. Indeed, Benedick is the first person after whom Beatrice enquires. The resourcefulness with which each attempts to outsmart the other is a kind of courtship or mating game, but it also arises from a fear of exposing their true, intimate feelings lest, having done so, they should be rebuffed or ridiculed – and, indeed, at one point Beatrice hints that she has, once, disclosed her love to Benedick but has been hurt. Their belligerent defensiveness could well have persisted indefinitely, leaving Beatrice in the state of perpetual spinsterhood to which she feels herself destined, and it needs the kindly intervention of their friends to convert it into the affection it actually conceals. Once the two of them have been induced to recognize their inner feelings, they make no attempt to resist them but allow themselves to be carried cheerfully on the tide of their newly released emotions:

> Contempt, farewell! and maiden pride, adieu!
> No glory lives behind the back of such.
> And Benedick, love on; I will requite thee,
> Taming my wild heart to thy loving hand.

Each of them feels possessed by a life force which exists even in such cool-headed, sophisticated characters as they appear to be. As Benedick declares, 'The world must be peopled.'

The two pairs of lovers are thus presented to us as opposites. Whereas Claudio undergoes a sudden infatuation, both Beatrice and Benedick fend one another off until they are enticed into loving. The enticement, moreover, consists in changing the way in which each sees the other. Having always imagined Beatrice to be scornful and waspish ('My Lady Disdain' is what he calls her), Benedick is persuaded that she is actually affectionate and easily hurt, and Beatrice is likewise induced to change her conception of Benedick. Then, as a result of their new impressions of each other, they themselves begin to change. Benedick shaves off his beard and starts to write love-poems, and the hitherto vigorous Beatrice falls mildly sick.

The moment at which they admit their love to each other is handled by Shakespeare with wonderfully controlled stagecraft. It occurs after the near-melodrama of Claudio's accusation of Hero and the outraged complaint made by Leonato at his daughter's supposed promiscuity. Left alone with Benedick, Beatrice for the first and only time in the play is overwhelmed with grief. She is at the same time incensed against Claudio for his callousness and powerless, as a woman, to strike back at him. She is at her most vulnerable, and it is her helplessness which induces Benedick to reveal his love for her and which allows her to admit her love for him. Yet there is still, in their frank declarations, a remaining touch of their former witty defensiveness:

| Benedick | I do love nothing in the world so well as you. Is that not strange? |
| Beatrice | As strange as the thing I know not . . . I was about to protest I loved you. |
| Benedick | And do it with all thy heart. |
| Beatrice | I love you with so much of my heart that none is left to protest. |

Her immediate command to Benedick, far from being the shock which some critics have believed it to be, in fact develops very logically from the preceding dialogue:

| Benedick | Come, bid me do anything for thee. |
| Beatrice | Kill Claudio. |

Having confessed to his dependence on her, Benedick discovers at once that he is no longer an easy-going bachelor but a man with responsibilities.

It is a feature of the careful construction of *Much Ado* that the turning points of both plots occur within moments of each other, and that the turning point of one follows as a consequence of the turning point of the other. In that one scene (Act IV Scene i), which occurs exactly three-quarters of the way through the play, Claudio, having revised his opinion of Hero, rejects her, and Beatrice and Benedick, having revised their opinions of each other, declare their love. The technique is what, in musical terms, is called an inversion. Moreover both these developments take place as a result of deliberate deceptions: as the malevolent plot of the wicked brother Don John causes the rejection of Hero, so the benevolent plot of the good-natured brother Don Pedro brings about the acceptance of Beatrice. Both plots take the form of eavesdropping: Claudio is made to observe the supposed Hero at her bed-room window and Benedick is made to overhear the conversation in the arbour. In fact the play is full of deceptions, both deliberate and accidental: Don Pedro pretends to woo Hero at a masked ball under the disguise of Claudio; his conversation is overheard and Don John claims that Don Pedro is actually wooing Hero for himself; Margaret the maid disguises herself as Hero, and Leonato deceives the young soldiers into thinking that Hero has died. The play opens and closes with a ball, a very appropriate gathering for this distinctively sociable play, and the guests are masked, a fitting device for this play of multiple deceptions and misleading appearances. Just before the various misconceptions are finally cleared away, there is one of the very few references to the natural world:

> Good morrow, masters; put your torches out;
> The wolves have prey'd; and look, the gentle day
> Before the wheels of Phoebus, round about
> Dapples the drowsy east with spots of grey.

It is a moment comparable to the breaking of dawn in *A Midsummer Night's Dream*. In both cases the arrival of the day is a signal to the audience that the confusions which have beset the characters are about to be resolved.

The slandering of Hero and Beatrice's commission to Benedick to kill Claudio produce a double crisis in the play which threatens to destroy both a marriage and a friendship. It is an episode comparable to the trial scene in *The Merchant of Venice*, a temporary cloud which overshadows the prospects of love and matrimony and, like the trial scene, it occurs in the fourth act. That the cloud is only temporary, however, is something of which the audience are aware, having already seen the arrest of the malefactors, Borachio and Conrade, Don John's henchmen. Our confidence that their villainy will be unmasked is qualified only by our doubts about the com-petence of the local police. Dogberry, the constable, and his dim-witted watchmen serve a number of functions in the play. For one thing they give us a glimpse of another part of the small community of Messina, as Bottom and his fellow-craftsmen fill out the picture of society in Athens. Like their social superiors, the watch are also involved in an eavesdropping and misinterpret what they overhear, not because the villains deliberately set out to deceive them but because they are incapable of understanding the truth when it is plainly delivered to their own ears, an error which, of course, occurs repeatedly in this play. Dogberry, the provincial officer, proud of his superior wisdom and authority, misconstrues words as Benedick and Claudio misinterpret character. Yet, in spite of his self-importance and dim-wittedness, Dogberry is a good-natured fellow, anxious that his colleagues should not disturb the peace even in the execution of their duties and, like Bottom, he has a kind of folk-wisdom which he expresses in traditional proverbial sayings, and to which his betters cannot rise. 'The ewe that will not hear her lamb when it baes,' he declares, 'will never answer a calf when he bleats', and he sizes up the villain Borachio sufficiently to tell him, 'I do not like thy look.' The difference between the intellectual gifts of the higher orders and the intuitive knowledge of the watch are pointed out by Borachio himself:

What your wisdoms could not discover, these shallow fools have brought to light.

*Much Ado About Nothing* is one of a number of Shakespearean comedies constructed on the belief that true knowledge is uncertain and that each individual perceives subjectively what he believes to be real. In *A Midsummer Night's Dream* the perceptions of the lovers are confused by the dim light of the forest and the magic potion dropped into their eyes by Puck; in *The Merchant of Venice* perceptions are distorted by social and religious prejudice: Shylock's view of the play is quite different from that of Antonio or Gratiano. The comedy Shakespeare wrote immediately after *Much Ado*, *As You Like It*, consists of little more than the juxtaposition of contrasting attitudes and, a few years later, in *Othello*, he rewrote the story of the successful soldier and the slandered woman, developing the shadowy villain Don John into the dominating character of Iago but without a Dogberry to bring the truth to light. In *Much Ado*, however, we are specifically instructed not to consider the villain or his ultimate fate. To the news that Don John has been captured, Benedick replies,

Think not on him till tomorrow. I'll devise thee brave punishments for him. Strike up, pipers.

# As You Like It

*As You Like It* is a comedy with practically no plot: it relies on its wit to keep it going. It was probably written in 1599, in the middle of Shakespeare's career as a dramatist, just before he embarked on the great tragedies. Seen in relation to his earlier works, it appears as the completion of a process whereby he gradually reduced the action of his comedies in order to concentrate more fully on the characters, their attitudes and relationships. Whereas the multiple plots of *The Comedy of Errors* (1592) and *A Midsummer Night's Dream* (1595) are intricately elaborate, the plot of *As You Like It* could almost be summarized on a postcard.

Such action as there is occupies the first act and the last six scenes, those parts of the play in which the malevolent characters, Oliver and Duke Frederick, either appear or make their influence felt. The events of the first act are primarily, though not entirely, a dramatic mechanism designed to propel Rosalind, Orlando and their companions into the forest; the concluding action provides a way of reconciling their differences and bringing them home again. This general movement of the play from the court to the country is one which Shakespeare also made use of in *A Midsummer Night's Dream*, *King Lear*, *Cymbeline* and *The Winter's Tale*, all of which are based on or derived from the popular works of fiction of Shakespeare's time known as romances. It was a form he used partly because it was ready to hand. In this play, such action as there is results from the tensions and animosities created at the court; the country is a place where people have the time and the freedom from social responsibilities to talk, sing and engage in the leisurely pursuit of wooing.

The action portrayed in the first act is not, however, merely a dramatic device. It creates an impression of inbred and unnatural hatred which contrasts strongly with the hospitality and love shown in the forest. Moreover, because the court is associated with unnatural animosities, we are induced to feel that to live at court is itself unnatural and that the forest allows people to behave more nearly according to their natures. Although life in Arden is far from comfortable, it is more congenial than the court: the winter wind is not so keen as man's ingratitude.

The predicaments of Orlando, a victim of a malevolent brother, and Rosalind, the victim of a ruthless uncle, are shown to be similar: he suffers the inhumanity of a brother; she of her father's brother. Moreover the motives of Oliver and Duke Frederick are also alike: both are guilty of envy, the most inhumane of all impulses. Oliver is envious of Orlando because the latter is popular, 'of all sorts enchantingly beloved' so that Oliver is 'altogether misprised'. Duke Frederick turns against Rosalind because her very virtues, 'her silence and her patience', outshine those of his own daughter. Both villains resemble Iago, whose envy of Cassio is derived from the 'daily beauty in his life' which makes Iago seem ugly. Moreover, Shakespeare shows us not only the cruelty inflicted on the hero and heroine but also their reaction to it: they respond to this unnatural hatred by displaying its opposite, a spontaneous and unselfish affection. Oliver and old Adam cling together in peril and Celia and Touchstone take flight with Rosalind out of pure love and sympathy. They discover that the uses of adversity are sweet. Their positive response to their plight forms a link with the central acts where it becomes one of Shakespeare's major preoccupations.

As well as having practically no plot, *As You Like It* has practically no setting and in this, also, it appears as the end of a development. The wood in *A Midsummer Night's Dream* is richly particularized and, when the characters are inside it, they constantly remind us of its features, the 'bushes', 'briars', 'cowslips', 'acorns', 'wild thyme', 'woodbine', 'ivy' and 'eglantine' which make up the landscape. By comparison the Forest of Arden is characterized by its lack of features. It is seldom referred to in any detail, and the word used most frequently to describe it is a 'desert': the banished Duke calls it 'a desert city', and Orlando a 'desert inaccessible'. It is, simply, a deserted place. Whereas the vegetation of the Wood near Athens forms a kind of dark maze within which the characters become entangled and confused, the Forest of Arden is little more than an open space. This setting was ideal for the Elizabethan theatre, consisting as it did of an empty platform thrust into a group of spectators. Here again, the absence of setting, like the absence of plot, leaves Shakespeare free to concentrate on the relationships between the characters. They respond to one another and not to the landscape. As a theatre historian has remarked, 'Shakespeare's is a drama of persons, not a drama of places.'

More significantly, the lack of setting enables each character to see in the forest whatever he is, temperamentally, inclined to see. It is not so much a place as a projection of the mind which enters it. Each character finds it 'as he likes it'.

The idea that the landscape is neither more nor less than what you make of it is conveyed immediately on the arrival of Rosalind and her companions:

*Rosalind*     O Jupiter, how weary are my spirits!
*Touchstone*   I care not for my spirits, if my legs were not weary.

| Rosalind | Well, this is the Forest of Arden. |
| Touchstone | Ay, now am I in Arden; the more fool I; when I was at home I was in a better place. |

These snatches of dialogue obviously tell us more about the speakers than about the subject of their conversation. Similarly, there is a complete difference between the exiled courtiers' reaction to rural life and that of Jaques. The former express their feelings in a song of praise:

> Come hither, come hither, come hither.
> Here shall he see
> No enemy
> But winter and rough weather.

The latter shows his disgust in, appropriately, a parody of the same song. The predicaments of Jaques and his companions are identical but each adapts himself to it quite differently and thereby reveals more of himself than of his situation. One reaction is balanced against another and the audience is amused by recognizing the discrepancy between the two.

The balancing and contrasting of one point of view with another is the way Shakespeare works in *As You Like It*. He offers us, instead of action, a series of arguments or debates. The little dialogue (Act III Scene ii) between Corin and Touchstone is no more than an informal debate on the virtues of the courtly and the country life:

| Corin | Sir, I am a true labourer; I earn that I eat, get that I wear; owe no man hate, envy no man's happiness; glad of other men's good, content with my harm; and the greatest of my pride is to see my ewes graze and my lambs suck. |
| Touchstone | That is another simple sin in you: to bring the ewes and the rams together, and to offer to get your living by the copulation of cattle; to be bawd to a bell-wether, and to betray a she-lamb to a crooked-pated, old, cuckoldy ram, out of all reasonable match. If thou beest not damn'd for this, the devil himself will have no shepherds. |

Their argument is never resolved because each is judging the situation by his own standards. As Corin points out, 'those that are good manners at the court are as ridiculous in the country as the behaviour of the country is mockable at the court'. Your judgement depends on the attitude you adopt.

To write dialogue of this kind must have come easily to Shakespeare because, as a schoolboy at the grammar school at Stratford-on-Avon, he almost certainly followed the course of study common to all schools of this kind during the renaissance, which included instruction in the arts of rhetoric and logic and the practice of debate or 'disputation' where both skills were brought into use. In the schools and universities of Shakespeare's time, the students were expected not to write essays or carry out scientific experiments but to deliver arguments for and against propositions set for them by their teachers. Touchstone shows his skill in this kind of exercise when he replies to Corin's question, 'How like you this shepherd's life, Master Touchstone?' Here he adopts not a single point of view – for the defence or the opposition – but keeps changing his position from one to the other, sentence by sentence:

Truly, shepherd, in respect of itself, it is a good life; but in respect that it is a shepherd's life, it is nought. In respect that it is solitary, I like it very well; but in respect that it is private, it is a very vile life. Now in respect it is in the fields, it pleaseth me well; but in respect it is not in the court, it is tedious. As it is a spare life, look you, it fits my humour well; but as there is no more plenty in it, it goes much against my stomach.

He more or less demonstrates that the country – or, indeed, anywhere – is good or bad depending on how you care to look at it. As Hamlet says, 'There is nothing either good or bad, but thinking makes it so.' Or, in the words of Pirandello, 'Right you are if you think you are.'

Once the exiles have settled in the Forest of Arden, they turn their attention from their new surroundings to the business of courtship and love, and, again, Shakespeare constructs dialogue out of the clash between points of view. Orlando's feelings for Rosalind are those of the ecstatic, idealistic lover and he expresses them in the exaggerated, figuratives language of poetry:

From the east to western Inde,
No jewel is like Rosalinde,
Her worth, being mounted on the wind,
Through all the world bears Rosalinde.
All the pictures fairest lin'd
Are but black to Rosalinde.

Touchstone's view of her is much more practical and prosaic, and he shows his derision of the love-sick Orlando by giving a parody of his verses:

If a hart do lack a hind,
Let him seek out Rosalinde.
If the cat will after kind,
So be sure will Rosalinde.
Winter garments must be lin'd,
So must slender Rosalinde.

Both are, obviously, describing the same woman but their impressions of her could scarcely be more different. Each man sees in her his own idea of Rosalind. By this simple and entertaining means, Shakespeare not only reveals the character of each speaker but also gives us several sketches of the same woman. That is one reason why Rosalind seems to us a complex character.

The characters in *As You Like It* are divided, more or less, into idealists and realists. The former are imaginative, spiritual, inexperienced, impractical and tend to express themselves metaphorically; the latter are pragmatic, experienced, disillusioned and speak literally. In the courtship of Phebe by Silvius, she is the realist, he the idealist. To Silvius's complaint that he has been wounded by her eyes (a suffering endemic among renaissance love poets), she retorts derisively that eyes are incapable of inflicting wounds:

> 'Tis pretty, sure, and very probable,
> That eyes, that are the frail'st and softest things,
> Who shut their coward gates on atomies,
> Should be call'd tyrants, butchers, murderers!
> Now I do frown on thee with all my heart;
> And if mine eyes can wound, now let them kill thee.

She is, of course, correct, if we take Silvius's words literally, but nevertheless he is wounded if only metaphorically. Words change their meaning depending on whether you are in love or not. To Silvius, Phebe is an ideal woman to be served and adored patiently, but to Rosalind she is no more than an arrogant, heartless, plain-featured woman, one of 'nature's sale-work', and she tries to cure the doting lover of his illusions:

> 'Tis not her glass, but you, that flatters her;
> And out of you she sees herself more proper
> Than any of her lineaments can show her.

In Rosalind's opinion, the beauty of Phebe exists only as an idea in her lover's mind, in the eye of the beholder.

Whereas Silvius is blinded by love, Touchstone is a realist. He cares not for his spirits if his legs were not weary. He has no illusions about the 'foulness' of Audrey, but is content to put up with it because she is the only available means of satisfying his sexual appetites. She is 'a poor virgin', 'an ill-favour'd thing', but his own. Nor does he have any high expectations of his marriage: he does not propose to be faithful to her, nor does he think she will be faithful to him. But even though he assumes that Audrey will betray him, nevertheless he embraces marriage cheerfully if only because it is better than remaining single:

A man may, if he were of a fearful heart, stagger in this attempt; for here we have no temple but the wood, no assembly but horn beasts. But what though? Courage! . . . As a wall'd town is more worthier than a village, so is the forehead of a married man more honourable than the bare brow of a bachelor.

This readiness to venture on marriage with a full knowledge of its hazards is a positive attitude which he shares with Rosalind. As a woman disguised as a young man, she is at the same time as passionate as Silvius and as pragmatic as Touchstone. Privately, to her cousin Celia, she can confess 'how many fathom deep' she is in love; in disguise, to Orlando, she shows the other side of her personality and becomes the brisk, commonsense Ganymede, dispelling his illusions about Rosalind and love in general:

| | |
|---|---|
| *Rosalind* | Now tell me how long you would have her, after you have possess'd her. |
| *Orlando* | For ever and a day. |
| *Rosalind* | Say 'a day' without the 'ever'. No, no, Orlando; men are April when they woo, December when they wed; maids are May when they are maids, but the sky changes when they are wives. |

She is the most subtle character in the play because she is intelligent enough to see everyone's point of view. She is also, like Touchstone, critical of herself and can mock the absurdity of her infatuation with Orlando even while she is possessed by it. She is ardent without being sentimental and inspires our confidence because she commits herself joyfully to love and marriage even though she recognizes their risks. She enjoys her protracted courtship by Orlando – 'Come, woo me, woo me; for now I am in a holiday humour, and like enough to consent.' At the same time she makes good use of her privileged position as Ganymede to try and cure her lover of his delusions: she wants him to marry her but in a realistic spirit similar to her own. More precisely, she wants theirs to be a 'marriage of true minds' in which her idea of Rosalind – as an unpredictable, fallible human being – will also be his.

It should by now be obvious that, although the dialogue in *As You Like It* is ostensibly about love and the country life, its implications are much broader. The idea that love is either ennobling or degrading depending on how you look at it can be extended to any experience, and indeed to human life in general. This partially accounts for the inclusion in the play of the one solitary figure, 'the melancholy Jaques'. Jaques is not a lover (he scoffs at the romantic Orlando) because he believes that love is an illusion, or, rather, that life is made up entirely of illusions. Whereas Touchstone, compared with the other characters, is a realist, Jaques is a cynic. His monologue on the seven ages of man is his manifesto. For him the world is a stage and man not merely an actor, but an actor in a drama which, from puking infancy to torpid senility, is futile. The lover's ardour is inspired merely by his mistress's eyebrow; the reputation for which the soldier strives is a mere 'bubble'; and man grows to maturity only to shrink back again into a second childishness, a regression to a more painfully ridiculous state than that from which he began.

That this is not Shakespeare's view of life is obvious from the eloquent arrival of Adam at the end of Jaques's monologue; the old servant's loyalty, generosity and self-respect have no place in the cynic's conception of man. Moreover, Jaques is a prejudiced and unreliable moralist. He believes mankind is depraved because he himself has been a libertine and, as the

Duke points out, attributes to others those vices of which he is himself guilty:

> all th' embossed sores and headed evils
> That thou with licence of free foot hast caught
> Wouldst thou disgorge into the general world.

As Silvius's view of Phebe is distorted by love, so Jaques's judgement of man has been corrupted by debauchery. Moreover, the love which variously motivates the other characters is itself a challenge to his cynicism. Whether they are prompted by blind infatuation like Silvius, or physical need like Touchstone, or a combination of love and worldly wisdom like Rosalind, all the wooers act on the assumption that marriage is a worthwhile enterprise. Jaques, whose attitude is contrary to everyone else's, makes it clear that to him such an undertaking is absurd. By distributing these different points of view among the various characters, Shakespeare portrays the paradoxes and complexities of love, its delights, its pains and its absurdities. Only Rosalind is acute and sensitive enough, and has the openness of mind, to appreciate all these things. We therefore trust her judgement as she takes on the responsibility of resolving the confusions of the lovers and bringing the play to an end.

With the appearance of Hymen, the god of marriage, in the final scene, Shakespeare introduces yet another point of view:

> Then is there mirth in heaven,
> When earthly things made even
> Atone together.

The union of man and woman in marriage delights the gods because they recognize that, in it, limited human beings approach as nearly as they can to the perfect harmony of heaven. Hymen's vision of this multiple marriage may be genuine but it is not the whole truth, as we can see if we survey the assembled company. Silvius's view of his marriage to Phebe is not the same as her view of her marriage to him: whereas he has won the woman he adores, she has accepted a second-best to Ganymede who has mysteriously evaporated. Touchstone does not intend his marriage to last and, in seizing Audrey, he has thwarted the hopes of the unfortunate and dim-witted William. Moreover, though Hymen may celebrate matrimony as a 'blessed bond', Touchstone, as befits his character, sees it as a gathering of the 'country copulatives', and Jaques sourly compares the couples to the beasts embarking in Noah's ark. Though the characters are united in marriage, their points of view remain unreconciled to the very end of the play. And, although the Duke himself welcomes his sudden restoration to power, we ourselves, in view of his former contentment in exile, may see this fresh turn of events as fortunate or unfortunate, depending on how we care to look at it. Even when all the characters appear to have achieved more or less what they want, and we may tend to be cheered by the general spirit of reconciliation and fulfilment, Shakespeare adds an epilogue to remind us that the world we have seen is merely a stage and all the men and women merely players, and he invites us, through Rosalind, to like as much of his comedy as has pleased us. We find it as we like it.

Obviously this is a much more complex and sophisticated play than it seems to be, but its popular success in the theatre shows that it can be enjoyed by people who are unaware of its implications. It is a comedy of incongruities: the prospect of Touchstone, the courtier, accommodating himself with difficulty to the rural life and exercising his wit on the uncomprehending Audrey, of Orlando unwittingly professing his love to the woman he adores, and of Rosalind uninhibitedly confessing her feelings to her less than romantic cousin, are entertaining in themselves. Moreover, in spite of its slender plot, *As You Like It* is full of variety. There is a wide range of characters, each with a distinctive language and style, and they are brought together in various combinations: Touchstone with Rosalind and Celia, with Corin, with Audrey, with Jaques, with William; Rosalind with Celia, with Silvius and Phebe, with Orlando, with Jaques. Rapidly moving, witty, colloquial dialogue is interspersed with long, formal speeches and songs. The audience's interest is constantly refreshed and revived. The predominant mood is confident and joyful, as the characters escape from the threats of their enemies, turn exile into a holiday, and gradually progress through courtship towards marriage. But although *As You Like It* is a romance, its effect is not merely romantic: it is unsentimental. The combination of a prevailing exuberance with a canny realism which distinguishes Rosalind is characteristic of the whole play. Shakespeare tactfully reminds us, largely through Rosalind, that, though men are April when they woo, they are December when they wed, that marriage, though a kind of ending, is also a beginning, and that life itself is but a flower in springtime. Perhaps Shakespeare's greatest achievement in this comedy is to recognize that life is a serious business but not to treat it too seriously. *As You Like It* has that quality which T. S. Eliot recognized in some seventeenth-century poetry, 'the alliance of levity with seriousness'.

# TWELFTH NIGHT

In his *Poetics*, the first true work of literary theory which we have and out of which all subsequent literary theory has grown, Aristotle says that whereas a tragedy should consist of one single and complete action, comedy may contain several actions. Whether Shakespeare was acquainted with the *Poetics* or not (and the strong likelihood is that he was), it is a fact that, with the exception of *King Lear*, his tragedies are formed out of one single plot and his comedies out of several interwoven plots. It is this mixture of plots which creates in each individual comedy its unique and distinctively complex tone. Hence, although the three comedies which Shakespeare wrote between 1598 and 1600, *Much Ado*, *As You Like It* and *Twelfth Night*, all deal with love and courtship and end in marriage, each contains its own distinct and special combination of feelings.

*Twelfth Night* is constructed from two very different kinds of plot, the romantic story of Viola's love for Orsino and the latter's infatuation with Olivia, and the robustly comic plot involving the deception and imprisonment of Malvolio. The former gives rise to the expression of a painfully unsatisfied love by all three of the major characters, as in Viola's concealed and stifled adoration of Orsino and Orsino's unrequited passion for Olivia:

> O, when mine eyes did see Olivia first,
> Methought she purged the air of pestilence.
> That instant was I turned into a hart,
> And my desires, like fell and cruel hounds,
> E'er since pursue me.

The latter plot, however, contains some of the best-constructed comic scenes Shakespeare wrote, such as Malvolio's interruption of Sir Toby's midnight festivities and his subsequent deception by the forged letter. In episodes like these, Shakespeare's comic writing comes as close as it ever did to farce.

It is the combination within this single play of such a wide variety of feelings and experiences that gives to *Twelfth Night* its distinctively complex, shifting tone. The play manages to encompass Sir Toby's crude and often forced high spirits, Sir Andrew's soulful, pathetic recollections of his wasted youth, Orsino's passionately demanding desire for Olivia, the desolation of the imprisoned Malvolio. As a consequence each production of this comedy – even each performance – can create a different kind of impression, depending on which of its elements a director chooses to emphasize and the extent to which any one of the actors tends to dominate the rest. More than most plays, its general effect on an audience will depend on which actors the director has chosen to cast in it.

It could, obviously, have been a fragmented work but in performance its various parts seem perfectly well integrated and it is worth considering how Shakespeare managed to weave its variously coloured strands into an entire fabric. He did so by his careful manipulation of the plots, his ability to organize the material in such a way as to link the plots together and, at the same time, to produce the maximum dramatic effect. His craftsmanship is apparent in his management of the conflict between Sir Toby and Malvolio from its inception to its complication and climax.

The two characters are rapidly established as opposites in social position, temperament and ways of life. Whereas Sir Toby is a knight, the uncle of the Countess Olivia, in whose house he appears to be a more or less permanent guest, Malvolio is by profession a steward, the highest member of the servant class and in charge of Olivia's domestic arrangements. Sir Toby, in spite of his relatively high place in society, is naturally irresponsible, coarse and thoughtlessly devoted to the social pleasures of food and drink. Malvolio, on the other hand, although a servant, has grandiose social ambitions and is guilty of the opposite form of excess, a natural hostility to enjoyment; he is, as Maria says, 'a kind of puritan'. Their differences are quite subtly revealed when each makes his first appearance: whereas Sir Toby engages in frank, blunt, easy conversation with the serving-woman Maria, Malvolio remains silently and stubbornly unresponsive to Feste's brave attempt to entertain his mistress and, when he finally speaks, addresses the Fool with a vicious and unwarranted contempt. The two characters are related to each other by contrast. Yet they are also surprisingly similar: each is, in his own way, egotistical and assertive. For all his superficial good humour, Sir Toby is actually consuming the fortune of his supposed friend, Sir Andrew, presumably in that 'quaffing and drinking' for which Maria reprimands him. As the dawn begins to break at the end of their night of revels, and the effects of drink begin to give way to hangover, he instructs Sir Andrew, 'thou hast need send for more money'. Sir Toby is apparently sponging on the man whose hopes of marriage he unscrupulously encourages and exploits. Malvolio, for all his superficial concern for social propriety, is actually hoping to exploit what he believes to be Olivia's love for him as a means of rising in society and becoming master of the household. Both attempt to profit from the people whose interests they pretend to serve.

Although the two characters are seldom on the stage together in the early scenes, the audience recognizes that they are so much at odds temperamentally that, sooner or later they will come into conflict, and we prepare, perhaps unconsciously, for the collision. It occurs in the middle of the second act at the point when Malvolio bursts in on Sir Toby's boisterous and forced festivities with Sir Andrew and Feste, and reprimands them ferociously:

My masters, are you mad? Or what are you? Have you no wit, manners, nor honesty, but to gabble like tinkers at this time of night? Do you make an alehouse of my lady's house, that you squeak out your coziers' catches without any mitigation or remorse of voice? Is there no respect of place, persons, nor time in you?

His attack on the revellers is entirely justified: it is now after midnight, and Sir Toby is a guest in what is a house of mourning. He and his companions have, indeed, no respect of 'place, persons, nor time'. What is offensive about Malvolio's reprimand is not his sentiments but the officiously self-righteous manner in which they are expressed. He is a servant and his words are addressed to a guest who is also socially his superior. Sir Toby's retort, 'Art any more than a steward?' is therefore equally justified. The episode does not consist of a simple encounter between puritanical virtue and the festive delights of cakes and ale (Sir Toby's view of the situation). Who would choose to have Sir Toby as a guest, or, for that matter, Malvolio as a steward? The former's callous irresponsibility is as unacceptable as the latter's pretentious self-assertiveness.

Now that the expected battle between the two characters has broken out, the audience assumes that Malvolio's opponents will retaliate and they do so at once by plotting to forge the letter. As the scene closes, Shakespeare makes us ready to witness the outcome:

For this night, to bed, and dream on the event.

In the concluding dialogue of this scene we are given the first intimations of the deception of Malvolio which is to follow. Similarly, the scene of Malvolio's deception by the letter ends with a promise of what we should expect as the plot develops further:

I thank my stars, I am happy! I will be strange, stout, in yellow stockings and cross-gartered, even with the swiftness of putting on.

Once more, Shakespeare whets our appetite for the sequel and this, in turn, is satisfied when Malvolio enters in his grotesquely inappropriate attire. The conclusion of each scene makes us eager to see the beginning of next.

Much of the comedy of *Twelfth Night*, unlike that of *Much Ado About Nothing* and *As You Like It*, arises from the violation of the audience's sense of social propriety. In this it resembles one of Shakespeare's earlier plays, *The Taming of the Shrew*, in which the heroine breaks a lute over her music master's head and the hero arrives for his wedding dressed in rags. The set-tings of both comedies are domestic households: the wealthy, middle-class establishment of Baptista in *The Shrew*, and the aristocratic houses of Orsino and Olivia in *Twelfth Night* with their respective servants, Cesario, Malvolio and Maria, and Olivia's guests. In such households the observation of social propriety is obviously important.

The various members of these establishments, though widely different in character, all find themselves in a similar kind of predicament: they are pos-sessed by desires which are unlikely to be fulfilled. Malvolio, by birth and profession a servant, performs his duties with an aggressively domineering manner which suggests that he regards himself as the head of the household, and we are not altogether surprised to discover that he already pictures him-self as Count Malvolio, condescendingly receiving the courtesies of his former superiors:

Toby approaches, curtsies there to me . . . I extend my hand to him thus – quenching my familiar smile with an austere regard of control.

He is neither satisfied in his present position nor capable of achieving that authority to which he aspires.

The feeble, easily duped Sir Andrew likewise lives on false hopes. He believes that he is a fashionable courtier, a master of all the social accom-plishments, and an eligible partner for Olivia. He claims to be 'dog at a catch', and thinks he has a 'strong' leg which 'does indifferent well in a dun-coloured stock', and that he has 'the back trick simply as strong as any man in Illyria'. But this is all pathetic self-deception. When he is forced to fight a duel he reveals his true cowardice, and ultimately he learns from his sup-posed ally, Sir Toby, that he is nothing but 'an asshead, and a coxcomb, and a knave – a thin-faced knave, a gull'. Both he and Malvolio have ambitions which they are temperamentally incapable of fulfilling.

It is not so much temperamental deficiencies as the force of circumstances which prevent Olivia and Viola from fulfilling themselves. Unlike Malvolio and Sir Andrew, both are highly eligible candidates for matrimony. Olivia is fortunate in being young, beautiful and capable of great tenderness, but she has been induced by the death of her brother to waste these gifts in retire-ment from the world:

> The element itself, till seven years' heat
> Shall not behold her face at ample view,
> But, like a cloistress she will veiled walk,
> And water once a day her chamber round
> With eye-offending brine; all this to season
> A brother's dead love, which she would keep fresh
> And lasting in her sad remembrance.

Her longing to keep alive her 'brother's dead love' is, of course, hopeless and Viola, whose reaction to the possible death of her own brother is much more realistic, rightly criticizes Olivia's chosen isolation as a waste of the gifts with which she has fortunately been endowed:

> 'Tis beauty truly blent, whose red and white
> Nature's own sweet and cunning hand laid on.
> Lady, you are the cruellest she alive
> If you will lead these graces to the grave,
> And leave the world no copy.

Instead of wasting her beauty in sterile isolation, Olivia should perpetuate it through marriage and the production of children. But even when Olivia is drawn out of her introspection by her sudden passion for Cesario, her new desire is, we know, a hopeless one because it is for a member of her own sex. But Viola, too, is trapped, throughout most of the play, in a state of unfulfilled desire. A gentlewoman by birth, she is forced to disguise herself and perform the functions of a man, to fight a duel, to act as a servant, and to woo her own rival on behalf of the man with whom she is in love. Her predicament is not dissimilar to that of her master, whose passion for Olivia is not reciprocated.

In the opening lines of the play, which establish the feeling of unfulfilled emotion, Orsino shows himself as willing to prolong his painfully enjoyable predicament as to end it. For him it is as good to have loved and lost as to have loved and won. Viola, on the other hand, is much more practical and extroverted. She undertakes the task of wooing Olivia on her master's behalf, 'so much against the mettle of her sex', with a determination which testifies to her loyalty to Orsino. Only once does she reveal, and then indirectly, the self-pity into which she could relapse if she allowed herself to do so. Her account of her imaginary sister is a confession of what she herself could easily become:

> She never told her love,
> But let concealment, like a worm i' the bud,
> Feed on her damask cheek. She pined in thought,
> And with a green and yellow melancholy,
> She sat like Patience on a monument,
> Smiling at grief.

Viola does not, however, abandon herself to such useless immobility. She expresses her devotion to Orsino by carrying out his wishes, and, in this menial undertaking, loses none of her natural dignity. Olivia, intrigued by this self-possessed messenger, significantly enquires about his social origins and asks, 'What is your parentage?' and, on being told by Cesario that he is 'a gentleman', acknowledges, 'I'll be sworn thou art.' Viola's gentleman-like

qualities are revealed, however, not in her impulse to dominate her inferiors as Malvolio does, but in her 'face, limbs, actions, and spirit', her
innate virtues, which her servant's disguise cannot conceal. She is a self-
effacing servant by whose ideal standard we measure Malvolio, and a
devoted lover by whose altruism we judge Orsino. She keeps her private
anguish to herself.

The apparently miscellaneous and varied characters of *Twelfth Night* are
connected by an elaborate pattern of similarities and contrasts. Malvolio
the steward is contrasted with Cesario the servant, Sir Toby the dissolute
knight is contrasted with Malvolio the ambitious commoner, Sir Andrew
the inept suitor is set off against Sebastian the eligible bridegroom, Olivia
the reclusive sister is paralleled with Orsino the reclusive lover and Antonio's intense male friendship is paralleled with Viola's feminine devotion.
But the unity of *Twelfth Night* is also one of feeling, the feeling of
prolonged and either painful or absurd frustration. Until the last scene the
desires of none of the characters seem likely to be fulfilled: it is impossible
that the steward should ever become the Count, Sir Andrew is an inadequate suitor for the warm-blooded Olivia, the Countess can never
bring her brother back to life, nor can she marry the entrancing Cesario.
Orsino's importunate demands on Olivia are never gratified and Antonio is
apparently betrayed by the man for love of whom he has risked his life.
The prevailing situation is one of immobility in which desire can neither
be satisfied nor abandoned. This uncomfortable tension is released only by
the arrival of Sebastian who, in marrying Olivia, makes it possible for some
of the characters to fulfil their hopes but permanently ruins the ambitions
of others.

The ending of *Twelfth Night* is, like the rest of the play, a subtle blend of
comedy and pathos. The gradual reunion of Viola with her brother is the
most purely moving episode in the play, but the various marriages do not
inspire as much confidence as those of, say, Beatrice and Benedick or
Rosalind and Orlando. The love at first sight of Olivia and Sebastian
should probably be taken at its face value as a convention of romantic
comedy, but though Viola gains the man she has served loyally it is less
certain that he is worthy of her devotion. Sir Andrew learns the truth about
himself, but the truth is so painful and ineradicable that it might have been
better for him to remain deceived; and Malvolio, unaware that he is
partially responsible for his own misfortunes, vows revenge on the whole
company. The resolution is only partial and the closing moments are like
the beginning of another play – *Malvolio's Revenge* perhaps.

The only major character who has undergone no emotional crisis is
Feste; even Sir Toby has been wounded by Sebastian. The Fool has no personal attachments and seems to have practically no character. His remarks,
when they are not the punning and ingenious logic of the professional

entertainer, consist of impersonal, general observations on the other characters or on mankind generally:

To see this age! A sentence is but a chevril glove to a good wit; how quickly the wrong side may be turned outward!

Unlike Malvolio and Sir Toby, he is careful to adjust his conduct to the company in which he finds himself, a social propriety he must maintain in order to stay in business. He must, as Viola remarks, echoing Malvolio,

> observe their moods on whom he jests,
> The quality of persons, and the time.

This is why his own character is so elusive. Whereas the others are predominantly introspective, Feste turns his attention outwards and thereby reveals more about other people than about himself. His closing song places the entire comedy in a new context which makes the adolescent frustrations of the lovers seem insignificant in comparison with the larger movement from childhood to youth and age, and the social catastrophes in Olivia's household seem insignificant compared with the wind and the rain which threaten outside and to which Feste is in continual danger of exposure. Though his social superiors have, in their way, undergone suffering, Feste's wisdom and perceptiveness seem to be the product of more radical, basic experience. The closing line of one of his earlier songs places this comedy of unrequited love in a disturbingly new light: 'Youth's stuff will not endure.'

# HAMLET

'If the dramas of Shakespeare were to be characterised, each by the particular excellence which distinguishes it from the rest,' wrote the first great English literary critic Samuel Johnson in 1765, 'we must allow to the tragedy of *Hamlet* the praise of variety.' Certainly this is the feature which distinguishes it from Shakespeare's other three major tragedies, and is one of the reasons why it has been a consistently popular play with theatre audiences. In *Othello* our attention is centred almost entirely on the psychological relationship between the two major characters; in *King Lear* on the extreme emotional pain suffered by the King, and in *Macbeth* on the moral disintegration of the hero. But, although our interest is always directed towards Hamlet (and in the few scenes from which he is absent he is the topic of conversation), nevertheless we are constantly seeing him in fresh kinds of situation and reacting to fresh kinds of people. The Prince dominates the foreground of the play but the background is filled with a large number and variety of other characters – Claudius, Polonius, Ophelia, the Player King, the Grave-digger, Osric – each one of whom has a strongly distinctive personality and speaks in a unique, characteristic style. This copious variety of character and style is a feature of some of the plays which Shakespeare had written during the years which preceded *Hamlet* (1601), especially the two parts of *Henry IV*. Hence, although the hero is always in the forefront of our minds, and the action is almost wholly confined to Elsinore, where he seems to be trapped (as Othello is apparently trapped with Iago in Cyprus, and Macbeth in Dunsinane), the audience is always being refreshed by changes of situation and mood, not to mention the variety of topics which the characters discuss, whether it be supernatural portents, the arts of acting and horsemanship, love, madness, death, or the ethics of suicide and revenge. One of Shakespeare's problems as he wrote this play must have been how to control and shape the potentially chaotic mass of material produced by his imagination. The limits of the three later tragedies are much more severely defined, though they are not for that reason the better plays.

The sheer variety of *Hamlet* is, presumably, not the only reason why it has been popular. The personality of the hero is the most complex in the whole of drama, and to attempt the role is the most testing challenge an actor can undertake. Hamlet adapts himself to every person and situation he meets and, hence, every character has a different opinion of him. With Claudius he is impertinent, with Rosencrantz and Guildenstern alternately genial and bitter, with Horatio affectionate, with the players courteous, with Ophelia full of pity, with Gertrude outraged, and with himself baffled and self-lacerating. He is ruminative in the graveyard, hysterical after the perform-ance of the play, and stoical as he accepts the challenge to the fencing match. Since every actor is inclined to emphasize those characteristics which strike him most forcibly, it is not surprising that there have been as many different Hamlets as there have been players to interpret him. His ceaseless changes of mood are a sign of his emotional instability but they are also a deliberate attempt to baffle, and he has succeeded in perplexing the critics as well as the other characters.

He is also 'the melancholy Dane', and his particular kind of melancholy may also explain why generations of readers have found him sympathetic and absorbing. When he first appears he is, we learn, a man who has recently and radically changed. Before the play opened he had been, as Ophelia says,

> The courtier's, soldier's, scholar's, eye, tongue, sword;
> Th' expectancy and rose of the fair state,
> The glass of fashion and the mould of form,
> Th' observed of all observers.

So variously has Shakespeare endowed the Prince's character that we can visualize the man he used to be without having seen him. Ophelia's praise does not seem excessive. By the time the play begins, however, he is already in a state of shocked disenchantment with human nature, for which he feels only disgust and disappointment:

> How weary, stale, flat and unprofitable,
> Seem to me all the uses of this world!
> Fie on't! Ah fie! 'tis an unweeded garden,
> That grows to seed; things rank and gross in nature
> Possess it merely.

The cause of this disillusionment, as he goes on to reveal, is in the first place his mother's remarriage, an act which has affected him profoundly for several reasons. Coming so swiftly after her first husband's death, Gertrude's remarriage seems to him to show a callous indifference to his father's memory, and her former expressions of love now appear false and hypocriti-cal. Moreover by marrying in middle age a palpably inferior man, she has revealed a desire for sexual gratification which her son finds repellent. As a result of what Hamlet sees as a betrayal of trust by the woman most intimately related to him, he becomes disenchanted with her, with women in general, and with humanity. In his first soliloquy he expresses a sense of outrage at the discrepancy between what his mother seemed to be, an ideally devoted wife, and what in his eyes she is, a faithless and incestuous woman. Hence he begins to doubt the certainty of all outward appearances, to feel he inhabits a world he can no longer trust, and he singles himself out as the only honest man in an otherwise dissembling world:

> Seems, madam! Nay, it is; I know not seems.

So movingly is Hamlet's melancholy expressed and so acute is his analysis of the other characters that it is tempting to assume that he is Shakespeare's own spokesman, the expression of the playwright's own disenchantment, and to look at the play through his eyes. But though Hamlet is sharply perceptive, the psychological shock he has suffered has also distorted his vision of other people. The violent expressions of disgust with which he assaults his mother, and particularly Ophelia, are scarcely deserved. Hamlet is at the same time more penetrating and more unbalanced than the other characters. Shakespeare allows us to understand him but also to judge him.

That men are not in fact what they appear to be is a truth which others in the play, especially Polonius, Laertes and the King, recognize and, indeed, accept without astonishment or protest. The worldly-wise Polonius simply assumes that Hamlet's protestations of love for Ophelia are false, a bait with which to seduce her, 'springes to catch woodcocks', and Laertes' opinion is much the same as his father's. The reason why Hamlet is horrified by that deceitfulness which others take for granted is, perhaps, that his expectations of his fellow-men have been greater, or that he has made the discovery late, suddenly and through intimately personal experience. The discovery that the world is less perfect than it seems is, I imagine, a realization undergone by most people, and Hamlet's eloquent expression of it is something with which we readily sympathize. By comparison, Shakespeare's other tragic heroes, such as Othello or Coriolanus, are remote, awe-inspiring figures. In a famous comment on the play, Coleridge confessed that he had 'a smack of Hamlet' himself, and I suspect that most people recognize a Hamlet within themselves. No one has confessed to having 'a smack of Othello'.

The return of his father's spirit from the grave serves simply to aggravate Hamlet's existing bitterness. His conviction that men are not what they seem – that 'one may smile, and smile, and be a villain' – is deepened by the Ghost's confirmation of Claudius's guilt, and his revulsion at his mother's betrayal of her marriage vows is intensified by the Ghost's own expressions of disgust:

> So lust, though to a radiant angel link'd,
> Will sate itself in a celestial bed
> And prey on garbage.

Yet it is in this state of renewed upheaval that Hamlet finds himself compelled to undertake an action of a very positive kind: to kill his father's murderer. His impulse hitherto has been to escape from a society he finds intolerable, to leave Denmark for the university in Wittenberg, or, failing that, to withdraw into the contemplation of his own thoughts, or, at its most extreme, to cease to exist, 'thaw and resolve into a dew'. He now finds himself required to undertake an extreme action at a time when his mind is un-balanced and in a world which he finds perplexing. He is immediately conscious of his own inadequacy for the task:

> The time is out of joint. O cursed spite,
> That ever I was born to set it right.

His desire to appear mad may come from a wish to escape his responsibilities by retreating into the security of the apparently insane.

The means whereby Hamlet eventually fulfils his promise to his father, and the attempts of Claudius to forestall him form, of course, the plot of the play, and Shakespeare was not so preoccupied with his hero's psychological condition as to neglect his control over the action. *Hamlet* is a brilliantly constructed drama of plot and counter-plot which holds the audience in continual suspense and expectation, a further reason for its success in per-formance. But what preoccupies both Hamlet and Claudius, at least until the end of the third act, is their need to penetrate into each other's minds. Hamlet needs positive proof of Claudius's guilt, and Claudius needs to uncover the cause of Hamlet's changed and potentially dangerous behaviour. The plot provides each of them with strong motives for wishing to do so. They are not, however, the only characters who try to pluck out the hearts of each other's mysteries. Polonius sends his servant to spy on Laertes in Paris; Claudius, prompted by Polonius, places Ophelia as a decoy for Hamlet; Rosencrantz and Guildenstern persistently question Hamlet and he them in order to search out their inner motives. The world of *Hamlet* is one in which character and motive are very difficult to fathom: the ghost of Hamlet's father may, or may not, be the devil; the Player weeps genuine tears for the death of a woman in whom he has no more than a professional interest; the King, apparently at prayer, is in fact incapable of praying; Hamlet may or may not be feigning madness; his changed behaviour may be the result of rejected love, as Polonius believes, or of thwarted ambition, as Rosencrantz and Guildenstern assume, or, as Gertrude suspects, of his father's death and her 'o'erhasty marriage'. 'I have of late,' says the Prince, 'but wherefore I know not, lost all my mirth.' He is unable, it seems, to understand himself, and devotes much of his soliloquies to self-analysis, vain attempts to grasp his own personality.

The truth is more difficult to ascertain in Elsinore because, there, decep-tion is practised as a matter of course: Ophelia, ostensibly reading a book, is actually a bait with which to catch Hamlet; the play, seemingly designed for the King's entertainment, is actually contrived to expose his guilt; the figure concealed behind the arras is not Claudius but Polonius; Hamlet is sent to England ostensibly for his safety but actually for his execution; the fencing match is proposed as a game but is conducted in earnest. As well as being a drama of suspense, *Hamlet* is also an expression of scepticism, a philosophical attitude current in Shakespeare's time, which assumes that 'all knowledge must always be in question and that enquiry must be a process of doubting'. Indeed the suspense in which the audience is kept throughout the first three acts, as Claudius and his spies sound out Hamlet and he, by means of the play, attempts to force the truth out of the King, depends on the assumption that the truth is hidden. Some of these doubts are, however, resolved. At the moment when, interrupting the performance of the play, Claudius calls for light and the two adversaries scrutinize each other's faces, Hamlet recognizes the King's guilt and Claudius recognizes the Prince's knowledge of it. Each now has a secure motive for action. It is only one of the many mischances which occur in this play which makes Polonius and not Claudius the victim of Hamlet's avenging sword. In stabbing the former, he gives the King a welcome pretext to despatch him to England and dispose of him, as he believes, for good.

The wide range of characters and the rapidly changing situations out of which Shakespeare created this tragedy – from the appearance of the ghost to the performance of the play, the interlude in the graveyard and the final duel – are given shape by a series of parallels and contrasts. Needless to say, the plot of 'The Murder of Gonzago' parallels the situation in the play as a whole, but there are other, less obvious links between characters and incidents. When the play opens, Fortinbras, like Hamlet, has recently lost a father who, like old Hamlet, bore the same name as his son. His military expedition, reported in the first scene, is an attempt to redress his father's defeat as Hamlet's plot against Claudius is an attempt to avenge his father's murder. This parallel is, in turn, reflected by the predicament of Laertes towards the end of the play. His father, like Hamlet's, has been murdered and he, too, is instinctively motivated to enforce justice and revenge. Indeed, Hamlet himself points out the similarity between their situations:

> I am very sorry, good Horatio,
> That to Laertes I forgot myself;
> For by the image of my cause I see
> The portraiture of his.

Shakespeare also invites us to see parallels between Hamlet and Ophelia. As he has suffered an emotional shock from the apparent transformation of his mother, so she is wounded and astonished by the radically changed behaviour of Hamlet. His former expressions of love for her are replaced by an embittered tirade against her and her whole sex, to which she submits with a horror and disappointment not unlike Hamlet's own. She becomes, as she says, 'of ladies most deject and wretched':

> Woe is me
> T' have seen what I have seen, see what I see.

And when her father, like Hamlet's, is also murdered, her mind crumbles into insanity and she escapes from the assaults of the world by the act of suicide which Hamlet had earlier contemplated. The effects of these parallels and contrasts is to provide a background against which the hero's personality and conduct stand out more clearly: unlike Fortinbras and Laertes, Hamlet has neither the singlemindedness nor the conviction to proceed unhesitatingly to his revenge, but, unlike Ophelia, he does have the stamina to withstand 'the slings and arrows of outrageous fortune' and to keep a hold on his sanity. Her genuine insanity contrasts with Hamlet's bouts of hysteria, and shows his supposed madness to be feigned. By contrast with these other characters, Hamlet stands out as the most rigorously intelligent person in the play, the one whose mind is tough enough to challenge conventional behaviour, the least willing to take any assumptions for granted.

His perplexity at the uncertainties and contradictions of life persist almost to the end. Even after his return from England he continues to be bemused by something which the Gravedigger takes for granted: that Yorick the jester should have become transformed into a decomposing skull, and that the mortal remains of Alexander the Great might stop a bung-hole. Yet, as the tragedy moves towards its conclusion, he does acquire a certain stability, a tranquillity of mind similar to that he admires in Horatio. Whereas previously he had tried to goad himself into positive action, to 'do such bitter business as the day would quake to look on', now he entrusts himself to the power of God, in the belief that

> There's a divinity that shapes our ends,
> Rough-hew them how we will.

It is with such trust that, in spite of his forebodings, he accepts Laertes' challenge to the duel:

There is a special providence in the fall of a sparrow. If it be now, 'tis not to come; if it be not to come, it will be now; if it be not now, yet it will come – the readiness is all. Since no man owes of aught he leaves, what is't to leave betimes? Let be.

Whether or not his faith in providence is justified by the events which follow it is hard to say. There is a certain justice in the ways in which his opponents come by their deaths: as Rosencrantz and Guildenstern have become the agents of their own executions, so Claudius is poisoned by the wine he has himself prepared, and Laertes is mortally wounded by the poisoned rapier he has intended for Hamlet. The words of the Player King look like a comment on the last stages of the tragedy:

> Our wills and fates do so contrary run
> That our devices still are overthrown;
> Our thoughts are ours, their ends none of our own.

Laertes, like the others, is 'justly killed by his own treachery'. Yet Hamlet's trust in providence can also be seen quite differently. In adopting this attitude he ceases to engage in those radical philosophical questionings which have hitherto made him superior to his fellow-men and, moreover, by submitting himself to a higher power he chooses to become passive at the very point in the play when action is most needed, for, as he seems to realize, his life depends on whether he or Claudius takes the initiative. In his passivity he allows himself to be destroyed. Whether or not there is a divinity at work in the closing scene is one of the many questions the play does not answer. It can be resolved only in that 'undiscovered country' which Hamlet had contemplated with curiosity and bewilderment, and to which he makes his exit.

# Troilus and Cressida

*Troilus and Cressida* stands out as one of the oddest of Shakespeare's works, the one which least resembles any of his other plays. Its first publication was accompanied by some unusual circumstances. It was described on the title-page of the first edition (the quarto volume of 1609) as 'The Historie of Troylus and Cresseida. As it was acted by the Kings Majesties servants at the Globe.' After some copies had been printed, however, this title-page was withdrawn and replaced by another which described the play as 'The Famous Historie of Troylus and Cresseid. Excellently expressing the beginning of their loves, with the conceited wooing of Pandarus Prince of Licia.' The reference to the play's having been performed at the Globe Theatre, the permanent home of the theatrical company for which Shakespeare wrote, had been removed. In addition to the new title-page, moreover, this second issue was supplied with a preface, probably written by the printer, which claimed that it was 'a new play, never stal'd with the Stage, never clapper-clawd with the palmes of the vulger'. Whether this statement meant that *Troilus and Cressida* had never been acted at all, or that it had been given performances only in private (such as those regularly given by Shakespeare's company before the lawyers at the Inns of Court or at King James's court itself) it is impossible to know for certain. It may be that the first title-page was correct, that the preface was a form of advertisement designed to increase sales, and that the play had been put on at the Globe but had been a failure and was no longer in the repertory.

The author of the preface recommends the play as 'passing full of the palme comicall' and consistently treats it as a comedy, notwithstanding the fact that it is still called a 'history' on the new title-page (though the two terms are not necessarily inconsistent since 'a history' could be used in the general sense of 'a story'). There were also odd circumstances surrounding the printing of the play in the First Folio of 1623, the first collected edition of Shakespeare's works. Bibliographical evidence shows that the printer originally intended to include it among the tragedies, immediately after *Romeo and Juliet*. After the first pages of type had been set up, however, the printing was stopped and the play, headed 'The Tragedy', was later inserted between the histories and the tragedies (more precisely, between *Henry VIII* and *Coriolanus*). It is not included in the Folio's list of contents. Though Shakespeare's printers had little concern for the precise distinctions between the dramatic forms, they do appear to have been sufficiently uncertain about *Troilus and Cressida* to have called it a history, a comedy and a tragedy. It has subsequently been described as a 'comical satire' and a 'heroic farce'. Literary critics are, of course, prone to the expression of extreme differences of opinion but seldom at such a fundamental level or at such an early stage in a play's history.

*Troilus and Cressida* differs from the comedies of Shakespeare in that it does not depict the processes of courtship and marriage which is the distinguishing feature of the comedies. On the contrary, Troilus's courtship of Cressida terminates abruptly in betrayal. Nor is the play dominated by a single character of the stature of Lear or Coriolanus with whose deaths those tragedies conclude. Hector, the most likely candidate for the role of tragic hero, is no more prominent than Achilles or Troilus and his death is not presented as the terminating climax of the drama. *Troilus and Cressida* does resemble the history plays to the extent that it creates the impression of a continuing action which has begun before the first scene opens and will continue after the final scene is over; it is also a dramatization of what were thought to be historical events. Unlike the plays classed as histories in the Folio, however, it does not deal with the history of England. Baffled by its uniqueness, one critic, F. S. Boas, invented a new category in which to place it (along with *Measure for Measure* and *All's Well That Ends Well*). He called it a 'problem play', a term which was popular for about half a century but is now being discarded.

It is clear, then, that we are dealing with a peculiar work, a drama from which the features which characterize Shakespeare's other plays are noticeably absent. Its own distinctive characteristics are most easily shown by an example.

When, in response to Hector's challenge to fight in single combat, Ajax waits eagerly in the Greek camp for his opponent to arrive from Troy (Act IV Scene v), his sense of expectation is animatedly described by his commander Agamemnon:

> Here art thou in appointment fresh and fair,
> Anticipating time with starting courage.

Agamemnon then commands Ajax to summon his challenger with a trumpet call:

> Give with thy trumpet a loud note to Troy,
> Thou dreadful Ajax, that the appalled air
> May pierce the head of the great combatant,
> And hale him hither.

Our sense of expectancy, already tense, is then heightened by the defiant language with which Ajax addresses the trumpeter:

> Thou trumpet, there's my purse.
> Now crack thy lungs and split thy brazen pipe;
> Blow, villain, till thy sphered bias cheek
> Out-swell the colic of proud Aquilon.
> Come, stretch thy chest, and let thy eyes spout blood:
> Thou blowest for Hector.

Ajax obviously requires a trumpet call powerful enough to express his notion of his own heroic stature and the reputation of his celebrated rival, and the trumpeter does his best to oblige. At this point, the audience expects Hector to make a spectacular entrance, but nothing happens. There is an uneasy pause; Ulysses, with some surprise, observes, 'No trumpet answers', and Achilles, embarrassed at the collapse of this belligerent ceremony, mutters, "Tis but early days.' Then a figure is discerned approaching from the direction of Troy, but it turns out not to be Hector but Cressida with Diomedes. Expectations have been built up only to be disappointed as the grandiose and defiant trumpetings of the Greeks collapse into silence.

The effect is typical of *Troilus and Cressida*, the construction of which consists of a series of anti-climaxes. The militaristic language of the Prologue, for example (who makes his appearance 'armed'), leads us to expect the play to open with a battle, or at least the kind of violent brawl with which *Julius Caesar* and *Coriolanus* begin, but what we are shown is Troilus, too enfeebled by love to fight, deciding to unarm. Even the much-heralded duel between Ajax and Achilles is abandoned almost as soon as it has begun. Having entered the enemy camp prepared to fight to the death, Hector finds himself invited to dinner. The first appearance of Helen, the cause for whom the war is being fought, is also an anti-climax. Earlier she has been described as 'a queen, whose youth and freshness / Wrinkles Apollo's', 'a theme of honour and renown', but when we actually see her it becomes obvious that, as one critic has put it, 'the face that launched a thousand ships belongs to a woman of extreme silliness and affectation'. Once again Shakespeare has shaped his material in such a way as to disappoint our expectations.

Thwarted expectation is also an experience undergone by many of the characters. It is the subject of the address with which Agamemnon opens the Greek council of war in the first act:

> The ample proposition that hope makes
> In all designs begun on earth below
> Fails in the promised largeness.

He makes this statement as though it were axiomatic, a fact of life, and certainly it applies to most of the events shown in the play. His specific reason for making it here is the failure of the Greek army, after seven years, to conquer Troy, and we begin to realize, as a meaning emerges from the verbose and inflated speeches with which the Greek staff officers habitually address one another, that the council has been called in order to diagnose the weaknesses in their campaign. Ulysses argues that the army is disunited and that the soldiers show no respect for their superiors. But, although he gives weight and solemnity to his argument by invoking the principle of 'rule' and 'degree' (or hierarchy) on which 'the heavens themselves, the planets and this centre' perform their appointed functions, it appears that he has one offender in mind, Achilles, who 'in his tent lies mocking our designs'. It is, again, typical of this play that a speech which began portentously with an account of the principles governing the universe should degenerate into a proposal to lure Achilles back into the fray by means of a trick. Nor does Ulysses' plan actually succeed. The generals proceed to treat Achilles with casual contempt and to praise his boorish rival Ajax in absurdly exaggerated terms:

> Thank the heavens, lord, thou art of sweet composure;
> Praise him that gat thee, she that gave thee suck;
> Fam'd be thy tutor, and thy parts of nature
> Thrice-fam'd beyond, beyond all erudition;
> But he that disciplin'd thine arms to fight –
> Let Mars divide eternity in twain
> And give him half.

The intention is that Achilles should be provoked into action in defence of his reputation and in envy of Ajax. The plot fails, however: Achilles continues to sulk and Ajax, convinced by the flatteries which have been heaped upon him, grows more intolerably vain. It is true that Achilles does, eventually, enter the field, but not in order to restore his reputation but in fury to avenge the death of Patroclus.

The 'sickness' which Ulysses perceives in Achilles arises from a contempt for the whole enterprise. It is this which keeps him with Patroclus 'upon a lazy bed the livelong day' and makes him such a willing audience for Thersites, the camp's resident satirist. When, moreover, the Trojans hold their family council, Hector, their best reputed warrior, reveals that he, too, has lost faith in the war. Although these two scenes of debate balance each other, they are devoted to different kinds of question. Whereas the Greeks are preoccupied with how to win the war, the Trojans ask themselves whether the war is worth fighting. Hector believes that it is not. It was, he maintains, undertaken in defence of Helen, but since Helen has turned out to be worthless, she should be returned to her husband and the war concluded:

> Let Helen go.
> Since the first sword was drawn about this question,
> Every tithe soul 'mongst many thousand dismes

> Hath been as dear as Helen – I mean of ours.
> If we have lost so many tenths of ours
> To guard a thing not ours, nor worth to us,
> Had it our name, the value of one ten,
> What merit's in that reason which denies
> The yielding of her up?

In other words, since Helen rightfully belongs to her husband Menelaus, the Trojan position is morally offensive and, moreover, the war is rationally indefensible since every soldier who has died was worth as much as Helen: 'she is not worth what she doth cost / The keeping'.

To Hector's rational argument, Troilus objects that war cannot be defended rationally:

> Nay, if we talk of reason,
> Let's shut our gates and sleep. Manhood and honour
> Should have hare hearts, would they but fat their thoughts
> With this crammed reason.

The value of Helen, for Troilus, lies not in her actual worth but in the heroism, the 'valiant and magnanimous deeds', which she inspires; she is herself less important than the idealism she arouses. It is clear that Hector's judgement of the war is the more sound, not least because the audience, unlike the characters, know in advance that the Trojans will lose and their city be destroyed. Nevertheless, as the debate concludes, Hector suddenly changes his mind, not because his brother's arguments have persuaded him but because he believes that if they give up, they will lose face:

> Yet, ne'er the less,
> My spritely brethren, I propend to you
> In resolution to keep Helen still;
> For 'tis a cause that hath no mean dependence
> Upon our joint and several dignities.

When he finally goes into battle, Hector acts not only in defiance of the prophecies of his sister Cassandra and the pleas of his wife, but of his own rational convictions. The field of battle which he enters is, moreover, not the scene of those 'valiant and magnanimous deeds' which Troilus had imagined, but of bloody slaughter. Hector meets his death unarmed and outnumbered by Achilles' pack of Myrmidons, and is butchered, fighting for a cause in which he has lost faith. Both his good sense and Troilus' idealism are shown to have been futile.

The romantic idealism of Troilus is also evident in his initial feelings for Cressida. As he waits, literally trembling with expectation, for the assignation which Pandarus has arranged for them, he looks forward to erotic delights so ecstatic that they will, he fears, annihilate him:

> Th' imaginary relish is so sweet
> That it enchants my sense; what will it be
> When that the wat'ry palate tastes indeed
> Love's thrice-repured nectar? Death, I fear me;
> Swooning destruction; or some joy too fine,
> Too subtle-potent, tun'd too sharp in sweetness,
> For the capacity of my ruder powers.

When Cressida comes to him he is speechless. No woman would be capable of fulfilling the expectations which Troilus has of her, and Cressida is not a very remarkable woman. She is young, immature, instinctively a flirt, but apprehensive about the affair on which she is embarking, uneasy about her capacity to live up to the hopes Troilus has invested in her, fearful to commit herself to the man towards whom she is already (egged on by Pandarus) committed. She is not one of Shakespeare's most striking characters, but she is created with a good deal of subtlety. She is sexually passionate yet half afraid of the emotions which possess her, not certain whether her apparent modesty isn't a kind of lure:

> My lord, I do beseech you, pardon me;
> 'Twas not my purpose thus to beg a kiss.
> I am asham'd. O heavens! what have I done?

It is to this knowing yet not fully adult woman that Troilus pledges his undying fidelity and, carried away on the wave of his ardour, she vows to be true to him for ever. The two protestations, though similar, are not identical. Troilus promises to be faithful:

> True swains in love shall in the world to come
> Approve their truth by Troilus.

Cressida, on the other hand, says that if she proves untrue, her name will become synonymous with the act of betrayal. The marked difference in her words suggests that she suspects, even as she makes her vow, that she may break it.

Her infidelity is, considering her shallowness and the circumstances in which she finds herself, entirely understandable. She is a victim of international diplomacy, powerless to prevent herself from being snatched away after her one night with Troilus, a vulnerable girl alone in an enemy camp, flattered by the attentions of the strong man, Diomedes, needing his protection, and as instinctively responsive to his sexual advances as she had been to those of Troilus. When she commits herself to becoming Diomedes' mistress, she does so not without a last thought for her former lover and a twinge of guilt:

> Troilus, farewell! One eye yet looks on thee;
> But with my heart the other eye doth see.

> Ah, our poor sex! this fault in us I find,
> The error of our eye directs our mind.
> What error leads must err; O, then conclude,
> Minds sway'd by eyes are full of turpitude.

She fails partly because she had no confidence in her strength to be constant. Having broken Troilus's heart, she disappears from the play.

The effect on Troilus of her betrayal is traumatic. The woman in whom he had placed his highest expectations has proved false and at first he is unable to recognize her as the woman he had worshipped:

> This she? No; this is Diomed's Cressida.
> If beauty have a soul, this is not she;
> If souls guide vows, if vows be sanctimonies,
> If sanctimony be the gods' delight,
> If there be rule in unity itself,
> This was not she.

He is unable to reconcile his impressions of what seem to be two different women:

> Instance, O instance! strong as Pluto's gates:
> Cressid is mine, tied with the bonds of heaven.
> Instance, O instance! strong as heaven itself:
> The bonds of heaven are slipp'd, dissolv'd and loos'd;
> And with another knot, five-finger tied,
> The fractions of her faith, orts of her love,
> The fragments, scraps, the bits, and greasy relics
> Of her o'er-eaten faith, are bound to Diomed.

Her betrayal creates a shock to Troilus' youthful idealism from which he never recovers. Unable to believe that she was unworthy of his love, or to understand that circumstances have changed and that she has adapted herself to circumstances, he finds relief for his pain only in revenge, and he plunges into battle determined to destroy his rival.

*Troilus and Cressida* is therefore made up of a series of disappointments. Ulysses' appeal to the universal principles of order and degree is disregarded and his attempt to revive Achilles fails; Hector's good sense is ignored even by Hector himself; Troilus' chivalric notions of love and war are shown to be false, and Cressida breaks her vow of constancy. In every case human ideals are shown either to be false or impossible to put into practice:

> The will is infinite, and the execution confin'd; the desire is boundless, and the act a slave to limit.

The repeated failures of which the play consists have persuaded some of its interpreters to conclude that it is an expression of Shakespeare's own disillusion, his belief that all ideals are no more than wishful thinking and that all actions are motivated by self-interest, the 'universal wolf' to which Ulysses refers. As though he foresaw such an interpretation, Shakespeare has, however, put into the play two characters who more-or-less hold this view, Pandarus and Thersites, the one a commentator on the love story, the other on the war.

Neither character could, by any stretch of the imagination, be called an idealist, but their pragmatism is of different kinds. Pandarus is a well-meaning old bawd, anxious to bring the two young people together for what he sees as a cosy night of love, but there is something gloating and prurient about the way he sets about it, as though he needs to be an onlooker at an activity of which he is himself incapable, and his busy, coaxing management of the affair shows that he has no notion of the high emotional fervour with which Troilus embarks on it. The dialogues between the ardent lover and the cheerful pimp are invariably comic as the idealism of the one conflicts with the practicality of the other:

> *Troilus*                               O gentle Pandar,
> From Cupid's shoulder pluck his painted wings,
> And fly with me to Cressid!
> *Pandarus*   Walk here i' th' orchard, I'll bring her straight.

Pandarus has the effect of bringing Troilus's idealism down to the merely physical, and doubt is cast on the attitudes of both men whenever they are together. Whereas Pandarus is a well-meaning sensualist, however, Thersites is a cynic who regards everyone with a gloating contempt:

Now they are clapper-clawing one another; I'll go look on. That dissembling abominable varlet, Diomed, has got that same scurvy doting foolish young knave's sleeve of Troy there in his helm. I would fain see them meet, that that same young Troyan ass that loves the whore there might send that Greekish whoremasterly villain with the sleeve back to the dissembling luxurious drab of a sleeve-less errand. A th' t'other side, the policy of those crafty swearing rascals - that stale old mouse-eaten dry cheese, Nestor, and that same dog-fox, Ulysses - is not prov'd worth a blackberry.

It is a brilliant performance, unparalleled in Shakespeare, except, perhaps, in the prolonged outpourings of disgust delivered by Timon of Athens. But Thersites is no Timon. Whereas Timon's diatribes against the bestiality of man are drawn from the depths of his own experience, Thersites is no more than a sick-minded, irresponsible exhibitionist, 'a deformed and scurrilous Greek', as the Cast of Characters describes him, and his grotesque caricatures of the Greek and Trojan warriors scarcely represent the people we actually see, incompetent and deluded though they may be. Thersites is, therefore, not the voice of Shakespeare, if only because he gives such a distorted account of Shakespeare's own characters, and since Thersites, if anyone, is a nihilist, *Troilus and Cressida* is not a nihilistic play, close though it comes to being so. It is a portrayal of a degenerate stage in a particularly futile war and is no more a commentary on the human condition generally than is any of Shakespeare's works. What Thersites fails to recognize is that the people he so despises do have ideals and do make some attempt to live by them, even though their attempts fail. To say that our actions fall short of our hopes is to utter a truism (Agamemnon utters it at length), and Shakespeare did not necessarily have to go through some kind of crisis of faith in order to discover it. What makes the play great is not the ideas which lie behind it but the human realities in which they are embodied, and the boldly experimental way in which they are presented to us, a way so unorthodox that it has only recently begun to be appreciated.

# ALL'S WELL THAT ENDS WELL

*All's Well That Ends Well* is a difficult, elusive play and theatre audiences have, understandably, never learned to like it. It offers few, if any, of the immediately easy pleasures to be found in Shakespeare's earlier comedies, the good-natured ironies of *Much Ado About Nothing*, the joyfulness of *As You Like It* or the romanticism of *Twelfth Night*. Its most accessible, boldly theatrical episode – the one in which Parolles' falsehood is exposed – is a scene of practical joking rather like the tricking of Malvolio by the forged letter, but the effect created even by this situation is not nearly as simple as the corresponding one in *Twelfth Night*. Parolles is not simply a boaster revealed as a coward but a traitor to his cause and his friends, terrified of what looks like imminent death, and as we laugh at him we are also made to pity and despise him. The mixed, complex reaction which this episode produces is typical of *All's Well*. It is most noticeable at the high points of the drama, the scenes in which Helena, by healing the King, manages to gain Bertram as a husband and in which, at the end, she wins him a second time and extracts from him a pledge of enduring love. In the first episode, we are inclined to admire the heroine for the more than human skill with which she has cured the King's disease and to share her satisfaction in gaining as a husband the one man she adores. But we also realize that she has trapped Bertram into marriage and can see the situation from his point of view, that of a man compelled, at a time when he has quite different ambitions, to marry a woman he neither loves nor respects. Helena creates as many problems as she solves and we are induced at the same time to applaud and protest against her achievement. By extracting herself from one predicament, that of the frustrated lover, she places herself in another, that of the rejected wife. This latter problem can be solved only by a change of heart by one or other of the characters: either Helena must learn to live without Bertram or he must develop a love for Helena. She herself attempts the first solution by leaving France, making a pilgrimage to Spain and spreading the false news that she is dead. But chance brings them together again and, through a combination of cleverness and opportunism Helena fulfils the apparently impossible tasks Bertram has imposed on her and forces out of him a public confession of his faults and a declaration that he will henceforth love her. It is here that the play ends. But the reunion of the hero and heroine does not arouse in us the unqualified relief and satisfaction we feel as the various couples are brought together at the end of *A Midsummer Night's Dream* or *As You Like It*. Bertram has again been the unwilling victim of Helena's manipulation and, having been publicly exposed as a liar and a corrupter of women, is forced into a situation where he has no choice but to take Helena back into his favour. His change of heart is brought about by public shame and embarrassment and, for this reason, we may wonder how genuine it really is. We probably expect from him a heartfelt declaration of fidelity, but Shakespeare gives him a single rhyming couplet and makes his vow depend on a hesitant, qualifying 'if':

> If she, my liege, can make me know this clearly,
> I'll love her dearly, ever, ever dearly.

It is scarcely surprising, after this cursory gesture of Bertam's, that the King looks to the future only with a guarded optimism:

> All yet seems well; and if it end so meet,
> The bitter past, more welcome is the sweet.

At none of these central points in the play does Shakespeare allow the audience to settle comfortably into a simple state of happiness or grief, acceptance or protest. The marriage of Bertram and Helena may or may not henceforth be successful. The audience has no means of knowing and very likely leaves the theatre bewildered.

Both the hero and the heroine are, in their different ways, strong-minded, independent people, determined to shape their own destinies and to achieve their own personal satisfactions, Helena in marriage and Bertram as a soldier. It is partly their strong-mindedness which makes them incompatible. When we first see them, in the opening scene, both are in the process of freeing them-selves from the obligations which have tied them to their parents: Bertram's father, like Helena's, has recently died and he is about to leave his mother and set out for the court. Neither of these young people shows much grief for the death of their parents; on the contrary, Helena seems liberated:

> I think not on my father;
> And these great tears grace his remembrance more
> Than those I shed for him. What was he like?
> I have forgot him; my imagination
> Carries no favour in't but Bertram's.

Her father's death at least gives her the freedom to make her way in the world, but, initially, she is thwarted by the difference in rank between herself and the man she loves: Bertram is now a count and she little more than a family servant:

> 'Twere all one
> That I should love a bright particular star
> And think to wed it, he is so above me.
> In his bright radiance and collateral light
> Must I be comforted, not in his sphere.
> Th' ambition in my love thus plagues itself:
> The hind that would be mated with the lion
> Must die for love.

By the end of the scene, however, she is no longer willing passively to accept her fate, but has summoned up a confidence in her own power to overcome the obstacles which prevent her happiness:

> Our remedies oft in ourselves do lie,
> Which we ascribe to heaven. The fated sky
> Gives us free scope; only doth backward pull
> Our slow designs when we ourselves are dull.

She believes in the power of her own will (or what she calls 'nature') to triumph over her circumstances (or 'fortune'):

> The mightiest space in fortune nature brings
> To join like likes, and kiss like native things.

It is in this optimistic state of mind that she sets out to cure the King. Her success, however, turns out to be a kind of failure, for although she gets the husband she wants, his desertion of her makes it unlikely that their marriage will be consummated.

It is, again, a youthful urge for independence which compels Bertram to desert his wife, disobey his guardian, the King, and escape to the wars. His motives are understandable. He is, as Coleridge says, 'a young nobleman in feudal times, just bursting into manhood, with all the feelings of pride of birth and appetite for pleasure and liberty natural to a character so circumstanced'. Yet he has no sooner left home than he is pursued, to his annoyance and embarrassment, by his mother's gentlewoman and, when the other young courtiers are setting off with excited hopes of battle, he is ordered to stay behind:

> I am commanded here and kept a coil with
> 'Too young' and 'The next year' and ''Tis too early'.
>
> I shall stay here the forehorse to a smock,
> Creaking my shoes on the plain masonry,
> Till honour be bought up, and no sword worn
> But one to dance with.

He escapes to the war in order to win honour, the reputation for bravery which his fellow-officers seek. But although he does distinguish himself as a soldier, he returns home more dishonoured than when he set out and, on his arrival back in Rousillon, finds himself accused of abandoning his wife, disobeying his guardian, seducing a virgin with false promises of marriage, and attempting to defend himself by lying. Moreover, in this shameful condition, he is brought under the judgement of his seniors, the Countess and the King, from whose domination he thought he had escaped. The impulsive attempts of the two central characters to fulfil themselves have a way of defeating their ambitions and producing results other than those they intend.

*All's Well* is very much about the attitudes of the young towards the old, their attempts to make their way in the world independently of their seniors. It is a play about the mistakes people make in the process of growing up, a condition in which they seem isolated and vulnerable. Helena makes her way into the French court, and embarks on her pilgrimage to Spain alone, and the only adviser Bertram, in his inexperience, will listen to is the treacherous Parolles.

But if the young have to suffer the penalties of inexperience, their seniors have to endure the frustrations of watching them go wrong. The older generation – the King, the Countess and Lafeu – often think regretfully of the dead – the late Count of Rousillon and Helena's father – and complain of the shallowness of those who have succeeded them. Bertram's late father, the King tells him,

> did look far
> Into the service of the time, and was
> Discipled of the bravest. He lasted long;
> But on us both did haggish age steal on,
> And wore us out of act. It much repairs me
> To talk of your good father. In his youth
> He had the wit which I can well observe
> To-day in our young lords; but they may jest
> Till their own scorn return to them unnoted
> Ere they can hide their levity in honour.

A man like Bertram's father, he goes on, 'might be a copy to these younger times';

> Which, followed well, would demonstrate them now
> But goers backward.

Both Helena and Bertram have to bear the responsibility of the expectations of their elders, the obligation to become a copy of their fathers, when they wish to be distinctively themselves. They are constantly forced to listen to advice and, more often than not, are told to imitate their seniors:

> Be thou blest, Bertram, and succeed thy father
> In manners, as in shape! Thy blood and virtue
> Contend for empire in thee, and thy goodness
> Share with thy birthright!

But Bertram, 'unseason'd courtier' that he is, fails to fulfil his mother's hopes and, as a consequence, grieves her and is himself made to feel inadequate and guilty.

During a performance of the play we are, naturally, absorbed in the struggles and frustrations of the characters, but Shakespeare also induces us to consider the problems which vex them in a more general, abstract way. *All's Well* is full of statements of a proverbial kind which arise out of the dramatic situation but are applicable in other contexts:

Moderate lamentation is the right of the dead: excessive grief the enemy to the living.

We wound our modesty, and make foul the clearness of our deservings, when of ourselves we publish them.

> Our rash faults
> Make trivial price of serious things we have,
> Not knowing them until we know their grave.
> Oft our displeasures, to ourselves unjust,
> Destroy our friends, and after weep their dust.

Of course Shakespeare does this kind of thing in all his plays, but in *All's Well* he does it much more frequently, which makes it a more overtly philosophical play than he usually wrote. In this respect it is, incidentally, like *Troilus and Cressida* and *Measure for Measure*, which he wrote at about the same time. The subject which most interests the characters is, however, what they call 'honour', a word which, together with what in Shakespeare's time was its synonym, 'honesty', they use very frequently. 'Honour', we are told, was the virtue which distinguished the parents of Bertram and Helena. It is the quality which the old hope the young will acquire, as when the King instructs his courtiers 'Not to woo honour, but to wed it'. It is also the achievement of which Bertram goes in quest when he sets out to become a soldier. 'Honour' is obviously a word which takes on a number of meanings and cannot be defined at all simply. Indeed, one of Shakespeare's intentions in writing this play seems to have been to explore its meaning. It is, in the first place, the reputation held by a nobleman by virtue of his rank, and which the young Count inherits automatically on the death of his father. But although Bertram is 'honourable' in this sense, he also dishonours himself by abandoning his wife and attempting to seduce Diana. Honour, therefore, can be a quality of character as well as of social position and, in this sense, corresponds to moral virtue, a quality which everyone except Bertram sees in Helena. At the moment when Bertram refuses to accept Helena as a wife, the two kinds of honour are brought face to face: the hero, a man of high rank and shallow character, rejects the heroine, a woman of great virtue but low birth, and his rejection prompts the King to deliver a formal speech (of the moralizing kind we have just noticed) on the superiority of Helena's kind of honour to Bertram's:

> Good alone
> Is good without a name. Vileness is so:
> The property by what it is should go,
> Not by the title. She is young, wise, fair;
> In these to nature she's immediate heir;
> And these breed honour. That is honour's scorn
> Which challenges itself as honour's born
> And is not like the sire.

Honour, he concludes, resides in what we are, not in the social rank to which we are born, and he uses his royal prerogative to raise Helena in wealth and social position knowing that she already possesses virtues which are innate and cannot be conferred.

The actions which display honour in a man are, however, different from those which reveal it in a woman, and the hero and heroine seek to acquire the honour appropriate to their sex. For Bertram this consists of the reputation for valour in the manly art of war and he earns it by his conduct in battle. Helena, on the other hand, is concerned about what used to be called her 'maiden honour', her virginity, which she discusses at length with Parolles in the middle of the first scene. Her love for Bertram eventually leads her to put her maidenhood to its proper use and, when she makes her appearance in the last scene of the play, she has not only fulfilled one of the tasks which Bertram has laid down as a condition of their reunion but has also fulfilled her role as a woman, paradoxically losing her virginity while remaining virtuous.

Whereas Helena as a devoted wife and Bertram as a soldier show their virtue, Parolles is exposed as a sham. His name (based on the French word 'paroles') indicates that he is a man of 'words' and not deeds. He is a social climber, eager to attach himself to the young count and to cut a fine figure at the court. But courtliness for him consists not in acting according to principle but in keeping up with the latest fashion in clothes and manners. Hence he advises the newly arrived Bertram to behave more effusively at court, as though courtesy were nothing more than a set of smart mannerisms:

Use a more spacious ceremony to the noble lords; you have restrained yourself within the list of too cold an adieu. Be more expressive to them; for they wear themselves in the cap of the time; there do muster true gait; eat, speak and move, under the influence of the most receiv'd star; and though the devil lead the measure, such are to be followed. After them, and take a more dilated farewell.

In his pretence to be an experienced soldier Parolles is obviously a sham, but when, blindfolded and bound, he finds himself – as he supposes – a captive in the enemy camp, he reveals that he is much worse than a coward, and the young aristocrats who have tricked him discover more than they had bargained for. Not only does he disclose all the military secrets for which they ask, but he paints such a scandalous picture of his colleagues' private lives that they have to be restrained from assaulting him. His comrade-in-arms, Bertram, whose friendship he had been so anxious to cultivate, he reviles as 'a foolish idle boy, but for all that very ruttish', 'a whale to virginity, and devours up all the fry it finds'. Parolles is a traitor to his friends as well as to his cause. In him Shakespeare depicts a man who has the outward appearance of honour but lacks the substance to support it. 'Now,' as the Second Lord says of Bertram, 'as we are ourselves, what things we are.'

To be able to see through Parolles is a sign of maturity in this play. Neither the Countess, Lafeu nor Helena is taken in by him, and when Bertram is made to recognize his treacherousness we know that he is beginning to grow up. Although Bertram behaves dishonourably he is never quite such a blackguard as Parolles. Yet when the latter is trapped and stands stripped of his pretensions, as Bertram does later before the King, he shows a readiness to face his faults squarely which makes him seem admirable. His will to survive – an instinct which he shares with Bertram and Helena – is undiminished:

> If my heart were great,
> 'Twould burst at this. Captain I'll be no more;
> But I will eat, and drink, and sleep as soft
> As captain shall. Simply the thing I am
> Shall make me live. Who knows himself a braggart
> Let him fear this; for it will come to pass
> That every braggart shall be found an ass.
> Rust, sword; cool, blushes; and Parolles, live
> Safest in shame. Being fool'd, by foolery thrive.
> There's place and means for every man alive.

This is a blackguard's creed, but Parolles can now at least face the fact that he is a blackguard.

Although, in general, Parolles is set up as a contrast to Helena and Bertram, he is, like them, a difficult character to judge, a mixture of weaknesses and strengths, or rather a man whose weaknesses may appear to be strengths depending on how we look at them. In a speech which sums up this characteristic quality of the play, the philosophical Second Lord observes,

The web of our life is a mingled yarn, good and ill together. Our virtues would be proud if our faults whipt them not; and our crimes would despair if they were not cherish'd by our virtues.

# MEASURE FOR MEASURE

*Measure for Measure* is one of the few plays of Shakespeare to which we can give a more-or-less precise date. In the account books of the Master of the Revels, the official responsible for providing entertainments for the monarch, there is an entry noting that a play called 'Mesur for Mesur' by 'Shaxberd' was performed in the banqueting hall at Whitehall on the night after Christmas, 1604, presumably as part of the seasonal festivities and in the King's own presence. If we compare this play with any of Shakespeare's previous comedies we can see at once that he was here experimenting in a new kind of drama. Whereas in the earlier comedies he had written chiefly about love, courtship and marriage, in *Measure for Measure* he writes about sex and fornication. It is also his only city comedy. It takes place in Vienna and as the action shifts from the ducal palace to the brothels, the convent, the courtroom and the prison it portrays the richly textured experiences of city life. It also conveys, like the greatest chronicles of the city, the novels of Dickens, the fragmentation of urban society. Just as in *Bleak House* the aristocracy exist in remote isolation from the crumbling, diseased tenements frequented by Jo the crossing sweeper, so in the opening scenes of this play the withdrawn, contemplative Duke, the fastidious scholar Angelo, and the ardent young novice Isabella live separate lives, unaware of Pompey, Froth and Mistress Overdone, whose haunts are the back streets and the brothels. And the high-principled solitaries discover, as they do in *Bleak House*, that their lives are linked with the criminal world in ways they had never supposed.

*Measure for Measure* was also, in its time, a topical play. Unlike Shakespeare's previous comedies it deals not so much with the problems of love and with domestic, household affairs, but with the problems of the community as a whole, with 'government', one of the very first words to be spoken in the dialogue. Its concern is specifically with the difficulties encountered by the ruler in his attempts to administer the law. This was the subject of a book which had been widely discussed during the year before the play was written, the *Basilicon Doron* (or 'Royal Gift'), the author of which was obviously the most prominent and noticeable member of the audience at that Christmastide production in 1604, James I himself. In his treatise on government, the King, who had come to the throne of England only a year previously, had observed that

Lawes are ordained as rules of vertuous and sociall living, and not to be snares to trap your good subjects: and therefore the lawe must be interpreted according to the meaning, and not to the literall sense.

These reflections are, as we shall see, particularly relevant to the crises which develop during the play. Moreover, the presence of the new monarch, who was also the author of a book of instruction in government, gave a topical significance to the Duke's opening speech:

> Of government the properties to unfold
> Would seem in me t' affect speech and discourse,
> Since I am put to know that your own science
> Exceeds, in that, the lists of all advice
> My strength can give you.

This is not simply a compliment addressed by Duke Vincentio to his faithful counsellor but, at the same time, a courteous tribute by Shakespeare to his King, the patron of his theatrical company, seated in the audience.

*Measure for Measure* was also a topical play, it has been suggested, in the choice of the rigidly moralistic Angelo as its central character,

> a man whose blood
> Is very snow-broth, one who never feels
> The wanton stings and motions of the sense,
> But doth rebate and blunt his natural edge
> With profits of the mind, study and fast.

His character was probably based on that of the strict puritans whose presence in English religious and social life was by then familiar. We may, today, assume that Shakespeare's introduction into the play of a law which defines fornication not simply as a sin but as a crime punishable by death was no more than a dramatic convention, highly improbable but necessary for the plot. In the early seventeenth century, however, it was far from improbable: the stricter puritans hoped to place such a law in the statute books if ever they came to political power.

It is with the problem of putting this law into effect that the action of *Measure for Measure* begins. Angelo, the newly appointed deputy for the Duke, is determined to revive this neglected statute and to enforce it absolutely, but finds himself, immediately he takes office, confronted with what we should now call a test case, the case of Claudio. Claudio is practically the only major character in the play who is an ordinary, average man. The rest are, in one way or another, extremists. The characters are divided, roughly, between the whoremongers – Lucio, Pompey and Mistress Overdone – and the celibates – Angelo, Isabella and the Duke. Claudio, however, belongs to neither side. He is guilty, certainly, of fornication and is an acquaintance of Lucio's, but he also loves Juliet and is betrothed to her. By consorting sexually with her before his actual marriage he is guilty, technically, of a capital offence yet one which any young man might commit. As the Provost sensibly remarks,

> All sects, all ages, smack of this vice; and he
> To die for it!

In a play characterized by its intractable moral dilemmas, the problem of applying the law fairly in the case of Claudio is the first dilemma.

Towards Claudio's offence, the various characters express widely differing, indeed opposing attitudes, all of them simple and extreme. Lucio, apparently Mistress Overdone's most regular client, sees it as trivial and regards Angelo's severity as absurd:

A little more lenity to lechery would do no harm in him . . . Why, what a ruthless thing is this in him, for the rebellion of a codpiece to take away the life of a man!

This is, of course, precisely the opinion we should expect from someone who spends his time in whorehouses and, moreover, Lucio has a special interest in the case of Claudio because if the latter is executed his own head will be at risk. Moreover lenity towards lechery has been the policy adopted by the Duke with disastrous consequences: the city has degenerated into anarchic licence, Vienna has spawned brothels like mushrooms and the topic of conversation in them, as we soon discover, is not the pleasures of fornication but its after-effect, syphilis, an infection much less easily cured in Shakespeare's time than in our own, and therefore more terrifying. To overlook Claudio's crime is, therefore, not a satisfactory solution and, indeed, the Duke's failure to enforce the laws, and its unhappy consequences, is one reason for his retirement in favour of the rigorous Angelo.

The Deputy's attitude towards Claudio's offence is precisely the opposite of Lucio's, though equally simple, extreme and, again, characteristic of the man who expresses it. His own moral restraint, his strict control over his sexual appetites, is a quality which all the characters recognize. To the Duke, for example, Angelo is 'a man of stricture and firm abstinence', one who 'scarce confesses that his blood flows, or that his appetite is more to bread than stone'. As a man of absolute continency himself, Angelo has no hesitation in condemning Claudio to the block. Yet his point of view is no more satisfactory than Lucio's. Not only are there, in Claudio's case, extenuating circumstances, but the imposition of the law against fornication will have effects on his subjects of which Angelo is unaware. The demolition of the brothels will, from what we see of the city, cause widespread unemployment in Vienna, and professional bawds such as Pompey and his mistress will lose their livelihood. Moreover, as the more realistic characters frequently point out, copulation is so general a vice that, as Lucio observes, 'it is impossible to extirp it quite . . . till eating and drinking be put down'.

The function of the law in any society is to protect its members against their own destructive or self-destructive appetites, whether for sexual satisfaction or for such obviously criminal activities as robbery or murder. This truth is grasped by the unfortunate criminal himself, Claudio, who neither denies his guilt nor is unwilling, at first, to endure the penalty:

> Our natures do pursue
> Like rats that ravin down their proper bane,
> A thirsty evil; and when we drink we die.

Although laws are, therefore, necessary for the survival of a society, there appears to be no wholly acceptable way of applying them. Moreover, since the two conflicting attitudes towards Claudio's predicament are expressed with great conviction by the characters, the audience is itself forced into a dilemma, made more acute by their recognition that the man on trial is their own representative, the average man.

These two extreme positions, the one of lenience, the other of rigidity, are brought into direct conflict in the two most intensely dramatic scenes in the play, the interviews between Isabella and Angelo (Act II Scenes ii and iv), which in turn give rise to a moral dilemma of a different kind. The basis of Isabella's plea to Angelo for mercy towards her brother is, yet again, consistent with what we know of her. As a young woman devoutly committed to the religious life, she invokes Christ's injunction 'Let him that is among you without sin cast the first stone', or, in her own words to Angelo,

> Go to your bosom,
> Knock there, and ask your heart what it doth know
> That's like my brother's fault. If it confess
> A natural guiltiness such as is his,
> Let it not sound a thought upon your tongue
> Against my brother's life.

No doubt we sympathize with her argument more strongly than with any other we have so far heard, yet Angelo's defence is also persuasive:

> It is the law, not I condemn your brother.
> Were he my kinsman, brother, or my son,
> It should be thus with him.

In other words, the law embodies principles which exist irrespective of the judge whose duty it is to safeguard them. Yet, although our sympathies may be divided between Isabella, who is, after all, trying desperately to save the life of her own brother, and Angelo who, however uncongenial personally, adheres to an irrefutable principle, neither is allowed to convince the other. For Isabella has, unknowingly, been testing Angelo at his weakest point: in the process of pleading for clemency towards Claudio's crime of adultery she has aroused the sexual appetite of Angelo himself, and we now understand the full significance of the Duke's earlier comment on him:

> Hence shall we see,
> If power change purpose, what our seemers be.

The underlying impulse behind Angelo's castigation of vice has been an unconscious sense of similar inclinations within himself. He has been punishing others for the weakness which he has, himself, with shame and difficulty repressed.

The first of these two great scenes, therefore, shows the testing of Angelo. The second shows the testing of Isabella, who is forced to make a choice between satisfying Angelo's lust, as the price for her brother's reprieve, and rejecting his advances, thereby voluntarily allowing Claudio to be executed. In short, she must choose between the sacrifice of her virginity and the sacrifice of her brother. In the first of the two scenes Isabella unwittingly tests Angelo's sexual restraint; in the second Angelo tests Isabella's sense of compassion, the very quality she had formerly tried to awaken in Angelo. But whereas the result of their first encounter is to break down Angelo's defences, the result of the second is to force Isabella into a more extreme religious and moral rigidity:

> Then, Isabel, live chaste, and, brother, die:
> More than our brother is our chastity.

Shakespeare has now shifted our attention from the apparently insoluble problem of Claudio to the intolerable dilemma of Isabella. Whether or not we support her resolution to protect her chastity at the expense of Claudio's life will depend very much on our own character and attitudes: the audience is again placed in the position of judge, and different readers have pronounced very different verdicts. The eighteenth-century critic Charlotte Lennox denounced Isabella as 'a mere vixen in her virtue' with 'the manners of an affected prude'. The nineteenth-century critic Mrs Jameson, on the other hand, saw in her 'a certain moral grandeur, a saintly grace, something of a vestal dignity . . . She is like a stately and graceful cedar, towering on some alpine cliff, unbowed and unscathed amid the storm.' Isabella's problem, like the case of Claudio, is one to which there is no wholly right solution.

Our attention is now transferred to the prison where Claudio is waiting to hear the result of his sister's intercession and, meanwhile, is being prepared by the Duke for death. Here, once more, we are shown two extreme and conflicting points of view, each consistent with the man who expresses it. In making the condemned man ready for execution, the Duke, in his disguise as a friar, argues that life is so inherently painful and insignificant that death should not be feared but welcomed as a release:

> Reason thus with life.
> If I do lose thee, I do lose a thing
> That none but fools would keep. A breath thou art,
> Servile to all the skyey influences,
> That dost this habitation where thou keep'st
> Hourly afflict. Merely thou art Death's fool;
> For him thou labour'st by thy flight to shun
> And yet run'st toward him still.

For the moment, the Duke's words of comfort convince Claudio that death is preferable to life, but when his sister announces that she has rejected Angelo's offer, he instantly changes his attitude from one of stoical resignation to terror and panic at the prospect of his imminent despatch into the unknown:

> Ay, but to die, and go we know not where;
> To lie in cold obstruction, and to rot;
> This sensible warm motion to become
> A kneaded clod; and the delighted spirit
> To bathe in fiery floods or to reside
> In thrilling region of thick-ribbed ice;
> To be imprison'd in the viewless winds,
> And blown with restless violence round about
> The pendent world; or to be worse than worst
> Of those that lawless and incertain thought
> Imagine howling – 'tis too horrible.

Having been persuaded, a few moments earlier, that life was not worth living, Claudio is now convinced that death is too terrifying to contemplate. Like all the major characters, Claudio is wrenched from one extreme attitude to its opposite and, as a result, finds himself in an insupportable dilemma. Neither death nor life appears to him acceptable. There is, needless to say, no other choice available to him.

The role of the Duke is the longest in the play and he dominates the last two acts. It is, as any actor who has played the part will confirm, a very difficult one to interpret with any psychological consistency. He is first shown to have been a dangerously indulgent ruler whose neglect of the law has allowed the city to become corrupt, and then to have foisted his problems on a substitute whose reliability is, as he himself suspects, uncertain. Although, to himself, he defends his actions as necessary for the moral education of Angelo, nevertheless the Deputy is tested at a very high cost: Claudio is made to believe that his execution is imminent and Isabella is allowed to think, almost until the end of the play, that Claudio is dead. On the other hand the Duke delivers a number of general observations on the nature of government of which, apparently, Shakespeare intended us to approve, and it is he who makes the most spectacular appearance 'like power divine' in order to dispense justice in the closing scene. It may be, however, that Shakespeare intended *Measure for Measure* to show the trial and education of the Duke as well as of Angelo and Isabella, and that this provides some explanation for the apparent inconsistencies in his character.

To begin with, the Duke appears self-assured and certain of his shrewdness in judging other people, his corresponding knowledge of himself, and his power to intervene and resolve any difficulties which may arise during his supposed absence. In all these respects he discovers he has been self-deceived. He assumes that Angelo, having spent the night with Mariana, will be a man of his word and pardon the condemned Claudio, whereas Angelo actually confirms the order for Claudio's execution. He prides himself as one who, in the words of Escalus, 'contended especially to know himself', yet discovers that his reputation, at least with Lucio, is quite different from what he had supposed: 'a very superficial, ignorant, unweighing fellow'. He imagines he can save Claudio from execution by placing Barnadine on the block instead, but discovers that Barnadine is not willing to co-operate. Deprived of his robes of office, he is less able to manipulate and control his people than he had imagined. And when, in his role as Duke, he reappears to pass formal judgement on the guilty, his attempts to resolve the problems he has created are not wholly satisfactory, for no such resolutions are possible.

When Angelo's guilt is finally exposed and he stands ashamed, repentant and begging for death, the Duke awards him life and marriage to the woman he has formerly rejected. The unfortunate Lucio is first condemned to death for slander but then allowed to live and compelled to marry a whore, a sentence which the accused regards as worse than death. To Isabella, the devout religious celibate, he proposes marriage, an invitation which, significantly, she greets with silence. Although *Measure for Measure* concludes, like the earlier comedies, with the prospect of several marriages, none of them seems likely to succeed. It is a comedy which seems designed to show the impossibility of writing comedy.

The underlying cause of the insoluble dilemmas which characterize this uniquely philosophical play is the essentially divided nature of man. Shakespeare recognizes that we are individuals with demanding impulses and desires of our own, but that we are also members of a community with an obligation to control our own wills for the sake of peace, stability and the common good. Whereas the unrestrained pursuit of personal appetite leads to anarchy, the rigid application of the law leads to injustice. Moreover, the presence of Isabella reminds us that we also have an obligation to God and that this may conflict with our obigation to our fellow-men. The unresolved conflicts in *Measure for Measure* arise because the human condition is itself one of conflict. The cumbersome, half-satisfactory resolution which the Duke supplies is, perhaps, in the circumstances, no worse than we can expect.

# OTHELLO

When, some time between 1602 and 1604, Shakespeare embarked on the composition of *Othello*, he was returning to a kind of story which he had dramatized four years earlier. In *Much Ado About Nothing* (1598) Claudio, a soldier newly returned from the wars, becomes engaged to be married to the young, innocent Hero. He is, however, persuaded by the malevolent Don John that Hero is sexually promiscuous, and during their wedding ceremony he denounces her as a whore. Stunned by her fiancé's accusation, Hero falls into a trance and is thought to have died.

The relationships between Claudio, Don John and Hero roughly correspond to those of Othello, Iago and Desdemona. This earlier play of slander and deception, must, however, have proved a much easier task for Shakespeare than the one presented by *Othello*. For one thing, Claudio is a man liable to be easily deceived. He is young – little more than an adolescent – shallow, inexperienced, and knows so little of his bride's character that he is as quickly disenchanted with her as he had formerly been infatuated. Moreover, *Much Ado About Nothing* is a comedy in which the audience's attention is dispersed among many characters, including the more lively Beatrice and Benedick, and hence our concern for the sketchily drawn Claudio is relatively slight. Othello, on the other hand, is a mature adult, 'advanced into the vale of years', a gifted, experienced, authoritative military commander whose personality is established with a force and complexity which commands our attention and respect, and he dominates the play to an extent which Claudio does not. In attempting to depict the process whereby this acknowledged public hero is reduced to a state of helpless rage and is finally transformed into a murderer and a suicide, Shakespeare set for himself an extremely difficult psychological and dramatic challenge. He had to make the extreme transformation in the hero's personality convincing. So successful was he that Samuel Johnson, the first great Shakespearean critic, recognized in the play a 'skill in human nature' superior to that of 'any modern writer'.

We can see how Shakespeare set about solving his problems by looking at the way the play is constructed. He placed the responsibility for Othello's deterioration heavily upon Iago, a far more fully developed character than Don John and whose role is by far the longest in the play; he made Othello the sort of man likely to fall prey to the persuasions Iago employs, and he depicted with great care the gradual process whereby Othello becomes ensnared. Furthermore, he chose to place the whole of the first act in Venice, thereby allowing himself to build up the characters of the two main protagonists very solidly before shifting them to Cyprus, where Iago starts to put his plans into effect. The first act scarcely advances the action at all; on the contrary it seems to set the tragedy off to a false start. But it is essential in preparing the ground for what is to follow.

During the first act Othello himself impresses us with the effortlessly natural power of his authority. He halts a street brawl with a few clipped, coolly ironical words, and goes before the senate to answer Brabantio's accusation that he has abducted Desdemona with the assured conviction that his known merit will be sufficient to defend him:

> My services which I have done the signiory
> Shall out-tongue his complaints.

His self-confidence proves entirely justified, for Brabantio's outraged accusations are very nearly brushed aside by the senators, preoccupied as they are with the threat from the Turks and the need to place Othello in charge of the defence of Cyprus.

We also learn during these early scenes that Othello's experience has hitherto been devoted exclusively to soldiering. He knows, as he says, little of the world 'more than pertains to feats of broil and battle'. Indeed it is his courage, his survival of 'hairbreadth scapes' and 'moving accidents by flood and field' that have drawn Desdemona to him. His accounts of the dangerous, exotic adventures he has undergone have revealed to her a more exciting way of life than that of the 'house affairs' to which she has so far been confined. Far from having been abducted, Desdemona has found herself irresistibly drawn to Othello. Each has opened for the other a door into hitherto unknown worlds and she has had as little experience of Othello's world as he has had of hers. The strangeness of each other's lives is a cause of their present joy and their ultimate tragedy.

The man on whom Othello depends for guidance in this new adventure is Iago, a tried soldier like himself but also apparently a man of the world and one whom everyone recognizes as trustworthy. In spite of Iago's seeming ingenuousness, however, he actually exploits to his own advantage the trust which others place in him. It becomes clear in the opening dialogue that he has already extracted money from Roderigo by pretending to further the latter's courtship of Desdemona. As Iago himself confides to us,

> Thus do I ever make my fool my purse;
> For I mine own gain'd knowledge should profane

If I would time expend with such a snipe
But for my sport and profit.

This ability to make use of others for his own advantage is one which he
practises time and again as the tragedy develops: he induces Brabantio to
accuse Othello before the senate; he allows Cassio to discredit himself by
becoming drunk; he gets Desdemona to plead for Cassio and thereby place
the two of them under suspicion; he forces Emelia to give him the handkerchief; he persuades Roderigo to assault Cassio in the hope that one or both of
them will be disposed of. In every case Iago plans the action but finds com-
pliant and unwitting accomplices to carry it out. If we should, then, doubt
his ability to make Othello the agent of his own tragedy, we have only to
observe that he has already worked undetected on practically everyone else.

As well as being an opportunist, a man who uses his insight into others in
order to employ them for his own ends, Iago has a strong sense of the military and social hierarchy and of his own inferior place in it. This is a play in
which the audience is made subtly and constantly aware of the class structure. Othello, by birth and race an alien in Venice, is nevertheless conscious
of his own authority, of the achievements by means of which he has earned
it, and of his descent 'from men of royal siege'. Cassio is a career officer, educated (as it might be at Sandhurst or West Point) in what Iago contemptuously calls 'the bookish theoric' of war, and Othello, who regularly addresses
him as 'Michael', regards him as socially his near-equal. Iago, on the other
hand, priding himself on his practical experiences in the field, appears to
have risen from the lower ranks to that of 'ancient', the equivalent of the
modern regimental sergeant major. He addresses Cassio by the ironically
respectful title of 'lieutenant' and, even when he holds Othello helpless in his
power, continues, dutifully, to call him 'sir'. No one is more alert than Iago to
the ironies of situations in which the man of inferior rank is actually controlling his superiors. The quick-wittedness with which he exploits every advantage that offers itself is consistent with his experience as a practical soldier.
Yet, conscious as he is of his inferior position, he envies the inherent virtues
of those placed above him which he is unable to acquire: Cassio's 'daily
beauty' or natural social graces, make Iago feel 'ugly' in his own eyes and
those of others. His malevolence towards Othello and Cassio is caused in part
by a desire to get even with them for possessing qualities which are beyond
his reach.

Iago's envy of his superiors is something which he generally keeps to himself. Outwardly he seems a stable, sociable man of good sense, a steady and
reliable pragmatist, and the word 'honest' which others use to describe him
(with growing dramatic irony) was used in Shakespeare's time to mean
'manly', 'direct' and 'sensible' as well as 'truthful'. As an earthy, hard-headed
man of the world, Iago claims to have no principles other than that of self-

interest, and he attributes to others the motives which he claims to see in himself. What Roderigo calls his 'love' for Desdemona, Iago dismisses as merely a 'carnal sting' or 'lust of the blood', and when Roderigo threatens to drown himself rather than suffer unrequited love, Iago advises him to take a more practical course:

Drown thyself? Drown cats, and blind puppies . . . Put money in thy purse.

This is the man who, when Cassio bemoans the loss of his 'reputation', retorts, 'I thought you had received some bodily harm.'

Iago's lack of idealism, his tendency to reduce all impulses to those of material self-interest, induces him to contemplate the marriage of Othello to Desdemona with a mixture of fascination, envy and cynical disgust. He sees their union as the coupling of 'an old black ram' and a 'white ewe', and warns Brabantio that his daughter is being 'cover'd with a Barbary horse'. Although he calls Othello 'sir' to his face, he refers to him as 'the Moor' behind his back, thereby calling attention to the colour of his master's skin, and to the reputation which the black races had for sexual potency. The only racist in the play is Iago and this is consistent with his general petty-mindedness. So obsessively preoccupied is he with sexual lust, which he claims to perceive in Roderigo, Cassio, Othello and Desdemona, that, as he confides to us as the first act concludes, he suspects his master of committing adultery with Emelia, his wife. It is, at least ostensibly, because he believes the 'lustful Moor' has 'leap'd into his seat' that he proposes to convince Othello of Desdemona's infidelity, an act of revenge whereby he will be 'even'd' with Othello, 'wife for wife'. Notwithstanding his claim to be thoroughly rational, Iago is actually driven by an entirely groundless, revengeful impulse to ruin Cassio and wreck Othello's marriage. He is the most irrational character in the play.

During the first act, then, Othello and Iago are shown to be total opposites. They belong to different races, they hold different ranks in the social and military system, the one is as conscious of his commanding position as the other is of his inferiority, and the romantic idealism of Othello is at odds with the mean-minded pragmatism of Iago. Neither is capable of understanding the other and the conflict between them is more-or-less predetermined by their natures. The innocent and bewildered victim of their combat is, of course, Desdemona, whose wit, charm and vivacity Othello, under the influence of Iago, mistakes for lasciviousness. For reasons beyond their control none of the three major characters has any comprehension of the others.

Despite the inevitability of the ensuing tragedy, we may be prompted to ask the question which Othello puts to Iago at the end of the play:

> Will you, I pray, demand that demi-devil
> Why he hath thus ensnar'd my soul and body?

It is a question to which Shakespeare's critics have supplied a variety of answers. Their disagreement arises not from an absence but an excess of motives. Coleridge, in a celebrated note on *Othello*, attributed to Iago a diabolical 'motiveless malignity' so darkly incomprehensible that it compelled the villain himself into 'motive-hunting'. Like all Shakespeare's complex characters, however, Iago is driven onward by a variety of impulses: a sense of unacknowledged merit, the contempt of the cynic for the idealist, the envy of the petty-minded for his natural superior, the urge to demolish the apparently impregnable, the pleasure of the Machiavellian in the exercise of his skill, the desire of the sexually suspicious man to infect others with his own obsession. These motives, we can imagine, might have rested dormant had not circumstances stirred them into action: the promotion of Cassio, the marriage of Othello to Desdemona and the removal of the four of them to Cyprus. In the tense, enclosed surroundings of the garrison town, a group of charaters, none of whom has any understanding of the others, is thrown into intimate and inescapable contact. Shakespeare succeeds not only in making the tragedy psychologically plausible: he convinces us that events could have fallen out in no other way.

The transformation of Othello takes place during the course of Act III Scene iii. At the beginning of that scene his devotion to Desdemona is absolute:

> Perdition catch my soul
> But I do love thee; and when I love thee not
> Chaos is come again.

By the end of the scene his loathing is no less extreme:

> Damn her, lewd minx! O, damn her, damn her!

Of the five hundred lines of dialogue during which this transformation takes place, Shakespeare devotes more than a third to the arousing of Othello's curiosity to know what thoughts Iago may be concealing in his mind. The process begins with Iago's seemingly disinterested and innocuous question,

> Did Michael Cassio, when you woo'd my lady,
> Know of your love?

Harmless though it seems, the question is sufficiently odd to provoke Othello's curiosity as to what, if anything, lies behind it:

> What dost thou think?

The ensuing dialogue consists of a series of repeated demands by Othello that Iago should speak his mind:

Show me thy thought.

I prithee speak to me as to thy thinkings.

The evasions with which Iago meets these demands culminate in an impasse:

Othello   By heaven, I'll know thy thoughts.
Iago   You cannot, if my heart were in your hand;
   Nor shall not, whilst 'tis in my custody.

Having thus aroused Othello's curiosity – or, in other words, having induced him to demand that he be fed with suspicions – Iago, ostensibly with reluctance and motivated by 'love and duty' to his master, grows more specific:

Look to your wife; observe her well with Cassio.

He can, of course, offer no actual proof of Desdemona's faithlessness, for none exists, but he makes good use of such circumstantial evidence as he can find: Venetian women, of whom Othello knows nothing, are habitually and furtively promiscuous; Desdemona, having hoodwinked her father, may now be deceiving her husband, and, moreover, her rejection of many suitors of her own race and class in favour, Iago hints, of a black alien, may be evidence of her lasciviousness and sexual perversity.

Having planted these hints in Othello's mind, Iago then cunningly withdraws, apparently unwilling to pursue any further a conversation which is distasteful to him, but actually in order to allow the seeds of jealousy to germinate in Othello's mind. The latter is so much the unwitting, even eager, collaborator that, left alone, he begins, of his own accord, to provide his own explanations for his wife's supposed promiscuity:

Haply, for I am black
And have not those soft parts of conversation
That chamberers have, or for I am declin'd
Into the vale of years – yet that's not much –
She's gone; I am abus'd; and my relief
Must be to loathe her.

The interlude half-way through the scene during which Othello is absent both allows time for Iago's 'medicine' to work and, fortuitously, provides the 'proof' which Othello had demanded in the form of the handkerchief. The 'evidence' of the handkerchief, together with what Iago calls 'the other proofs' (which are, needless to say, non-existent) aggravates Othello's loathing into a desire for vengeance, the compulsive violence of which seems to astonish even Iago. The motive force which drives the tragedy onwards has now passed from Iago to Othello and, as it does so, it gains a momentum greater, perhaps, than its instigator had foreseen.

The state of mind to which Othello has been reduced and the impulses

which drive him to the murder of Desdemona are clearly articulated by the
Moor himself (Act IV Scene ii lines 48–65). He could, he declares, have suffered physical pain, no matter how extreme, with equanimity; he could, perhaps, have tolerated the scorn of being thought a cuckold; but to have been
betrayed by the woman he not only loved but in whom he had invested the
very purpose of his being is insupportable:

> But there, where I have garner'd up my heart,
> Where either I must live or bear no life,
> The fountain from the which my current runs,
> Or else dries up – to be discarded thence!
> Or keep it as a cistern for foul toads
> To knot and gender in! Turn thy complexion there,
> Patience, thou young and rose-lipp'd cherubin –
> Ay, here, look grim as hell.

As he enters Desdemona's bedchamber, he sees himself as the solemn and
deliberate agent of justice, intent not on murder, an act of personal retribution, but on sacrifice 'lest she betray more men'. In fact he assumes the role of
judicial assassin only in order to enable him to retain a belief in his own
rectitude as he destroys the woman with whom he is still, in some sense, in
love. He has become the unresisting agent of Iago who has aroused in him a
sense of injured dignity, of loss of that reputation which Cassio had also
prized, and, above all, of betrayal by the person to whom he had dedicated
this latter part of his life.

According to Aristotle, the founder of our theories of tragedy, the tragic
hero is an otherwise admirable man who is ruined by some fatal flaw in his
personality. Shakespeare's tragic heroes, however, are destroyed by qualities
which, in any situation other than the one in which fate has placed them,
would appear virtues. Othello, from the start of the play, is distinguished by a
magnanimity, a 'free and open nature' which even Iago acknowledges. This
capacity for trust, for taking his fellow-men at their word, is in itself laudable; it becomes a liability only when it has to deal with Iago. The Moor also
has a justifiable sense of his own dignity, derived as it is from achievements
which are admired by almost everybody. When he feels this dignity has been
undermined, that he has become

> The fixed figure for the time of scorn
> To point his slow unmoving finger at,

the power which had sustained his self-assurance is turned against his
supposed betrayer. Othello is also one of many Shakespearean heroes –
including Hamlet, Lear, Troilus, Posthumus, Leontes and Prospero – who,
having suffered a real or imagined betrayal by someone intimately dear to
them, undergo not simply a personal but what might be called a metaphysi-

cal crisis. Desdemona having proved false, chaos is come again. Othello's personality is destroyed by Iago but, unlike Lear, he is given no time to build a new identity out of the ruins of the old. In his last, formal speech, in which he delivers what he sees as his own funeral oration, he revives in himself the memory of the greatness he once possessed, but only in order to brace himself for suicide. His death is as spectacular as his life and the impression with which we are left is one of waste.

*Othello* is the most tightly constructed of all Shakespeare's tragedies. Unlike *Macbeth* or *King Lear*, it is a 'domestic' tragedy in the sense that it scarcely touches on political issues but it centred almost exclusively on the intimate relationships between husband, wife and servant. Othello's personal tragedy has no effect on the state of Venice of the kind that Macbeth's has on Scotland or Lear's on Britain. This reduction of the scope of plot and character allows Shakespeare to direct our attention to Othello and Iago and to create out of their relationship a sustained and increasingly powerful suspense from which he offers very little relief. The suspense is created by a relentless dramatic irony unparalleled elsewhere in Shakespeare's work and which arises from the audience's insight into Iago's character and intentions, an insight of which the other characters are incapable. By allowing Iago to confide in us, in his soliloquies, more frankly and intimately than he does in his associates, Shakespeare compels us, however reluctantly, to become complicit in Iago's designs. We are trapped spectators, able to foresee the impending catastrophe yet powerless to prevent it. Hence we are moved by that pity and fear which Aristotle identified as the characteristically tragic emotions and, at the same time, are conscious of the superlative control over his material by means of which Shakespeare arouses them.

# KING LEAR

Although *King Lear* is a dramatization of a series of events which supposedly happened during a very early period of British history, its plot is radically different from those of Shakespeare's other English history plays such as *Richard II* or *Henry V* in that whereas the latter are for the most part derived from actual historical events, such as the deposition of Richard or the Battle of Agincourt, the former originated in ancient folk-tale and myth. The story of the father who has three daughters (or, in some versions, three sons) of whom only the youngest, at first misjudged, proves loyal and honest, is part of the folklore of many countries. Moreover, although Shakespeare may well have believed that Lear had once been a real historical figure – his reign was, after all, described along with those of more recent kings in Holinshed's *Chronicle* – nevertheless he treated his story in such a way as to emphasize and bring out its mythical qualities.

One of the ways in which he created this effect was by setting the tragedy in a distantly remote and deliberately undefined historical period. According to Holinshed, 'Leir the sonne of Baldud was admitted ruler over the Britains in the year of the world 3105, at what time Joas reigned in Juda', which is as much as to say that it happened 'once upon a time'. Whereas in *Macbeth*, which also depicts an early and barbaric period of history, the audience is given some precise historical bearings and a consequent sense of authenticity by the references to Edward the Confessor, in *King Lear* no such reassuring context is provided. The names of the gods on whom the various characters call in times of stress suggest that this is a pagan, pre-Christian era:

> For, by the sacred radiance of the sun,
> The mysteries of Hecat and the night;
> By all the operation of the orbs
> From whom we do exist and cease to be;
> Here I disclaim all my paternal care,
> Propinquity and property of blood,
> And as a stranger to my heart and me
> Hold thee from this for ever.

Indeed, in this invocation, Lear assumes the roles not simply of a fa[...]
monarch but of an ancient priest-king, the intermediary between [...]
jects and the elemental deities of primitive nature worship. Moreo[...]
pre-Christian setting of the play makes credible the frequent attempt[...]
characters to conjecture from the limited evidence of their own exper[...]
what kind of supernatural beings control their destinies. Having no knowledge of the Christian gospels, they are compelled, with incomplete and
inadequate evidence, to form tentative, provisional notions of what kind of
beings the gods may be.

Not only the historical period but the location of the play is significantly
indistinct. Very early in his career Shakespeare had shown himself capable of
evoking in the minds of his audience a vividly specific sense of place, such as
the wood near Athens in *A Midsummer Night's Dream* or the Capulet household in *Romeo and Juliet*, but *King Lear* is characterized by its notable lack of
location. Although it opens, presumably, in Lear's castle and moves later to
the home of Gloucester, we are given no indication of what these establishments are like or even where, exactly, they are, and when Lear, hurt and
enraged at his treatment by his daughters, impetuously rushes off, he goes,
simply, into a storm:

> Alack, the night comes on, and the high winds
> Do sorely ruffle; for many miles about
> There's scarce a bush.

There is, in this play, none of the kind of descriptive writing which would
limit its significance to any specific place. The only passage of particularized
description is Edgar's account of Dover Cliff, from the top of which crows
seem as small as beetles and fishermen the size of mice. Yet, paradoxically,
the place does not exist; it is fabricated by Edgar in order to deceive his blind
father. The actual drama is enacted in a much less precise context. The
empty, unadorned platform, of which the stage at the Globe Theatre
basically consisted, not only allowed Shakespeare to set his plays in any location and to shift rapidly from one to another (from Alexandria to Rome, for
example, or the court to the tavern in East Cheap), but also to put them in no
particular setting. He could thus leave himself free to draw the attention of
the audience to the essentials: a king dividing his territory; a son leading his
blind father; a naked beggar in a storm; a father kneeling to his daughter. It is
the timeless, elemental nature of stage images such as these which gives to
*King Lear* its unusual power and has ensured its survival.

It is in the nature of myths, whether classical like the story of Proserpine
which deals with death and rebirth, or biblical like the tale of Adam and Eve
which portrays the loss of a golden age, to describe not so much the fate of a
specific individual as experience common to mankind, and *King Lear*,
uniquely among Shakespeare's plays, has a breadth and generality of

significance. The tragedies of Othello and Coriolanus are special, not representative cases, but *King Lear* repeatedly portrays the restless intolerance of the young towards the old, the powerlessness of virtue in the face of craft, the helpless vulnerability of old age, the fragility of the bonds which hold families and communities together, and the hidden nature of the supernatural beings, if they exist, which govern our lives.

It is also characteristic of myths to be repeated, like rituals, passed on from one community or generation to another, and in *King Lear* Shakespeare not only dramatized a tale which had already been told in many different versions, but provided in the tragedy of Gloucester another version of the same tale. Like Lear, Gloucester fatally misjudges his own children; like Lear, he discovers his error only when it is too late to avoid its consequences; both pay a price which is monstrously disproportionate to their initial errors and both find ultimate, though temporary, consolation in their reunion with their rejected children. At the point where the two tragedies intersect, when the blind Gloucester meets the mad Lear, Shakespeare provides one statement of the bleak advice which is, perhaps, the only comfort the play has to offer:

> I know thee well enough; thy name is Gloucester.
> Thou must be patient.

Yet although the two tragedies often run in parallel (and thereby contribute to the play's myth-like generality and breadth of significance) there are also some telling differences between them. The initial passivity of Gloucester, his readiness to accommodate himself to the new regime of Goneril and Regan, contrasts strongly with Lear's wilful determination to have his own way despite his lost authority; Lear's inner anguish, the emotional pain he suffers as a result of his daughters' contempt, is of a different order from the physical violence inflicted on Gloucester, and the latter's desire to terminate his suffering by suicide serves to emphasize Lear's extraordinary toughness and fortitude, his gradually acquired capacity for 'patience'. Most striking are their differences in death: whereas Gloucester has the consolation of being rescued from despair by his son, in whose presence he dies "twixt two extremes of passion, joy and grief", Lear dies as a result of his discovery of the dead Cordelia, a shock the brutality of which even his patience cannot endure. Hence, though the fate of Gloucester may satisfy, in however rough and ready a way, our notions of justice, those of Lear and Cordelia do not. The play refuses to accommodate itself to any moral or theological generalizations we may be tempted to draw from it, and challenges any simple assumptions about loyalty and justice we may be inclined to hold.

This is, in fact, the effect on Lear of the experiences he undergoes in the first two acts. Repeatedly during this first section of the play his most cherished assumptions are proved to be false. In casting off the burden of government he hopes to enjoy a comfortable old age but in the event exposes himself to extreme mental and physical discomfort; he expects from Cordelia a declaration of love even stronger than those of her sisters, but is met with the apparently brutal and perverse 'Nothing'; he arrives in Goneril's household expecting that obedience to his whims to which he has presumably been accustomed ('Let me not stay a jot for dinner; go get it ready'), only to discover that he must subject himself to his daughter's will and dispense with half his retinue. Thwarted and enraged though he is at this rebuff, he consoles himself that he has 'another daughter' who is 'kind and comfortable', but finds Regan as stony and intransigent as Goneril. The greatest shock he undergoes, the death of Cordelia, is thus only the last, the least expected and the least tolerable of these challenges to his expectations.

His reaction to these repeated shocks is, initially, one of sheer disbelief, as his incredulous questions indicate:

> Are you our daughter?

> Does any here know me? This is not Lear.
> Does Lear walk thus? speak thus? Where are his eyes?
> Either his notion weakens, or his discernings
> Are lethargied. – Ha! waking? 'Tis not so. –
> Who is it that can tell me who I am?

As the reality of his daughters' callousness becomes plainer to him, however, his incredulousness turns into an incensed desire for vengeance. But since he has abdicated all power and is incapable of putting his impulses into effect, his threats become increasingly pathetic:

> You unnatural hags,
> I will have such revenges on you both
> That all the world shall – I will do such things –
> What they are yet I know not; but they shall be
> The terrors of the earth.

The only retaliation which he has the power to muster is, with difficulty, to retain his composure, to fight off his tears, and defiantly to reject the meagre hospitality which is all they offer him by going off into the storm. Having been rejected by them, he tries to regain the initiative by rejecting them.

Thus the drama of the first two acts consists of the gradual removal from Lear of those props which had supported his sense of identity as king. He gives away his kingdom; he is refused all visible manifestations of love by his daughters; his retinue is taken from him and, as the second act concludes, he wilfully refuses to shelter himself against the elements. He is now 'nothing' and, as he strips off his garments, he makes the final gesture which reduces him to the level of that 'unaccommodated man' which the naked Edgar seems to him to represent.

During the storm of the third act, Lear is torn between conflicting impulses, each one of which gains temporary ascendancy. He

> Strives in his little world of man to outscorn
> The to-and-fro conflicting wind and rain.

At first he resolutely defies the tempest in the spirit in which he had previously challenged his daughters. Then self-pity overcomes him as he is forced to recognize his vulnerability:

> Here I stand, your slave,
> A poor, infirm, weak and despis'd old man.

Finally he attempts to resist these assaults upon his dignity with the only resource which is left to him, an inner, stoical refusal to be moved:

> No, I will be the pattern of all patience;
> I will say nothing.

Behind this determination to bear his afflictions with patience lies his fear of madness, the irresistible and helpless loss of control over his mind, his identity, the possibility of which intermittently troubles him during the first half of the play. The madness of Lear, like that of Ophelia, sets in when the assaults he suffers become so violent a challenge to his view of himself and his fellow-men that he is compelled, instinctively, to see them as other than they really are. Unable to tolerate reality, he retreats into a world fabricated by his crazed imagination in which he is restored to his former power, arraigning Goneril and Regan, and, supported by the 'learned justicers', Poor Tom and the Fool, sits in judgement over them. At this point he has lost even that identity which he had struggled tenaciously to preserve.

Other major characters in the play undergo a loss of identity though in different senses and by different means from Lear. Having followed the dictates of his own compassion for the King and tried to rescue him, Gloucester is deprived of his eyes and, hence, of that contact with his fellow-men on which our sense of our own personality depends. Then, as Lear retreats helplessly into the fantasies of madness, Gloucester tries to make the most desperate escape by ending his own life. His expectations, like those of so many of the characters, are, however, thwarted:

> Is wretchedness depriv'd that benefit,
> To end itself by death? 'Twas yet some comfort
> When misery could beguile the tyrant's rage
> And frustrate his proud will.

He is cheated even of the meagre comfort of suicide. When he returns, as he believes, from the very brink of death, he recognizes that he can rely only on that fortitude which the King had tried vainly to sustain:

> Henceforth I'll bear
> Affliction till it do cry out itself
> 'Enough, enough' and die.

– a fate which finally overtakes Lear.

Kent and Edgar are forced to change their identities but in a less radical way. Kent, banished by the King yet determined to go on serving him, can do so only by concealing his identity. Unlike Lear and Gloucester, however, he undergoes no inner collapse; on the contrary, he remains stubbornly plain-spoken, boldly loyal to his master, and retains his cheerfulness even when forced to suffer the indignity of imprisonment in the stocks, a punishment, as Gloucester points out, usually given for 'pilferings and common tres-passes'. Kent already has the kind of sturdy patience the others are forced painfully to acquire.

Edgar's concealment of himself under the disguise of the half-witted vagabond Poor Tom is also forced upon him by circumstances. Wrongly accused of plotting the murder of his father and proclaimed a criminal, he is compelled to take refuge by assuming the identity of 'the basest and most poorest shape / That ever penury in contempt of man / Brought near to beast'. But whereas Kent, despite his new appearance, keeps his resilient personality intact, Edgar so loses himself in his new role as to let it possess him completely:

> Edgar I nothing am.

Indeed, until this moment he has had little or no distinguishing character. He speaks only ten lines, most of them in response to the questionings of Edmund, of whom he is merely the dupe. When he makes his next, pathetic entrance in the storm he seems to have become so broken by exposure and neglect as to have become the character he feigns. Nevertheless, in response to the plight first of Lear and then of Gloucester, he begins to develop a new personality and it is a naively buoyant one, determined to make the best of his degraded condition:

> Who alone suffers suffers most i'th' mind,
> Leaving free things and happy shows behind;
> But then the mind such sufferance doth o'erskip
> When grief hath mates, and bearing fellowship.

The notion that the sight of others' pain reduces his sense of his own is, how-ever, yet another of those false consolations with which the characters in this tragedy attempt to reconcile themselves to hardship. The sight of his father, blinded and thrust out into the storm, gives him absolutely no sense of com-radeship in adversity. On the contrary it comes as a horrifyingly painful shock to a man who thought he had already experienced the worst:

> O gods! Who is't can say 'I am at the worst'?
> I am worse than e'er I was.

Henceforth Edgar is deprived even of the slender consolation of believing that life holds no worse torments for him. He realizes that he must rely on that patient endurance by which Kent survives and on which his father rests:

> Men must endure
> Their going hence, even as their coming hither:
> Ripeness is all.

Thus, though the action of the play lurches forward from one unforeseen disaster to another, and though the dialogue breaks down to a level at which it is scarcely intelligible, Shakespeare himself remains in control of the chaotic drama he has created. He does so by organizing the characters and actions in a series of parallels and contrasts. The initial fortitude of Lear runs parallel to the steadfastness of Kent and contrasts with the passivity of Gloucester; the vulnerability and solitude of Gloucester in his blindness resembles the helplessness of Lear in his madness; the assertive individualism of Edmund is set off against Edgar's self-effacement and compassion. Lear, Gloucester and Edgar are all three subjected to humiliations far more painful than they could have foreseen and in which they are left with nothing to sustain themselves but their own powers of endurance, and in Lear's case even this ultimate support collapses.

Their sufferings are brought about by the callousness of Goneril, Regan and Edmund, which is released by their parents' credulousness and misplaced trust. In spite of the anguish which they cause, however, they are not quite the monsters Lear believes them to be. Edmund, deprived of all rights of inheritance by the bastardy for which he is not responsible, and treated (if we may judge from the scrap of dialogue with which the play opens) with a kind of genially prurient condescension by his father, at least has some cause for asserting himself. The fact that his resolution ruthlessly to prosper in the world is an act of deliberate choice shows that he does have some moral sense if only because he consciously determines to act in opposition to it. His death-bed instinct to do some good despite his own nature is therefore consistent with his awareness of his former inhumanity. Goneril and Regan, on the other hand, are given no motive for their callousness. As Lear tells Cordelia,

> Your sisters
> Have, as I do remember, done me wrong.
> You have some cause; they have not.

They are by nature unfeeling and egocentric. They are attracted to Edmund by their own lust and each destroys the other in her eagerness to possess him.

Yet, like Edmund, they do have a kind of pragmatic good sense which, if it were not so unfeeling, would seem laudable. Their father with his wayward and domineering whims and his hundred knights is, no doubt, an intolerable guest and one can sympathize with their desire to be rid of him:

> Regan                                    Shut up your doors.
>             He is attended with a desperate train;
>             And what they may incense him to, being apt
>             To have his ear abus'd, wisdom bids fear.
> Cornwall    Shut up your doors, my lord; 'tis a wild night.
>             My Regan counsels well. Come out o'th' storm.

Their treatment of Lear appears unnatural largely because they are his daughters and because of the consequent effect it has on him.

The character who is least astonished by their unfeeling self-interest is the Fool, whose riddles, conundrums and snatches of song and folk-sayings obliquely reveal that he has nothing to learn of the ingratitude of men. From the start he tells Lear what the latter fears but does not wish to know:

> The hedge-sparrow fed the cuckoo so long
> That it's had it head bit off by it young.

Let go thy hold when a great wheel runs down a hill, lest it break thy neck with following; but the great one that goes upward, let him draw thee after.

He is scarcely a character but the mouthpiece of disinterested paradoxical and proverbial observations. He comes into the play as though from nowhere and his disappearance half-way through is unexplained; he has no past, no future and no home, and he undergoes no crisis of identity because he seems to have no identity to lose. He receives no shocks because he holds no false assumptions and he knows from the start what Lear, Gloucester and Edgar gradually discover.

Whereas the Fool remains unperturbed by the unfeeling egotism of the younger generation, others find it so incompatible with their view of human nature that they conclude it must be the effect of some malevolent supernatural agency. Kent can account for the difference in character between Cordelia and Lear's two other daughters only by attributing it to the influence of the stars:

> It is the stars,
> The stars above us, govern our conditions,
> Else one self mate and make could not beget
> Such different issues.

Gloucester, blind and reeling from the pain inflicted on him by Cornwall, sees himself the victim of some fiendishly malicious deities:

As flies to wanton boys are we to th' gods –
They kill us for their sport.

Albany, on the other hand, sees the murder of Cornwall by his own servant as evidence of the essential justice of the gods:

This shows you are above,
You justicers, that these our nether crimes
So speedily can venge!

Lear, yet again, baffled and shocked by his daughters' hard-heartedness, tries in his madness to locate and identify its source as though it were a malignant virus:

Let them anatomize Regan; see what breeds about her heart. Is there any cause in nature that makes these hard hearts?

The most obvious feature of these and other metaphysical speculations in the play is their subjectivity and, consequently, their inconsistency. Shakespeare, through the medium of the play, shows the attempts of his characters to penetrate into the heart of darkness, but he himself gives us no answer to the questions which his characters raise. Indeed, he could scarcely do so. Nor does he provide an answer to the most deeply anguished question which Lear asks as he holds the dead Cordelia in his arms:

Why should a dog, a horse, a rat have life,
And thou no breath at all?

It is a question to which no answer could possibly be given.

# MACBETH

In *Macbeth* Shakespeare explored more fully and deeply than in any of his other plays the nature and effects of evil. It is portrayed in the action, particularly in the murder of Duncan and of Macduff's family, in the characters, most obviously that of Lady Macbeth, and in the dark, oppressive images which convey the impression of evil as a palpable, substantial presence:

> Light thickens, and the crow
> Makes wing to th' rooky wood;
> Good things of day begin to droop and drowse,
> Whiles night's black agents to their preys do rouse.

> Now o'er the one half-world
> Nature seems dead, and wicked dreams abuse
> The curtain'd sleep; now witchcraft celebrates
> Pale Hecate's offerings; and wither'd murder,
> Alarum'd by his sentinel, the wolf,
> Whose howl's his watch, thus with his stealthy pace,
> Moves like a ghost.

The potential for evil is present in the whole of creation: in nature, the animals and in man, all three of which are linked together in this second passage. It is also a supernatural force and, as such, is invoked by the witches in their spells and by Lady Macbeth when she calls upon the 'spirits that tend on mortal thoughts' to possess her totally.

Shakespeare, unlike Poe or the gothic novelists, does not portray evil in some vague, mysterious and seductive way but in specific, concrete and repellent terms, as when Lady Macbeth visualizes the knocking out of her child's brains or Macbeth looks with revulsion on his bloody hands. Shakespeare is able to do so because he has a very full and precise understanding of it morally and theologically. Evil in Macbeth consists of the disruption of the instinctive and necessary allegiances which hold society together. It manifests itself in the violation of the bonds which link parent with child, ruler with subject, husband with wife. It is, in the literal sense of the word, 'unnatural' or contrary to nature. Hence, in calling up the spirits of night, Lady Macbeth invites them to transform her milk into poison, and, in response to Duncan's murder, his horses 'turn wild in nature', 'contending 'gainst obedience' and devour each other.

The opening chapter of the book of Genesis describes how God created order out of chaos by separating the night from the day, the land from the waters and the fowls of the air from the fishes of the sea, but it is in the nature of evil, as portrayed in *Macbeth*, to demolish this order. In murdering Duncan, Macbeth destroys a man to whom he owes a natural allegiance as his subject, kinsman and host, and, on the day following this unnatural act, the sun is 'strangled' by the night. Evil is therefore the manifestation of Antichrist, of the devil; it tends towards anarchy. The witches are neither wholly male nor female; they look like women and yet have beards, and their element is 'the fog and filthy air', an amorphous substance at once palpable yet intangible. The stew they boil in their cauldron is repellent because it is made up of the dismembered parts of unrelated, incompatible objects:

> Liver of blaspheming Jew,
> Gall of goat, and slips of yew
> Sliver'd in the moon's eclipse,
> Nose of Turk, and Tartar's lips,
> Finger of birth-strangled babe
> Ditch-deliver'd by a drab.

The ingredients are either poisonous, unnatural (like the 'birth-strangl'd babe'), or pagan (like the Jew, Turk and Tartar), and the thick gruel which they constitute is an image of the formless confusion towards which the devil always works. Its larger image is Scotland, a country ruled by a murderer, where unprotected innocents are killed by hired assassins and truth has been supplanted by lies, and which collapses into civil war. The force of evil is unleashed by Macbeth and his wife and gradually spreads from them to possess the whole kingdom.

The first impression we receive of Macbeth is a disturbingly ambiguous one. His defeat of the rebellious Macdonwald is described by the Sergeant (who, since he is bleeding, seems to have brought evidence of the ferocious battle with him) in strikingly barbaric terms:

> Brave Macbeth – well he deserves that name –
> Disdaining Fortune, with his brandish'd steel
> Which smok'd with bloody execution,
> Like valour's minion, carv'd out his passage
> Till he fac'd the slave;
> Which ne'er shook hands, nor bade farewell to him,
> Till he unseam'd him from the nave to the chaps,
> And fix'd his head upon our battlements.

Duncan's delighted reaction, 'O valiant cousin! worthy gentleman!', is scarcely appropriate. Macbeth, as described in this passage, is at the same time heroically courageous in the defence of his king yet pitilessly violent, a man capable of an extreme brutality which is, for the moment, employed for a laudable purpose.

His first words, 'So foul and fair a day I have not seen' ('foul', presumably, in its actions yet 'fair' in its outcome), pick up and sustain this ambiguity. They also echo the earlier words of the witches, 'Fair is foul and foul is fair', and thereby associate him with them in a way which is troubling but as yet unspecific. His immediate response to the witches is oddly unexpected, considering the favourable prophecies they deliver. As Banquo comments in surprise, Macbeth starts and seems to fear things which sound fair, as though he recognizes in the witches' words some fearful impulse which he has already, half-consciously, sensed within himself. The witches in no way compel him to action. They merely address him as Thane of Glamis, Cawdor and as the future King, but his reaction suggests that they have awakened in him an idea which fills him with dread and, in an unguarded moment, the idea declares itself:

> My thought, whose murder yet is but fantastical,
> Shakes so my single state of man
> That function is smother'd in surmise
> And nothing is but what is not.

It is Macbeth, not the witches, who has supplied the idea of murder and it is characteristic of his complex, divided nature at this stage of the play that he should both conceive of murder and yet be terrified by it.

Shakespeare shows us two other reactions to the prophecies which contrast strongly with Macbeth's own response and thereby call attention to it and define it more sharply. Banquo, theologically correct according to the beliefs of Shakespeare's time, very properly reminds himself that

> oftentimes to win us to our harm
> The instruments of darkness tell us truths,
> Win us with honest trifles.

For this reason he remains guarded, detached and sceptical, as though waiting to discover how events will turn out. Lady Macbeth, on the other hand, on reading her husband's account of the witches, embraces the news eagerly and, resolving unhesitatingly on Duncan's murder, calls upon the supernatural agents of the devil to stifle all human feeling in her in order that she may unflinchingly perform it:

> Make thick my blood,
> Stop up th' access and passage to remorse,
> That no compunctious visitings of nature

> Shake my fell purpose nor keep peace between
> Th' effect and it.

In a literal sense she implores the forces of evil to possess her and to transform her into that unnatural creature, an unfeeling woman. Her prayer is consistent with the theological views of Shakespeare's contemporaries who believed that the devil could not take possession of his victims against their wills. Lady Macbeth invites him in.

By contrast, Macbeth responds neither sceptically nor willingly to the witches. He is both fascinated and repelled by them. His wife's assessment of his divided character is shrewdly accurate:

> Thou wouldst be great;
> Art not without ambition, but without
> The illness should attend it. What thou wouldst highly
> That wouldst thou holily; wouldst not play false,
> And yet wouldst wrongly win.

As she perceives, Macbeth is not lacking in ambition (the real lust for power is hers) yet is too humane to give way wholeheartedly to its promptings. As the carefully balanced clauses in her speech reveal, Macbeth is at this stage in a condition of tense, unstable equilibrium, a potential murderer who is as yet incapable of carrying out the deed. His equilibrium is upset firstly by Duncan's sudden nomination of Malcolm as his immediate heir, which places an obstacle between Macbeth and the throne. The effect of this announcement is to revive in Macbeth the thought of murder and its concomitant fearful sense of guilt:

> That is a step
> On which I must fall down, or else o'erleap,
> For in my way it lies. Stars, hide your fires;
> Let not light see my black and deep desires.
> The eye wink at the hand; yet let that be
> Which the eye fears, when it is done, to see.

Macbeth is in a literal sense divided within himself, his eye unwilling to look at the act his hand wishes to perform, and it is while he is in this state that Duncan suddenly decides to come at once to Macbeth's castle at Inverness, thus providing him with the opportunity to act swiftly on his wife's persuasions.

Hence Macbeth is prompted partly by his own violent nature, partly by the more dominant, ambitious personality of his wife and partly by circumstances. Had any of these circumstances not been present he could, we feel, have resisted the temptation to murder. What makes him a tragic and not merely a treacherous man is, however, that he grasps the moral significance of the deed but acts in defiance of his own moral understanding. He is his own most acute judge. He knows that the effects of the murder must eventually recoil back on

himself, though in ways which he cannot, for the time being, precisely specify.
He seems to see himself as provoking an act of revenge:

> But in these cases
> We still have judgement here. We but teach
> Bloody instructions, which being taught return
> To plague th' inventor.

He also realizes that in killing Duncan he would violate the most fundamental
laws on which society rests:

> He's here in double trust:
> First, as I am his kinsman and his subject –
> Strong both against the deed; then , as his host,
> Who should against his murderer shut the door,
> Not bear the knife myself. Besides, this Duncan
> Hath borne his faculties so meek, hath been
> So clear in his great office, that his virtues
> Will plead like angels, trumpet-tongu'd, against
> The deep damnation of his taking off.

There is no doubt in Macbeth's mind that he would literally suffer 'deep dam-
nation' were he to commit the deed. What holds him back, however, is his own
inherent humanity. It is only by stifling his natural feelings that Macbeth can
turn himself into an assassin.

Lady Macbeth, on the other hand, having already deliberately stifled her
humanity, assists her husband to do the same. She does so by accusing him, a
soldier, of cowardice. His retort is, in the terms established by the play, absolutely correct:

> I dare do all that may become a man;
> Who dares do more is none.

Although by the end of the scene Macbeth has given way to his wife's incite-
ments, he already foresees that in order to carry out the murder he must force
himself against his own better nature. He must compel his hands to perform an
act on which his mind is now set, and the guilty sense of revulsion which overwhelms him after the murder is already present in him before he actually carries it out:

> I am settled, and bend up
> Each corporal agent to this terrible feat.
> Away, and mock the time with fairest show;
> False face must hide what the false heart doth know.

Paradoxically he is the most sensitive as well as the most destructive character
in the play.

Ironically, the murder which Macbeth compels himself with such loathing to perform brings him no satisfaction. On the contrary, it brings him only fear, anxiety, sleeplessness, a guilty conscience, despair and, eventually, death. The assaults he suffers from others are trivial compared with the torment he endures within. His restless, chaotic mind is possessed by the evil he has initiated; his 'bloody instructions' do indeed 'return to plague the inventor'. From the moment when he returns from Duncan's bedchamber he is beset with guilty fears; an owl's hoot and a sudden knock on the door fill him with panic. He knows that he has given the 'eternal jewel' of his soul to the devil and that he will be damned in the next world, but his more pressing concern is with his security in this world and, in order to protect himself, he finds himself compelled to eradicate Banquo. He is trapped in the consequences of his own crime, 'cabin'd, cribb'd, confin'd', forced again to embark on the murder of a man whose royalty of nature he recognizes and from which his instincts there-fore recoil. Already the promptings of conscience which he had managed to quell during the assassination of Duncan reassert themselves in the form of terrible dreams to the extent that he now envies his victim:

> Duncan is in his grave;
> After life's fitful fever he sleeps well.

These are not, however, the worst consequences which Macbeth has to endure. His conscience, at this stage, is very much alive, as his vision of the dead Banquo's invasion of the feast reveals. But, as he is obliged to commit one crime after another, he becomes so habituated to evil that his capacity for fear, and the sense of right and wrong to which it bears witness, becomes atrophied. By now his humanity is not stifled but smothered. Having forfeited all sense of morality, even all sense of guilt, he becomes a mere husk of a man wearily act-ing out a life which offers no satisfaction, nor even any interest for him. His life has no meaning because he has himself removed the meaning from it:

> Tomorrow, and tomorrow, and tomorrow,
> Creeps in this petty pace from day to day
> To the last syllable of recorded time,
> And all our yesterdays have lighted fools
> The way to dusty death.

He sees himself as an actor forced to take part in a drama composed by a lunatic:

> Life's but a walking shadow, a poor player,
> That struts and frets his hour upon the stage,
> And then is heard no more; it is a tale
> Told by an idiot, full of sound and fury,
> Signifying nothing.

By destroying others he has destroyed his essential self. The man who is cor-nered and killed at Dunsinane is, really, already dead.

Lady Macbeth, for all her resolution and strength of will, is the lesser of the two characters because she has none of her husband's moral imagination. She is from the start portrayed as an unnatural woman, a virago, like Volumnia in *Coriolanus* and Queen Margaret in *Henry VI*, and her influence, like that of those other domineering women, is irresistible and destructive. Any tenderness she has ever been capable of is effectively destroyed in the moment when she steels herself to the murder and invites the agents of hell to possess her. From then onwards she is concerned not, as her husband is, with the ethics of murder, but with the practical details of getting it done. It is she who knows that Duncan's journey will have tired him and who thinks of first drugging the King's attendants and then using their daggers. In her practicality she is monstrously efficient:

> I laid their daggers ready;
> He could not miss 'em.

Her reaction to Macduff's outraged cry of discovery,

> Our royal master's murder'd!

seems to be spontaneous and genuine:

> Woe, alas!
> What, in our house?

Her first concern is not for the murdered king but for her own reputation. Yet there are signs that she is not quite the unfeelingly ambitious shrew she appears to be. She does, after all, find it necessary deliberately to cast out all 'compunctious visitings of nature' before putting her plans into effect and, as she looks at the sleeping Duncan, she betrays the first hint that there is more to her than her impregnable exterior:

> Had he not resembled
> My father as he slept, I had done't.

Her function is to strengthen her husband's will to commit the murder. Once that has been done she gradually disappears from the play. The killing of Duncan brings Macbeth and his wife together in a sickening intimacy but, once it is over, Macbeth continues on his brutal course alone, not only planning the murder of Banquo himself but concealing his intention from her. She has initiated him into evil and her pupil now no longer needs her. In the aftermath of the murder she is left in a state of sad, deflated fearfulness similar to Macbeth's:

> Nought's had, all's spent,
> Where our desire is got without content.
> 'Tis safer to be that which we destroy,
> Than by destruction dwell in doubtful joy.

When, some considerable time later, she makes her final appearance, alone, in a trance, ceaselessly washing her hands, obsessed with the sight and smell of blood, she is a pitiful, vulnerable woman but no longer a morally trivial one. Whereas Macbeth loses his moral imagination, Lady Macbeth gains hers and, as her suicide implies, it is intolerable.

Macbeth's 'bloody instructions' return to plague him in the form of fearfulness, guilt and despair, and also in the form of Malcolm, Macduff and their army of invasion. His cruelty creates its own opposition in that his subjects first take flight and are then impelled by a sense of outraged justice to rise up against him. The murder of Lady Macduff and her children is an act of gratuitous butchery and shows the extent to which Macbeth has become steeped in blood, but its effect is to provoke Macduff into action. His grief converts to anger and his tears become 'the whetstone of his sword'. The chain of murders, far from strengthening Macbeth's position as he hopes, directly activates the forces, both outward and within himself, which unseat him. Hence England, as Shakespeare portrays it, becomes the centre of both the military and the moral opposition to the usurper. It is the seat of Edward the Confessor, the saintly monarch, who, in contrast to the 'devilish' Macbeth, possesses the miraculous power of healing,

> And sundry blessings hang about his throne
> That speak him full of grace.

'Grace' is here used in the specific, theological sense of 'the grace of God', and it is in England, too, that we hear from Malcolm of the 'king-becoming graces', the moral positives in the play which, in the context of the prevailing images of evil, take on an extraordinary force:

> As justice, verity, temp'rance, stableness,
> Bounty, perseverance, mercy, lowliness,
> Devotion, patience, courage, fortitude.

It is as the defenders of these virtues that Malcolm and Macduff rebel against the tyrant in what amounts to a religious crusade. When Birnham Wood appears to advance on Dunsinane, it is as though nature itself has risen up in outrage against a man who has violated its laws.

*Macbeth* is the last of Shakespeare's four major tragedies and by far the shortest. The writing is unusually compressed and densely packed so that practically every line is charged with meaning and none is redundant. Its brevity also contributes to its dramatic effect: no sooner has Macbeth conceived the idea of murder than the opportunity comes for him to act on it, and no sooner is the murder committed than its consequences follow thick and fast. He is given no opportunity to enjoy the satisfaction of the power he has seized, but the evil which he and his wife have knowingly let loose in the world takes root and grows like a virulent disease. It was a disease which

Shakespeare examined with increasing fascination during the course of his major tragedies. In *Hamlet* it preoccupies the imagination of the hero, who contemplates with disgust the rottenness in the state of Denmark; in *Othello* it is present in the mind of Iago who transfers it to Othello himself, and in *King Lear* it spreads outwards from the circle of the family to erupt in civil war. Only in *Macbeth*, however, is Shakespeare so exclusively preoccupied with evil and only in this play does he contemplate it in its supernatural, metaphysical form as well as in the individual, in nature and in society. The powers which the witches conjure up in the opening scene seem to hover over the rest of the play even though we can perceive them only in their effects. Having completed *Macbeth*, Shakespeare turned his mind to completely different things. He returned to Plutarch and the history of Rome. He felt, perhaps, that he had carried this particular enquiry as far as he could. No other English writer has pursued it further.

# ANTONY AND CLEOPATRA

The materials out of which Shakespeare made his plays were not only those of the poet – language, rhetoric and the expressive rhythms of blank verse – but also of the dramatist – sharply contrasted characters, plots so constructed as to hold the attention of an audience, and visual impressions created by the placing of characters in relation to one another on an otherwise empty stage. His plays are full of expressive stage pictures, such as the scene in *The Winter's Tale* where Hermione's statue, raptly observed by her husband and daughter, slowly begins to breathe human life, or the moment in *Richard II* when the King holds the crown suspended between his own head and that of the usurper Bolingbroke.

*Antony and Cleopatra* is also a very visual play in which the stage pictures can often sum up the meaning of the drama at a particular stage. In the opening scene, two Roman soldiers in the foreground look on contemptuously as Antony and Cleopatra enter with 'her Ladies, the Train, with Eunuchs fanning her' and we immediately recognize the infatuation which the lovers feel for each other, the oriental luxury with which it is associated, and its violation of the Roman ideals of military self-discipline represented by the soldiers. The opening dialogue does little more than expand what the picture has already told us. Again, towards the end of the tragedy, when we see Cleopatra, surrounded by her maids, holding the body of Antony in her arms, we recognize her desolation, her vulnerability now she has lost her protector, and we share her feeling that the play has come to a halt now that the man who motivated both her and it lies dead.

These are, however, momentary static tableaux in a play which more often creates an impression of motion and change. No sooner have the two lovers embraced in the first scene than a series of messengers interrupt and separate them with demands that Antony should return to Rome; no sooner has Antony's marriage to Octavia been arranged than we are forewarned by Enobarbus that it will soon break up; Antony's confident embarkation on the sea fight is quickly followed by defeat, whereas his subsequent, less promising encounter on land is followed by unexpected victory. No situation, no relationship, in this play remains stable and fixed but is shown to be in a cease-less state of motion, transformation and flux.

   This impression is also created by the frequent and rapid shifts of location. Throughout the first three acts the scene alternates between Alexandria and Rome, a dramatic device which induces the audience to view the characters and situations from different and conflicting points of view. One impression melts into another in such a way that the characters themselves are made to seem indistinct or to appear transformed. Again, in the fourth act, as the for-tunes of war waver unpredictably between the two sides, we are presented with a rapid succession of short episodes showing the conflict first through Antony's, then through Octavius's eyes and we are forced to keep reassessing the situation. It is only in the final section, which is confined entirely to Cleo-patra's monument, that the action reaches a point of rest with Antony's death and Cleopatra's resolution to commit suicide, a deed which, as she says, 'shackles accidents and bolts up change'.

   The impression of instability is also conveyed by the violent, sudden shifts in the moods of the characters, especially those of Cleopatra, on whose whims the fates of the others depend. It is in her nature never to rest in one state of mind for more than an instant, much to the perplexity of her lover. Indeed she deliberately makes use of her instability in order to baffle, charm and keep her control over him. As she tells her maid,

> If you find him sad,
> Say I am dancing; if in mirth, report
> That I am sudden sick.

On hearing of Antony's decision to return to Rome she changes from one extreme to another within two lines:

> Cut my lace, Charmian, come!
> But let it be; I am quickly ill and well.

As she tries in vain to occupy the time while he is absent, her impulse is first to hear music, then to play billiards, then to go fishing; and, on hearing of her lover's marriage to Octavia, she first threatens to whip the messenger with wire, then commends him as a fellow of 'good judgement'. It is the capacity for change that Enobarbus regards as her distinguishing quality:

> Age cannot wither her, nor custom stale
> Her infinite variety.

All her emotions are felt with extreme intensity and the only feeling of which she seems incapable is that of stillness. Her ability to feel passionately is so strong that it takes on the quality of a moral virtue: she has the power, through the sheer violence of her emotions, to 'make defect perfection', and those qualities which in other people would be vices in her appear like virtues. She is a queen

> Whom everything becomes – to chide, to laugh,
> To weep; whose every passion fully strives
> To make itself . . . fair and admir'd.

When, with Antony's death, the world has become merely 'dull' she decides it is time to leave.

As a result of her instability, Antony, whose very being depends on her, is allowed no emotional rest. Depending on how she treats him he is alternately submissive, irritable, apologetic, adoring, enraged or tender. She dictates how he will feel by forcing him to respond to her moods. Antony is, of course, made the more unstable by his divided loyalties. From the beginning he is torn between his devotion to Cleopatra, through whom alone he feels fulfilled, and his responsibility to Rome, the security of which depends on his support. Both Cleopatra and Caesar equally require his loyalty and are therefore rivals for his attention: the former needs him as her protector and the object of her passion, the other as his aid in the defence of Rome against its enemies. Pulled first one way and then the other, Antony is allowed no rest. His military obligations call him away from Alexandria and the potency of Cleopatra draws him back from Rome. Like her, he finds repose only in death, or in that life he imagines after death where he will be released from 'the strong necessity of time'.

For their own particular reasons, both Cleopatra and Octavius need to keep Antony steadfastly loyal to themselves. As Octavius declares,

> It cannot be
> We shall remain in friendship, our conditions
> So diff'ring in their acts. Yet if I knew
> What hoop would hold us staunch, from edge to edge
> O' th' world I would pursue it.

Whereas Cleopatra tries to secure Antony's fidelity by exercising her charm, Octavius appeals to his sense of duty, an obligation which becomes personal as well as political once he has married Caesar's sister. The marriage is arranged, as Agrippa explains, in the hope that the two leaders will remain in 'perpetual amity':

> To make you brothers, and to knit your hearts
> With an unslipping knot, take Antony
> Octavia to his wife . . . Her love to both
> Would each to other, and all loves to both
> Draw after her.

The marriage fails not simply because, in comparison with Cleopatra, Octavia is 'of a holy, cold, and still conversation', but because, in the world Shakespeare has created, nothing is capable of permanence.

The impression of instability and continual flux is also created by the distinctive language Shakespeare used in the writing of this play. It is full of references to the processes of melting and decomposition, to objects which mysteriously transform themselves into their opposites or, like water or mist, slip through the fingers as we attempt to grasp them. It is in language of this kind that Antony refers to the instability of the empire:

> Let Rome in Tiber melt, and the wide arch
> Of the rang'd empire fall! Here is my space.
> Kingdoms are clay.

Again, on hearing the news of his wife Fulvia's death, he observes how easily both our loathings and desires can change into their opposites and pleasure can sicken even as we indulge in it:

> What our contempts doth often hurl from us
> We wish it ours again; the present pleasure,
> By revolution low'ring, does become
> The opposite of itself.

Assets have a way of transforming themselves into liabilities. This paradoxical, contradictory effect is also created by Cleopatra's servants, the 'pretty dimpled boys' who wait on her in her barge. The breeze created by their 'divers-colour'd fans'

> did seem
> To glow the delicate cheeks which they did cool,
> And what they undid did.

The most fully developed of these references to transformation and elusiveness occurs just after Antony's last battle in which he has been defeated and believes that Cleopatra has induced his soldiers to desert to the enemy. The two ideals to which he has devoted himself – his soldiership and his love – have thus apparently failed him and, as a consequence, he feels that his personality, his identity, is evaporating:

| | |
|---|---|
| *Antony* | Sometime we see a cloud that's dragonish; |
| | A vapour sometime like a bear or lion, |
| | A tower'd citadel, a pendent rock, |
| | A forked mountain, or blue promontory |
| | With trees upon't that nod unto the world |
| | And mock our eyes with air. Thou hast seen these signs: |
| | They are black vesper's pageants. |
| *Eros* | Ay, my lord. |
| *Antony* | That which is now a horse, even with a thought |
| | The rack dislimns, and makes it indistinct, |
| | As water is in water. |
| *Eros* | It does, my lord. |
| *Antony* | My good knave Eros, now thy captain is |

> Even such a body. Here I am Antony;
> Yet cannot hold this visible shape, my knave.

He had declared in the opening scene that he was 'himself' only when 'stirred' (or 'inspired') by Cleopatra. Now that he has been betrayed by her he no longer has any 'self'.

Cleopatra, on the other hand, develops a new kind of identity once Antony is dead. Recognizing that the only life she can hope for is as Caesar's prisoner, she resolves to commit suicide and, in so doing, acquires a stability of purpose:

> My resolution's plac'd, and I have nothing
> Of woman in me. Now from head to foot
> I am marble-constant; now the fleeting moon
> No planet is of mine.

She is convinced that after death she will be immune to the fluctuations of fortune which have governed her life, and her emotions reach a stability in her determination to be reunited with Antony in another world.

Shakespeare creates on his audience an effect of change and elusiveness not simply by his portrayal of character and actions and his use of certain kinds of language, but also by compelling us continually to revise our judgements of what we see on the stage. As the location shifts from Egypt to Rome and back again, so we are induced to assess the situation first from the Egyptian, then from the Roman point of view. Hence, for Antony, the embraces of Cleopatra are an expression of 'the nobleness of life', whereas for Caesar Antony has abandoned himself to 'lascivious wassails'. Their points of view are in such absolute opposition that they amount to two alternative and conflicting sets of principles or ways of life. The Roman attitude, expressed by Octavius, is one in which public duty takes precedence over private pleasure, in which the highest virtues are those of martial valour and success can be measured tangibly in terms of victories won or territory added to the empire. The character who displayed these virtues most fully was the Antony who existed before the beginning of the play, whom Octavius recalls with admiration and whose present degeneracy he bewails:

> When thou once
> Was beaten from Modena, where thou slew'st
> Hirtius and Pansa, consuls, at thy heel
> Did famine follow; whom thou fought'st against,
> Though daintily brought up, with patience more
> Than savages could suffer . . . On the Alps
> It is reported thou didst eat strange flesh,
> Which some did die to look on. And all this –
> It wounds thine honour that I speak it now –
> Was borne so like a soldier that they cheek
> So much as lank'd not.

The Roman virtues (which are also to be found in Shakespeare's other Roman heroes, Brutus and Coriolanus) are those of patriotism, self-discipline, physical prowess and a stoical control of personal emotions. Cleopatra, on the other hand, embodies everything that Rome is not. For her, emotions are not to be controlled but welcomed and cultivated. Whereas Octavius is dispassionately calculating, she is powerfully spontaneous. Success for her is measured in terms of intensity of experience. Hence she will, if necessary, sacrifice all her subjects in order to convey her love to Antony:

> He shall have every day a several greeting,
> Or I'll unpeople Egypt.

But, to save her own skin, she also deserts Antony in the sea battle and, in terror at his wrath, sends him the false news that she is dead.

Torn as he is between his enthralment to Cleopatra and his sense of obligation to Octavius, Antony is placed in a situation in which he is forced to betray the one or the other. By marrying Octavia he appears false to Cleopatra and by deserting Octavia he betrays both her and the Rome which her brother governs. It is his inability to reconcile these demands which destroys him. He is, however, not the only character divided between conflicting loyalties: as the sister of Octavius and wife of Antony, Octavia is uncertain where her sympathies should lie when the two men are at odds with each other, and Enobarbus finds himself unwittingly caught up in the kind of moral dilemma which characterizes this play. Like Antony, Enobarbus is a Roman who can willingly adapt himself to the life of Egypt. He obviously relishes the delights of Cleopatra's court and, as his enraptured account of her arrival on the River Cydnus shows, he can appreciate her theatricality and the magic of her character. He is also a professional soldier who is practical and shrewd enough to foresee the folly of the sea battle and the absurd histrionics of Antony's challenge to fight Caesar in single combat. With his capacity to adjust himself to both the worlds of the play he is a smaller version of Antony. Yet, as a minor figure in Roman politics, he is able, for most of the time, to remain on the sidelines of the action, an amused observer of the personal and political crises in which his master is engaged. It is this apparent detachment which enables him, when Antony's defeat seems inevitable, to get out while the going is good:

> I see still
> A diminution in our captain's brain
> Restores his heart. When valour preys on reason,
> It eats the sword it fights with. I will seek
> Some way to leave him.

It is only when he has actually deserted to the enemy, and is told that Antony, far from condemning him, has sent his treasure after him, that Enobarbus realizes he is no longer a mere spectator. Unable to return to the defeated

Antony, yet morally incapable of forgiving his own treachery, he embraces death as the only solution to his dilemma. Shakespeare's portrayal of the tragedy of Antony contains the lesser tragedy of Enobarbus. Both arise from a failure to reconcile conflicting loyalties. In following the dictates of common sense, Enobarbus has betrayed his sense of personal fidelity.

The deaths of both Antony and Enobarbus are pitiful. The former botches his attempt to end his life in a grand, stoical gesture of suicide; the latter dies cursing his own disloyalty. Cleopatra, on the other hand, stage-manages her death in such a way that it appears less like a defeat than a triumph. It is her last and most spectacular attempt to 'make defect perfection'. Whereas in the fourth act Shakespeare compresses a great deal of action into a short space of time, he devotes the entire fifth act to Cleopatra's slow resolution and preparation for death. By concentrating our attention entirely on her, in one of those mysterious transformations characteristic of *Antony and Cleopatra*, Shakespeare almost alters our impression of the entire play. The process begins with her expression of contempt for the merely worldly success which Octavius has accomplished:

> 'Tis paltry to be Caesar:
> Not being Fortune, he's but Fortune's knave,
> A minister of her will.

Realizing that she is defeated, she convinces herself that victory is not worth winning. She then lavishes on Dolabella her magnificent eulogy of the Antony whom, in her idealizing imagination, she remembers:

> His legs bestrid the ocean; his rear'd arm
> Crested the world. His voice was propertied
> As all the tuned spheres, and that to friends;
> But when he meant to quail and shake the orb,
> He was as rattling thunder.

The demi-god of her imagination is scarcely the very human Antony we have actually seen and, indeed, Dolabella does not believe he existed. But, by now, Cleopatra has persuaded herself that it is preferable to be reunited with Antony in a life beyong death than to remain a prisoner in this 'vile world'. Dressed in her crown and robes of state, she makes her death seem like a spectacular entrance into a 'better life', and the intensity of her conviction and the lyrical power of the poetry Shakespeare has written for her may compel us to believe her. Whether her suicide is the victory she thinks it is, or merely her last splendid delusion, we have no means of knowing. 'The crown o' th' earth doth melt', but into what?

# CORIOLANUS

The opening scene of *Coriolanus* is so brilliantly constructed and tells us so much about the play it introduces that it is worth looking at in some detail. It immediately arouses the interest of the audience and then proceeds to sustain that interest with increasing intensity; it is a subtle expository scene which conveys information – about Roman politics and society, about Coriolanus himself – without appearing to do so, and, as it concludes, Shakespeare introduces the action (the invasion of Rome by the Volscians) which is to occupy the following scenes.

Like another of Shakespeare's Roman plays, *Julius Caesar*, *Coriolanus* opens with the spectacle of the mob in a state of dangerous turmoil. The fact that both these plays begin with the mob is significant because it will be they who will determine the course of Roman history – or rather, not the mob themselves, but those demagogues who by their oratory are capable of harnessing to their wills the mob's potentially destructive energy. Brutus in *Julius Caesar* failed to carry through his coup d'état because Mark Antony and not he was the more effective orator, and Coriolanus fails to hold the consulship because the tribunes are more skilful manipulators of the mob than he is. In Rome to control the plebeians is to control the city. The explosion of the mob onto the stage in the first moment of the play is one of the features which creates the impression of its 'Romanness'. Mob violence is very seldom a feature of the English histories.

Another distinctively Roman feature of *Coriolanus* is the preponderance of public, oratorical speeches. We are only fifty lines into this first scene when the populace are addressed by Menenius and they are harangued by Coriolanus shortly afterwards. But these are by no means the only formal, public speeches in the play: Coriolanus addresses his troops before the gates of Corioli, the plebeians are subjected to the rabble-rousing speeches of the tribunes, Cominius delivers a long, formally constructed eulogy of Coriolanus in the capitol and, even in private, Coriolanus, Aufidius and Volumnia address their fellows in extended, logically constructed speeches as though addressing a public audience. Oratory is of great importance in the Roman plays because, in an oral as distinct from a written culture, one which was largely illiterate and had no printed books, it was the only method of political debate and, of course, for Shakespeare, versed as he was in the orations and rhetorical treatises of Cicero from his days as a schoolboy at Stratford-on-Avon, Rome was the nurse of rhetoric. Oratory is not such a predominant feature of his English history plays.

Another important part of the first scene of *Coriolanus* is the sketchy but vivid characterization of the two leading citizens. First Citizen is rebellious, bold, determined and violent. It is he who attempts to make himself the leader and spokesman of his discontented companions:

First, you know Caius Martius is chief enemy to the people . . . Let us kill him, and we'll have corn at our own price. Is it a verdict?

He is also an intelligent, perceptive man who diagnoses Coriolanus's character and motivation with what later turns out to be precise accuracy:

I say unto you, what he hath done famously he did it to that end; though soft-conscienc'd men can be content to say it was for his country, he did it to please his mother, and to be partly proud, which he is, even to the altitude of his virtue.

These three motives – patriotism, the desire for public reputation (or what Volumnia later calls 'honour', which is the same thing) and the need to satisfy his mother's ambitions are, indeed, the impulses which drive the hero first to victory and then to destruction. Second Citizen, on the other hand, is a worried, cautious, tolerant fellow:

Consider you what services he has done for his country? . . . What he cannot help in his nature you account a vice in him. You must in no way say he is covetous.

It is he, unlike First Citizen, who thinks well of Menenius ('one that hath always lov'd the people'). The two men are so sharply contrasted that Shakespeare has given, even to his small-part actors, characters they can develop and work on. The differentiation between the two characters, moreover, serves to make a point which will be very significant as the tragedy unfolds. It makes us, the audience, recognize that, although these people constitute a mob, they are not simply a faceless rabble. The mob is composed of a number of distinctive, individual human beings and, for this reason, when they say they are hungry we are inclined to believe and sympathize with them. The individuality of each member of the mob is something of which Coriolanus is totally unaware. When he addresses them he always does so as though they were indistinguishable one from another:

> What's the matter, you dissentious rogues
> That, rubbing the poor itch of your opinion,
> Make yourselves scabs?

The words with which he describes them are all undiscriminating, collective nouns expressing both his contempt for them and his inability to regard them as even human. He calls them 'curs', 'hares', 'geese', 'slaves' and 'rabble'. Having already observed the distinctiveness of their personalities, the audience knows that he is wrong. Hence we are induced, from the very start of the play, to regard Coriolanus in an unsympathetic, critical, even hostile way. He seems to us arrogant, imperceptive, blinded by his aristocratic contempt for his social inferiors.

Menenius, privately, shares Coriolanus's contempt for the people: 'Rome and her rats' is his real view of them; they are what he later calls 'the multiplying spawn'. In public, however, and when political expediency requires, he can treat them with a certain jocular condescension:

| Menenius | What do you think, |
|---|---|
| | You, the great toe of this assembly? |
| 1st Cit. | I the great toe? Why the great toe? |
| Menenius | For that, being one o' th' lowest, basest, poorest, |
| | Of this most wise rebellion, thou goest foremost. |

No doubt this riposte produces the derisory laughter at the expense of First Citizen that Menenius requires. He knows that if he can turn First Citizen into a figure of fun he is half-way towards quashing the rebellion of which the latter is the leader.

It quickly becomes apparent in the first scene, therefore, that Menenius is – and prides himself on being – an astute politician. Temperamentally and by conviction and birth he is a patrician. He worships Coriolanus and shares the hero's loathing both for the people and for their elected representatives the tribunes, but in public he is prepared to appear good-natured, genial, even, self-indulgently, to mock his own weaknesses. He is a temporizer, a believer in expediency and, when the situation demands it, a hypocrite. His political astuteness throws Coriolanus's ineptitude into sharp relief. The hero's intransigence shows up more strongly by contrast with the acumen of Menenius. Or, to put it another way, Coriolanus's integrity, the honesty on which he prides himself, contrasts favourably with Menenius's capacity for dissembling, for this is a play in which, although the characters are quite simple and easy to understand, they are people about whom it is hard to make moral judgements. In totally different ways, both Coriolanus and Menenius are at the same time sympathetic and alien to us.

When Menenius offers to instruct the citizens by means of a 'pretty tale', First Citizen is quick to protest that he must not try to fob off their disgrace with a tale. Yet this is precisely what Menenius does. His fable of the belly is an account of the well-ordered, interdependent, productive society in which each part carries out its function for the benefit of the whole. It is, however, no more than a vision of the ideal state. The real Rome falls pitifully short of it, for the Rome of this play is a catastrophically split society in which each social class – the plebeians, the tribunes and the patricians – attempts to assert its own will over the rest. It is this class warfare, coupled with his own political ineptitude, which precipitates the hero's exile and death. Menenius's fable of the belly is not the description of Roman society he pretends it is. It is merely a means of distracting the citizens' attention and thereby defusing a rebellion. If, as he says they are, the senators are the belly of the body politic, what do they actually contribute to the good of the whole? Far from sending food through 'the rivers of your blood, / Even to the court, the heart, to th' seat o' th' brain', they actually withhold the very corn which is all the citizens are demanding. Menenius's tale is really an irrelevance masquerading as a parable, and it is characteristic of Shakespeare to have given this vision of the ideal community to a character who does not believe in it and who exploits it for his own immediate ends. The possibility of such an ideal state is undermined by the character and motives of the man who describes it.

Furthermore, Menenius's subtly timed oration fails to achieve its purpose, for no sooner has he finished than Coriolanus enters and instantly fans the flames of revolt which Menenius had laboured to extinguish, thereby thrusting the citizens into the hands of the tribunes, who are only too delighted at this opportunity to exploit them for their own purposes. The entry of Coriolanus is well prepared for. His is the first name to be mentioned in the play; it is he who has been singled out as 'chief enemy to the people', and, but for the intervention of Menenius, he might have been assassinated. When he does enter, he explodes onto the scene like a cannonball. His sudden arrival, his immediate and scathing tirade against the citizens, his destruction of the calm which has been so carefully created, are all characteristic of him. Indeed the effect of his entrance tells us something about Coriolanus even before he speaks: that he is rash, impetuous, insensitive, politically naive. He monopolizes the scene instantly and the next sixty lines are a more-or-less unbroken tirade against the mob. What is the basis for this contempt? It is the contempt of a member of the ruling class for those who, he believes, have ideas above their station, and the scorn of the professional soldier for the soft, cowardly civilian:

> What would you have, you curs,
> That like not peace nor war? The one affrights you,
> The other makes you proud. He that trusts to you,
> Where he should find you lions, finds you hares;
> Where foxes, geese.

It is also the contempt for the inconstant, easily manipulated multitude of a man who, throughout most of the play, sees himself as the embodiment, the model, of constancy:

> You are no surer, no,
> Than is the coal of fire upon the ice
> Or hailstone in the sun.
>
> With every minute you do change a mind
> And call him noble that was now your hate,
> Him vile that was your garland.

These are, of course, prophetic words, but the interesting thing about Shakespeare's stagecraft at this point is that he allows us to perceive the kind of man Coriolanus is, the virtues he admires, not by letting him voice them openly but by making him express them by implication. We discern what Coriolanus believes in by hearing what he most despises. Unlike the inconstant mob, Coriolanus is, as one of his soldiers later tells us, 'the rock, the oak, not to be wind-shaken'.

The virtues which Coriolanus embodies are, for Shakespeare, distinctively Roman virtues. It is these, above all, which give to the play its Roman flavour. These qualities – his sense of his own patrician worth, his fearlessness, his military prowess, his loyalty to his city, and his constancy – are summed up in the Latin word *virtus*. They are predominantly masculine, public virtues; he is a man with practically no private life. He never radically changes during the course of the play. He flashes before us in the first scene – confident, arrogant, fearless, brutally honest – and remains so until his death. In this he is unlike Othello, Lear and Macbeth who, at their deaths, have been totally transformed from their earlier selves. If our judgement of Coriolanus changes from scene to scene it is not because he himself is transformed but because Shakespeare has placed him in different kinds of situation. His fortitude, patriotism and desire for honour are soldierly virtues and Shakespeare shows us in some detail how he has acquired them. In one of the play's few domestic scenes, his mother explains to his wife, Virgilia, how she has deliberately instilled them into him:

When yet he was but tender-bodied, and the only son of my womb . . . I, considering how honour would become such a person . . . was pleas'd to let him seek danger where he was like to find fame. To a cruel war I sent him, from whence he return'd his brows bound with oak.

Coriolanus, for all his pride in his self-sufficiency ('as if a man were author of himself and knew no other kin'), is in fact the creation of his mother. She made him and he is therefore dependent on her. These soldierly virtues are, however, not simply irrelevant but catastrophic in peace, where their opposites – humaneness, patience, a sense of community – are essential, and the victor over the Volscians is also the man who enflames the mob. His assets in war become liabilities in peace, and one of Shakespeare's minor preoccupations in *Coriolanus* is the difference between peace and war, or rather the different qualities of character required in each. Aufidius refers to this difference in what is probably the crucial interpretative speech in the whole play, a summing up of the hero's character towards the end of the tragedy which parallels First Citizen's summary at the beginning. Coriolanus, he reflects, is in part the victim of his own personality, his

> nature,
> Not to be other than one thing, not moving
> From th' casque to th' cushion, but commanding peace
> Even with the same austerity and garb
> As he controll'd the war.

'So our virtues,' he concludes, 'lie in th' interpretation of the time.' In other words, the very assets which Coriolanus displays in war are liabilities in peace. He is, therefore, a man whom we can neither praise nor blame unreservedly.

The reason why Coriolanus finds himself caught up in politics is that his mother, and not he, has political ambitions. Having seen him return in triumph from his victory over the Volscians, Volumnia declares triumphantly,

> I have lived
> To see inherited my very wishes,
> And the buildings of my fancy.

And she adds, at what proves to be a turning point in the tragedy,

> Only
> There's one thing wanting, which I doubt not but
> Our Rome will cast upon thee

(meaning, of course, the consulship). Her son, however, has no such desire. This moment marks the split between Coriolanus's ambition and those of his mother. From this point onwards he becomes a divided man, unwilling to demean himself before the mob by showing his dependence on them, and yet unwilling to fail his mother, whose hopes he has hitherto always satisfied. This division in his personality becomes the focus and creates the tensions in two of the most powerful scenes in the play.

The first scene (Act III Scene ii) is the one in which he is, with great reluctance, persuaded to return to the plebeians and ask yet again for their support. To beg for their votes a second time is totally alien to his character, for he prides himself on his independence. Yet he does agree to do so, not because it is expedient, nor because it will fulfil his political ambitions (for he has none), but because his mother threatens to disown him:

> At thy choice, then.
> To beg of thee, it is my more dishonour
> Than thou of them. Come all to ruin. Let

> Thy mother rather feel thy pride than fear
> Thy dangerous stoutness; for I mock at death
> With as big heart as thou. Do as thou list.
> Thy valiantness was mine, thou suck'dst it from me;
> But owe thy pride thyself.

By virtually disowning him, she wins him over.

The tension created in this scene arises from the fact that it is one of painfully protracted choice. Coriolanus is here faced with the necessity to choose between two principles which had not hitherto been in conflict: his aristocratic sense of honour and honesty and his obligation to his mother. As the scene ends, it is the latter which is, for the moment, in the ascendant:

> Pray be content.
> Mother, I am going to the market place;
> Chide me no more. I'll mountebank their loves,
> Cog their hearts from them, and come home belov'd
> Of all the trades in Rome.

Once he leaves Volumnia, however, and comes face to face with the tribunes, it is his own sense of independence and his inability to dissemble which take over and, as a result, he is forced into banishment.

It is a similar dilemma in which he finds himself in the climactic scene of the play (Act V Scene iii). His alliance with Aufidius and his advance on his own city is, essentially, an act of vengeance, an attempt to wipe out the people who, he believes, have failed to appreciate and be grateful for the services he has done them. His invasion of Rome is the supreme expression of the contempt for the mob he revealed in the opening scene. Attempts are made to persuade him to call off the attack but he is totally deaf to the pleas of his fellow-patricians. His old comrade in arms, Cominius, tries in vain to dissuade him; Menenius, his closest friend, makes a second attempt but is dismissed. The third, final attempt is made by Volumnia, and the scene in which she and his wife and child approach him is one of unusual dramatic tension because we already know (from our experience of the earlier scene) that she is the only person who might be able to influence him.

His dilemma is precisely the same as it had been in the third act. He has a simple choice between two alternatives. He can either obey the dictates of his own integrity and destroy those who have affronted it, or he can obey the pleas of his mother and call off the invasion. Moreover, as in the earlier scene, whatever choice he makes must constitute a betrayal. If he invades Rome he must betray his filial loyalty; if he calls off the invasion, he must betray those principles which are an essential part of his nature – principles which, ironically, he has acquired from his mother.

He gives way to her persuasions, and it is worth noticing the kind of arguments she uses. If he pursues the attack he will, as she says, 'reap . . . such a name / Whose reputation will be dogged with curses.' She then appeals to his sense of patrician honour:

> Think'st thou it honourable for a noble man
> Still to remember wrongs?

These pleas are, however, unavailaing, though no doubt they wear down his resistance. She succeeds only when she appeals to him in the most intimately personal terms, as a mother to her son. She once more disowns him:

> Come, let us go.
> This fellow had a Volscian to his mother;
> His wife is in Corioli, and his child
> Like him by chance.

She threatens to desert him and, in so doing, touches his feelings at their deepest level. That is the one wound he cannot bear to receive and, in the very moment of conceding to her, he recognizes the consequences of his choice:

> O my mother, mother! O!
> You have won a happy victory to Rome;
> But for your son – believe it, O, believe it! –
> Most dangerously you have with him prevail'd,
> If not most mortal to him.

The man who had, throughout the play, prided himself on his absolute autonomy is in this moment exposed as dependent on his mother's esteem, her respect for him. Far from being the stoical warrior, impervious to pain and the contempt of others, he is deeply vulnerable.

Does this vulnerability make him a more or a less sympathetic man in our eyes? It obviously makes him the more human. His mother's influence is the source both of his strength and his weakness. It is she who has shaped his character and she who brings about his destruction. What happens in this scene is simple enough; what is complex is the judgement Shakespeare compels us to make of him. Coriolanus has halted an invasion and that is, needless to say, commendable. He has displayed a very human weakness and that brings him closer to us. But at the same time he has signed his own death warrant and has betrayed that distinctively Roman constancy which made him so exceptional. His moment of weakness is perhaps also his moment of greatest strength.

# TIMON OF ATHENS

*Timon of Athens* has always been one of the least read and least performed of Shakespeare's plays. This may be because it lacks the variety of style and characterization which distinguishes more popular works such as *Hamlet*, *Twelfth Night* and the two parts of *Henry IV*, and because its hero excites less admiration, respect or pity than Lear, Othello or even Macbeth. Timon, in both his initial prosperity and later exile, is a remote figure whose feelings have few resemblances to our own, and the long crescendo of hate of which his speeches in the last two acts consist removes him steadily further from our sympathy. The play does, however, contain a certain kind of Shakespearean poetry at its most violent and intense, that invective motivated by a disgust at the depravity and inhumanity of man to which Hamlet, Coriolanus and Leontes give voice in moments of psychological and moral crisis:

> Matrons, turn incontinent.
> Obedience fail in children! Slaves and fools,
> Pluck the grave wrinkled Senate from the bench
> And minister in their steads. To general filths
> Convert, o' th' instant, green virginity.
> Do't in your parents' eyes. Bankrupts, hold fast!
> Rather than render back, out with your knives
> And cut your trusters' throats. Bound servants, steal:
> Large-handed robbers your grave masters are,
> And pill by law. Maid, to thy master's bed:
> Thy mistress is o' th' brothel. Son of sixteen,
> Pluck the lin'd crutch from thy old limping sire,
> With it beat out his brains.

Though much of the last two acts is written in this savage tone, *Timon* is also full of a penetrating and often comic irony at the expense both of the hero and of his time-serving acquaintances, and in the scene where his servants take their leave of one another, Shakespeare creates a sense of pathos at the final parting of friends. The dramatic writing is actually more varied than it seems. The play's greatest achievement, however, is to be found in its con-struction. Every part of it fulfils a function in the play as a whole.

The plot could scarcely be more simple. Timon, an Athenian aristocrat, feels a general affection for all his fellow-men which he expresses by enter-taining them lavishly, and indiscriminately showering on them munificent gifts. When, as a result of his liberality, he runs deeply into debt, he appeals to his friends for help but they refuse him. Their betrayal destroys his faith in mankind and, disillusioned, he takes refuge in a desolate place where, having delivered a series of embittered tirades against humanity, he dies. His career, his transformation from generous benefactor to solitary misanthrope, is summed up by Apemantus:

The middle of humanity thou never knewest, but the extremity of both ends.

Shakespeare had read about Timon in Sir Thomas North's English transla-tion of the *Lives of the Noble Grecians and Romans* by the Greek biographer Plutarch, a book which also supplied him with the material for *Julius Caesar*, *Coriolanus* and *Antony and Cleopatra*. But Plutarch, and the other sources which Shakespeare may have used, describes only the latter part of Timon's life. This play differs from all previous accounts by showing his early pros-perity, and one reason why Shakespeare chose the subject may have been a desire to explore the process whereby a man can be reduced to a state of absolute loathing for mankind.

It was in Plutarch's *Lives* that Shakespeare also read about Alcibiades, the central figure in the sub-plot, which is equally simple. Alcibiades, a success-ful commander in the Athenian army, begs the Senate to pardon one of his soldiers whom they have condemned to death for murder. They not only ignore his pleas but banish Alcibiades himself who, affronted by their appar-ent ingratitude for his services to the state, leaves the city, assembles an army and advances on Athens, threatening to destroy it. In response to the senators' pleas for mercy, however, he calls off the invasion.

There are obvious connections between the two plots. Both Timon and Alcibiades are shown at the beginning of the play in a state of prosperity; each leaves Athens as a result of what he believes to be the ingratitude of those men who have formerly benefited from his services, and each expresses his consequent hatred by assaulting his fellow-citizens, the one with curses, the other with military force. But whereas Timon dies solitary and unforgiv-ing, Alcibiades is persuaded to be tolerant and rejoins the community. The features of one man's character and conduct emphasize those of the other either by similarity or by contrast. *Timon of Athens* is so simple in outline that it might appear to create no problems of interpretation. In fact it does con-sistently raise one central and difficult question, and that is how we should react to and judge the central character. Is he an admirably generous man betrayed by the meanness and ingratitude of his friends, or is he a reckless

spendthrift who is ruined by his own naive trust and profligacy? These questions are actually raised within the play itself and are given different answers.
Flavius, the conscientious and loyal steward, places on Timon's perfidious
friends most of the blame for his master's downfall:

> Poor honest lord, brought low by his own heart,
> Undone by goodness! Strange, unusual blood,
> When man's worst sin is he does too much good!
> Who then dares to be half so kind again?
> For bounty, that makes gods, does still mar men.

Apemantus, the cynic, on the other hand, despises Timon's generosity as
blind and stupid:

O you gods, what a number of men eats Timon, and he sees 'em not! It grieves me
to see so many dip their meat in one man's blood; and all the madness is, he cheers
them up too.

Their conflicting opinions help to define the problem but take us no further
towards a solution, because each character assesses Timon in a way which is
consistent with his own personality and assumptions: the devoted steward is
naturally inclined to think well of his master and the professed cynic naturally regards everyone with contempt. Neither character expresses Shakespeare's own opinion. Moreover, the uncertain feelings created in us by
Timon's initial benevolence give way to a different kind of uncertainty
towards his later misanthropy. Is his hatred of men justified by the treatment
they have given him, or is it no less narrow and obsessive than his former
love? Again, the play itself offers different opinions. To Apemantus, Timon
was formerly 'a madman', now 'a fool'. To Flavius, on the other hand, he is
the innocent victim of ingratitude:

> What viler thing upon the earth than friends,
> Who can bring noblest minds to basest ends!

These two extreme and differing assessments of the central character have
been repeated by the Shakespearean critics, some of whom have taken
Flavius's view and idealized him, while others have seen in his very munificence a certain egotism and self-indulgence. The answers to these questions
can best be found by looking closely not at the characters but at the way the
play is constructed. By so doing we can estimate the kind of reactions Shakespeare hoped to produce from his audience and can also, incidentally,
discover how carefully he put it together.

The play opens with the entrance of a poet, a painter, a jeweller and a
merchant, all of whom are waiting to offer Timon their wares. The first of
them describes the contents of his poem in such fullness of detail that his

speech forms a kind of prologue or synopsis of the ensuing play. Shakespeare invites us to look at the play in the light of the poem:

> I have upon a high and pleasant hill
> Feign'd Fortune to be thron'd. The base o' th' mount
> Is rank'd with all deserts, all kind of natures
> That labour on the bosom of this sphere
> To propagate their states. Amongst them all
> Whose eyes are on this sovereign lady fix'd
> One do I personate of Lord Timon's frame,
> Whom Fortune with her ivory hand wafts to her;
> Whose present grace to present slaves and servants
> Translates his rivals.

As long as Timon is favoured by Fortune and remains prosperous, the poet continues, his associates flock solicitously to him. They

> Follow his strides, his lobbies fill with tendance,
> Rain sacrificial whisperings in his ear,
> Make sacred even his stirrup, and through him
> Drink the free air.

But, once his fortune changes and he falls from power, everyone abandons him.

The instability of Fortune was one of the most popular subjects of medieval art and literature because it was thought to represent the common vicissitudes of life, and, indeed, the painter remarks that he could produce 'a thousand moral paintings'

> That can demonstrate these quick blows of Fortune's
> More pregnantly than words.

As he says, "tis common'. And, as if to warn us that Timon, now enjoying the favour of Fortune, will eventually be cast down, Shakespeare here brings his central character onto the stage for the first time. From the start of the play, the dramatist induces us to regard Timon's prosperity as insecure and risky, and to foresee that those acquaintances whom we see flocking to him will later abandon him. We are made to feel less confident than he is himself and to look with suspicion on the friends he unhesitatingly trusts.

Shakespeare then introduces Apemantus, whose sour comments strengthen our suspicion that Timon's associates may not be as good-natured as they seem. As Timon and his guests exchange elaborate greetings, Apemantus mutters his contempt:

> Aches contract and starve your supple joints!
> That there should be small love amongst these sweet knaves
> And all this courtesy. The strain of man's bred out
> Into baboon and monkey.

To him, such displays of affection are mere hypocritical sham.

The inconsistencies between these two views of the situation – those of Timon and Apemantus – continue into the next scene where, at the banquet, warmed by the adulation of his guests, Timon is moved to tears, a spectacle which by now we cannot help but observe with a certain amount of irony, especially since he is confident that he can call on his friends in time of need:

We are born to do benefits; and what better or properer can we call our own than the riches of our friends? O, what a precious comfort 'tis to have so many like brothers commanding one another's fortunes! O, joy's e'en made away ere't can be born! Mine eyes cannot hold out water, methinks. To forget their faults, I drink to you.

The spectacle which arouses gratitude in Timon, however, provokes disgust in Apemantus:

> I wonder men dare trust themselves with men.
> Methinks they should invite them without knives:
> Good for their meat and safer for their lives.

Shakespeare consistently invites us to balance one opinion against another, to give our assent neither to Timon's gratitude nor to his friends' apparent affection, nor to Apemantus's evident revulsion. We treat all of them with a certain hesitancy or even mistrust.

Our impression of Timon is now made even more complex by the introduction of an entirely new character, Flavius, the steward, who casts yet another light on the situation. Flavius reveals for the first time that Timon is, in fact, bankrupt. He refuses to be told that he is impoverished and is, moreover, deeply in debt to the very guests he entertains:

> He commands us to provide and give great gifts,
> And all out of an empty coffer;
> Nor will he know his purse, or yield me this,
> To show him what a beggar his heart is,
> Being of no power to make his wishes good.
> His promises fly so beyond his state
> That what he speaks is all in debt; he owes
> For ev'ry word. He is so kind that he now
> Pays interest for't; his land's put to their books.

What may so far have looked like misplaced benevolence now begins to seem like thoughtless profligacy and, in case we should still not recognize Timon's rashness, Shakespeare immediately shows him squandering his possessions yet more recklessly. Each act of generosity is more thoughtless than the last. Timon began by paying a friend's debts and thereby freeing him from prison, a humane and laudable gesture; he then generously helps his own servant to a wife; but now he gives away a horse to a nameless lord simply because the latter has spoken well of it. By shaping his material in this way, by balancing one character's opinion against another's, and by warning us to be critical of Timon's deeds before he actually performs them, Shakespeare compels us constantly to readjust our impression of him so that, by the end of the first act, his munificence has been made to seem rash, foolhardy and self-indulgent.

The process of readjustment continues in the second act. Flavius, the most reliable witness, warns us that his master now has neither the means to support his lavish way of life nor the will to change it: he will neither 'know how to maintain it' nor 'cease his flow of riot'. He also predicts that, in this moment of financial crisis, Timon's friends will desert him. It is with this foreknowledge of their perfidiousness that the audience is then shown the refusal of three of the friends, Lucullus, Lucius and Sempronius, to help Timon in his need. Shakespeare's irony which in the first two acts was increasingly directed against Timon, is now directed against his friends. The third act, like the rest of the play, is organized in a neat and simple pattern: each friend receives a similar request and, in turn, gives a similar, predictable answer. It is, however, not in the least repetitive and contains the most subtly ironical and psychologically acute writing in the play. The interest of this section lies in the different kinds of ingenuity with which each character wriggles out of his obligations. Lucullus, self-satisfied and censorious, argues that, since Timon ignored the advice of his friends, he has only himself to blame:

> Many a time and often I ha' din'd with him and told him on't; and come again to supper to him of purpose to have him spend less; and yet he would embrace no counsel, take no warning by my coming. Every man has his fault, and honesty is his. I ha' told him on't, but I could ne'er get him from't.

Lucius, with a hypocritical show of remorse, blames himself not for refusing Timon his assistance but for failing to put aside money with which to provide it, and Sempronius, apparently indignant, claims to be insulted that he is not the first to have been approached for help. All three manage to evade their responsibilities while retaining a comforting sense of integrity and self-esteem. If there is any point at which we feel compassion towards the hero it is now when, deserted by his friends, his love turns into loathing. And it is at this point that Shakespeare places Alcibiades at the centre of the stage and shows the rejection of his pleas by the senators. Shakespeare's intention – that we should draw a parallel between the two men – could scarcely be clearer.

In spite of the uncurbed violence of Timon's curses during the last two acts, they are, again, carefully organized. Shakespeare's hero seems uncontrolled but his creator's art is not. For one thing, Timon's cries of hatred and disgust become steadily more manic and wider in their scope. At first his wrath is directed simply against the city of Athens, but his discovery of gold prompts him to deliver a tirade against the venality of mankind in general:

> This yellow slave
> Will knit and break religions, bless th' accurs'd,
> Make the hoar leprosy ador'd, place thieves
> And give them title, knee, and approbation,
> With senators on the bench.

The arrival of Apemantus then serves as a challenge to him and provokes the two cynics to engage in a contest of curses in which each tries to outdo the other in nihilism, and Timon's apocalyptic vision extends beyond mankind to embrace the whole animal kingdom and, finally, the universe itself:

> The sun's a thief, and with his great attraction
> Robs the vast sea; the moon's an arrant thief,
> And her pale fire she snatches from the sun;
> The sea's a thief, whose liquid surge resolves
> The moon into salt tears; the earth's a thief,
> That feeds and breeds by a composture stol'n
> From gen'ral excrement – each thing's a thief.

Throughout the tirade, which, astonishingly, Shakespeare manages to sustain for the course of almost two acts, Timon never radically changes. He simply becomes more singlemindedly and intensely himself. Our impression of him does, however, alter, and Shakespeare creates this effect, as he did in the first part of the play, by introducing a series of contrasting characters, each one induced by curiosity or the hope of gain to visit Timon in his misanthropic exile, and each one persuades us to alter our impression of him. The first is Alcibiades, whose justified hostility towards the Athenians tends to reinforce Timon's own bitter sense of betrayal. The second is Apemantus, whose habitual contempt for mankind Timon now shares. In their mutual exchange of insults, however, Apemantus appears the more shallow, for, as Timon points out, the philosopher has no personal cause to hate his fellowmen whereas his own disenchantment has grown out of experience, out of a deeply personal betrayal which Apemantus has never suffered. The comparisons we make between Timon and these first two visitors incline us to sympathize with his misanthropy, to see that his predicament is not unique and to appreciate its causes. The next arrival, Flavius, however, affects us differently. Timon fails even to recognize his old steward and, when he is reluctantly persuaded of the latter's continued loyalty, he wilfully refuses to abandon his convictions: the whole human race, with the exception of Flavius, is still abhorrent to him:

> I do proclaim
> One honest man – mistake me not, but one;
> No more, I pray – and he's a steward.
> How fain would I have hated all mankind!

And thou redeem'st thyself. But all, save thee,
I fell with curses.

As the last section of the play develops, our impression of the central character undergoes a series of changes comparable to those created in the first
section and brought about by a similar method. Each new arrival casts fresh
light on him and as, at the same time, Timon's own virulence grows in scope
and intensity, so he appears increasingly stubborn, egotistical and paranoid.
It is odd to recall that the nineteenth-century romantic critics of Shakespeare
saw the play as an expression of the dramatist's own misanthropy, a cry of
despair wrung from him by some hypothetical crisis in his private life. By the
time Shakespeare's hero has offered the Athenians a tree on which to hang
themselves he has become both terrifying and ridiculous. That Timon has
gradually moved beyond his creator's sympathy is most apparent in the final
scene where Alcibiades, financed by Timon's gold, arrives in Athens with his
army, resolved to carry out his revenge. He is the agent both of Timon's and
his own hatred, about to express it in physical action. But whereas Timon
was scarcely moved by his steward's display of affection, Alcibiades listens to
the appeals of the citizens, calls off his invasion and is welcomed back as a
member of the community. Moreover it is at this point that Shakespeare
chooses to announce the news of Timon's death and of the final curse
recorded in his epitaph:

Here lies a wretched corse, of wretched soul bereft;
Seek not my name. A plague consume you wicked caitiffs left!

The difference between the two men could scarcely be more strongly
pointed: Alcibiades lives and the Athenians have been saved; Timon dies a
victim of his own inflexible and fruitless misanthropy.

To the questions with which this enquiry began there can clearly be no
straightforward answers. Our impression of Timon is modified as one
episode flows into another. It is obvious, however, that Timon is neither, as
some nineteenth-century critics once thought, the voice of Shakespeare's
personal disillusionment nor, as more recent critics have believed, the butt of
his satire, but a character, however simple, whom we are induced to look at
in a complex way, with whose initial good will we can only partially sympathize and whose final pessimism we must reject.

If this were all the play had to offer, however, it would not be worth very
much. Its achievement lies not in what it tells us (that mankind is neither
wholly lovable nor unworthy even of our contempt) but in the way it affects
us: by its strongly contrasted dramatic images of opulence and desolation, by
the force of its rhetoric and, in a way which is surprising with a work distinguished by its extremity of feeling, by the subtlety and firmness with which
Shakespeare places his characters in relation to each other.

Most scholars now believe that *Timon of Athens* was printed directly from Shakespeare's own manuscript, or a transcript of it, where he had left it in an unfinished state, and they are probably correct. The text as we have it suggests that there was work still to be done: two of the characters, a Fool and a Page, make one single, apparently irrelevant appearance and are left undeveloped; the verse is often irregular and passages of prose suddenly shift into verse. There also seems to be some missing material: we never see the soldier whom the senate has condemned to death, nor do we learn precisely what services Timon has performed for Athens for which he is offered the captainship. Apart from these loose ends, however, the play not only hangs together and makes good sense but shows that Shakespeare, an experienced writer for the stage, was entirely in control of his material.

# PERICLES

Since *Pericles* was not included in the first collected edition of Shakespeare's plays, the First Folio of 1623, the only text we have which approximates to Shakespeare's original manuscript is the First Quarto of 1609. The texts of the other editions printed during Shakespeare's own lifetime were all of them taken directly or indirectly from the 1609 Quarto and it is on that edition that all others must necessarily be based. The Quarto is, however, filled with errors which create a great many problems for scholars, directors and actors. In the first place it was incompetently printed. Entire scenes which were obviously written in blank verse are printed as though they were in prose, and passages written in prose with no regular metrical stresses (such as the dialogue between the fishermen at the beginning of the second act) are set out as though they had been written in badly composed verse. Some of the blank verse passages, moreover, are very irregular and have defeated the attempts of the editors to make them scan regularly; essential stage directions are missing, the punctuation follows no known or consistent principles, and some of the dialogue makes no sense whatever.

Why it was that Pericles came to be printed so badly it is hard to say. Scholarly tests have shown that three different typesetters worked on it in two different printers' shops, but though this would account for inconsistencies, it does not explain the large number of errors. Shakespeare and his company, whose property it was, can hardly have given their consent to a publication as faulty as this, and it is likely that the printer, Henry Gosson, hoped to make money from what was a very popular work and that he got hold of the text by illicit means. He may have obtained it from some of the actors who took part in the production but, if this was what happened, their manuscript must have been not only inaccurate but hard to decipher and the printers may have had to make what sense they could out of partially illegible handwriting.

Even allowing for these errors, moreover, it is obvious that the quality of the writing is very uneven. Much of the first two acts is written in a monotonous rhythm and with little feeling for the expressive powers of the language:

> Then thus it is: the passions of the mind,
> That have their first conception by misdread,
> Have after-nourishment and life by care;
> And what was first but fear what might be done
> Grows elder now, and cares it be not done.
> And so with me.

On the other hand, there are short passages to be found in the midst of this inferior writing which stand out with unusual expressiveness, and from the opening of the third act onwards the poetry is of a very high quality indeed:

> Thou god of this great vast, rebuke these surges,
> Which wash both heaven and hell; and thou that hast
> Upon the winds command, bind them in brass,
> Having call'd them from the deep! O, still
> Thy deaf'ning dreadful thunders; gently quench
> Thy nimble sulphurous flashes!

> The seaman's whistle
> Is as a whisper in the ears of death,
> Unheard.

It does not take a literary critic to recognize that much of the dialogue, especially in the last three acts, was written by a great dramatist who, since his company performed the play and his name was printed on the title-page, was presumably Shakespeare.

How did this collaboration between Shakespeare and a third-rate dramatist come about? One possibility is that there was, originally, a complete play of *Pericles* written by a minor author and that Shakespeare set about the task of revising it but became fully engaged in the process only by the time he reached the third act. Another possibility is that he arranged to work together with the other dramatist and that they split the task between them. What actually happened we do not know, nor has the identity of the collaborator been discovered, though various candidates have been suggested. These include William Rowley, who also worked in collaboration with other Jacobean dramatists such as Middleton, Webster and Fletcher; Thomas Heywood, who himself claimed to have worked on over two hundred plays; John Day, who is known to have collaborated with other playwrights; and George Wilkins, whose novel *The Painful Adventures of Pericles Prince of Tyre* was published a year before the First Quarto and was actually based on the play. Every one of these possible collaborators has had his supporters but which of them it was we do not know.

In spite of the uneven quality of the dialogue, however, the plot and construction of *Pericles* hang together consistently. If Shakespeare simply completed a play which had been left unfinished, he did remain faithful to the original conception and plan. It is one of only two Shakespearean plays (the other is *Henry V*) in which a Chorus or presenter plays a frequent and important role. The Chorus in this case is John Gower, the fourteenth-century poet, whose reputation was quite high in Shakespeare's time and from whose long poem the *Confessio Amantis* the dramatist took most of the material for his plot. Gower introduces himself at the beginning as a figure returned from the very distant past and whose purpose is to retell a story which was old even in his own time. In order to create the impression that Gower is an 'ancient' poet, the dramatist (who, for the sake of convenience, will now be called 'Shakespeare') has written his lines in a monotonous rhyming verse of four stresses, the octosyllabics which Gower himself habitually used. It is an attempt to create an archaic-sounding, medieval style:

> To sing a song that old was sung,
> From ashes ancient Gower is come,
> Assuming man's infirmities,
> To glad your ear and please your eyes.

It is, moreover, the antiquity not only of Gower but of the tale itself which is emphasized:

> It hath been sung at festivals,
> On ember-eves and holy-ales;
> And lords and ladies in their lives
> Have read it for restoratives.

Shakespeare makes it plain from the start, then, that what he is offering his audience is not a realistic drama such as *Julius Caesar* or *Henry IV* in which once living characters are shown in actual historical situations which are made as credible as possible, but a version of a story so familiar that it has the quality of a myth or folk-tale. If we compare the opening of *Pericles* with that of, say, *Hamlet* or *Coriolanus*, we can see how deliberately unrealistic it is, and, as Gower returns to fill in the gaps between the acts, we have the impression of watching something which is not so much a play as a series of illustrations of an old story, a narrative. This effect is also created by the number of episodes which are played in mime or dumb show, such as the delivery of the letter to Pericles at the beginning of the second act, his departure with Thaisa from Pentapolis and the announcement of the supposed death of Marina. These silent tableaux are visual illustrations of Gower's narrative. Ben Jonson scathingly called the play 'a mouldy tale' and you can see what he meant.

The emphasis on the narrative becomes more obvious if we consider how many of the ingredients we might expect to find in a Shakespearean play are absent from this one. You might think that the playwright who had recently completed *Antony and Cleopatra* and *Coriolanus* would continue to create fully-realized, interesting, life-like characters but this is not the case. Pericles himself is, simply, a good man of many talents who suffers a series of misfortunes. He has the intelligence to solve Antiochus's riddle which has baffled his daughter's previous suitors, the skill in arms to win the tournament at Pentapolis, the composure to endure his misfortunes patiently and a fair-mindedness which has won the respect of his subjects, but he undergoes no internal moral or mental conflict and has no faults or weaknesses. We must therefore agree with him when he says,

> My actions are as noble as my thoughts,
> That never relish'd of a base descent.

Another reason why he appears a simple character is that generally he does not act but is acted upon. He leaves Antioch in order to escape a plot against his life; he is the helpless victim of the sea which casts him on the shores of Pentapolis, where he meets and marries his wife, then deprives him of her in the very moment of childbirth, then drives him to Mytilene where, by sheer chance, he is reunited with his lost daughter. He is guilty of no errors of judgement such as those by which Lear and Othello brought tragedy upon themselves, nor does he in any way deserve the troubles which fall upon him. He is a virtuous man who is the victim of powers too large for him to resist:

> A man whom both the waters and the wind
> In that vast tennis-court hath made the ball
> For them to play upon.

Nor does the power of Fortune to which he is subjected act on any consistent principles. It is, indeed, in the nature of Fortune to be inconsistent, arbitrary, unpredictable and hence, when Pericles has lost everything except his life, then

> fortune, tir'd with doing bad,
> Threw him ashore to give him glad.

We can make no more sense of his misfortunes than he can.

Although Marina is a powerfully moving character, her strength is revealed largely from the effects she has on others, especially when, towards the end of the play, she draws her father gradually back into life. Her virtue shines out by contrast with the brutality and degeneracy of the murderers, pirates, prostitutes and bawds into whose company she is thrown. She is the embodiment of duty, chastity and patience in a corrupt, tempestuous world, more purely saint-like than any other character in Shakespeare.

Far more realistic are the minor characters, the fishermen and whores among whom Pericles and his daughter find themselves, and some of the best writing is in the prose scenes where ordinary people are shown plying their trades and chatting casually in a way that still sounds like easy conversation. It is the kind of dialogue that Shakespeare wrote for the tapsters and ostlers of the history plays or the country folk of *The Winter's Tale*:

*1 Fisherman*    Alas, pour souls! It grieved my heart to hear what pitiful cries they made to us to help them, when, well-a-day, we could scarce help ourselves.
*3 Fisherman*    Nay, master, said not I as much when I saw the porpas how he bounc'd and tumbled? They say they're half fish, half flesh. A plague on them! They ne'er come but I look to be wash'd. Master, I marvel how the fishes live in the sea.
*1 Fisherman*    Why, as men do a-land – the great ones eat up the little ones.

Such characters, of course, have no psychological depth, but their language and the rhythm of their sentences sound authentic and they have a kind of proverbial wisdom which is timeless. Sometimes, moreover, Shakespeare's imagination begins to work and he begins to visualize and fill in the background of these minor characters so that we catch a glimpse of the lives they are supposed to lead when they are off the stage:

*Bawd*     The stuff we have, a strong wind will blow to pieces, they are so pitifully sodden.
*Pander*   Thou sayest true; they are too unwholesome, o' conscience. The poor Transylvanian is dead that lay with the little baggage.
*Boult*    Ay, she quickly poop'd him; she made him roast meat for worms.

Dialogue like this has no other function than to provide a realistic context in which the major characters may move and to make the minor characters entirely credible.

Since it is an episodic play, a series of incidents linked only by the Chorus and the two main protagonists, Pericles has little dramatic suspense. Each episode is self-contained and creates little or no impression of a development moving steadily with increasing intensity towards a catastrophe of the kind we find in *Othello* or *Coriolanus*. The lack of dramatic tension arises from the lack of dramatic irony. It is true that, unlike Pericles, the audience knows that his wife Thaisa has survived her burial at sea, and that Marina is not dead, but these ironies are not sustained in any way. They are not kept at the forefront of our minds but, knowing that father, mother and daughter are all alive, we are left simply to wait with the kind of patience they themselves display until they are reunited. The reunion with Marina, moreover, is not brought about by any deliberate action on either part. Pericles is simply 'driven by the winds' until he arrives 'where his daughter dwells'. Considering how frequently and brilliantly in his earlier plays Shakespeare had built up the dramatic intensity of an episode by preparing the audience for it and raising their expectations, it would seem that the lack of such preparation is quite deliberate. Hence the audience is not allowed to become emotionally engaged in the events. We are simply asked to watch them.

It is clear, therefore, that *Pericles* was an experimental play, unlike anything that Shakespeare had previously written. It does, however, have interesting similarities to the medieval religious pictures with which he must certainly have been acquainted. Time and the Civil War have effaced most of the paintings with which the walls of English churches were formerly decorated and most of our medieval stained glass has gone, but in Shakespeare's time our churches were full of mural paintings showing scenes not only from the life of Christ but also of the Virgin Mary and the saints. The picture of the Last Judgement which survives on the wall of the Guild Chapel at Stratford-on-Avon, just across the road from New Place, the house which Shakespeare bought in 1597, was originally only one of a series painted in the sixteenth century. Six scenes from the life of St Catherine can, however, still be seen in the Tropenell Chapel at Great Chalfield in Wiltshire and at Broughton in Oxfordshire there are the remains of a series of episodes from the life of the Virgin. Some idea of what they might have been like may perhaps be formed from the European religious paintings which are still more-or-less in their original state, such as the scenes from the life of St Ursula which Memling painted for the Hôpital Saint Jean at Bruges or the hundreds of medieval narrative paintings depicting episodes in the life of Christ. Consisting as they do of significant events in the life of the central character, such pictures are necessarily episodic. Nothing, moreover, is done to explain why the character experiences suffering or happiness, nor does his or her face display any distinguishing features. Like Marina and Pericles, they reveal nothing more than the passive virtue and simplicity of the saintly person. The blandness of the major figure contrasts strongly with the expressive, even grotesque, features of the common people, the usurers, soldiers or torturers by whom they are afflicted and the sick whom they heal, and all the smaller narrative scenes are grouped round a central panel which displays the climactic moment in the figure's life: the resurrection of Christ or the assumption of the Virgin or saint. This central picture may be compared to the concluding scene of *Pericles* where husband, wife and daughter are brought together in the Temple of Diana in what appears to be a miraculous experience. It may be that Shakespeare wrote what, for him, was a distinctively medieval drama and that its medieval qualities are to be seen not simply in the figure of Gower but in the way the whole work is constructed and the characters portrayed.

*Pericles* is a play which contains a good deal of inferior writing, some of which is almost certainly not by Shakespeare, and which offers us few of the pleasures we receive from his other works. Why was it apparently so popular at the time of its first performance and what can we gain from a modern revival?

It is a play which depicts the most basic and elemental of feelings – the bonds of love which unite husband with wife, parent with child, the ultimate dependence of man upon the elements, and the mystery of the supernatural powers which control us:

> Wind, rain, and thunder, remember earthly man
> Is but a substance that must yield to you;
> And I, as fits my nature, do obey you.

Moreover Shakespeare has expressed these most radical feelings in poetry of an extraordinary tenderness, as when, in the midst of the tempest, Pericles is shown the body of his wife, dead in childbirth:

> A terrible childbed hast thou had, my dear;
> No light, no fire. Th' unfriendly elements
> Forgot thee utterly; nor have I time
> To give thee hallow'd to thy grave, but straight
> Must cast thee, scarcely coffin'd, in the ooze;
> Where, for a monument upon thy bones,
> And aye-remaining lamps, the belching whale
> And humming water must o'erwhelm thy corpse,
> Lying with simple shells.

Such emotions are, as we should expect, felt with the greatest power in the two scenes of reunion, the first between Pericles and Marina, the second between Pericles, Marina and Thaisa, where Shakespeare's creative powers are again roused and he expresses an extraordinary violence of feeling:

> O Helicanus, strike me, honour'd sir;
> Give me a gash, put me to present pain,
> Lest this great sea of joys rushing upon me
> O'erbear the shores of my mortality,
> And drown me with their sweetness.

These are among the most deeply expressive passages Shakespeare wrote.

The predominant impression made by the play is, however, that of a story and there was clearly something about this particular story which made it unusually compelling, ensuring its survival from the ninth century and earlier, inducing the medieval scribes to go on copying it time and again before it finally reached Shakespeare in a printed book of Gower's poetry. The tale of Pericles has several features which recur frequently in myth, folk-tale and romance. It tells of a beautiful woman who can be won only by solving a riddle, of a stranger who arrives from nowhere poorly dressed but who wins the love of a princess, and of death by water and resurrection. The ultimate source of this and similar folk-tales was probably in religious myth or ritual, told or enacted 'at festivals, on ember-eves and holy-ales', and, like the story of Christ's resurrection, 'the purchase is to make men glorious', as

Gower tells us. It may be that, in the retelling, it stirs in us some latent religious impulse. Indeed the very primitive nature of the construction and much of the writing allows this mysteriously moving story to work on us directly. Shakespeare does not come between us and the tale he tells.

# CYMBELINE

Samuel Johnson, the first great Shakespearean critic, could find little to admire in *Cymbeline*. He admitted that it had 'many just sentiments, some natural dialogues, and some pleasing scenes', but complained that these were obtained 'at the expense of much incongruity'. He then proceeded contemptuously to dismiss the play as a whole:

To remark the folly of the fiction, the absurdity of the conduct, the confusion of the names and manners of different times, and the impossibility of the events in any system of life, were to waste criticism upon unresisting imbecility, upon faults too evident for detection, and too gross for aggravation.

Violent though Johnson's attack undoubtedly is, his opinion should be considered seriously. He judged a piece of writing by its 'truth to nature', the extent to which it gave an accurate and faithful account of human character and behaviour. To him, a work of literature was of value to the extent that it taught him something about himself and his fellow-men. Hence he is able to appreciate in *Cymbeline* those parts which seem to him true to life, the 'just sentiments' and 'natural dialogues', but he rejects it as a whole because of the extreme improbability of the plot. A play the events of which bear no resemblance to our own lives was, for Johnson, a play from which we could learn nothing.

Judged by Johnson's standards of probability, *Cymbeline* is certainly unacceptable. As he points out, each of the main plots – the war against the Romans and Iachimo's deception of Posthumus – takes place in a different historical period and the two periods are separated by some fourteen centuries. Whereas the leader of the Roman army, Caius Lucius, is a general serving under Augustus Caesar, Iachimo is a sophisticatedly devious Italian of the kind associated with Machiavelli and it is clear that Shakespeare visualized him in a renaissance setting. The bedroom in which he observes the sleeping Imogen with its silken tapestries, carved chimney piece and gilded ceiling is decorated in the style of that period and, indeed, Shakespeare took the plot in which Iachimo is involved from a story by Boccaccio, the fourteenth-century novelist. The two sets of events could never have taken place during the same period.

Quite apart from this historical inconsistency, however, there are, as Johnson saw, other kinds of improbability. Imogen, when disguised, is consistently mistaken for a man, even by her own husband; she in turn mistakes the disguised body of Cloten for Posthumus; taking flight into the Welsh mountains, she is fortuitously received as a guest by her own disguised and long-lost brothers, who are equally unaware of her identity. In due course the brothers and their guardian succeed in defeating the entire Roman army and, as the play reaches its conclusion, all the characters are conveniently assembled at Milford Haven, where every one of the play's multiple errors and misconceptions is cleared up. Earlier in his career, Shakespeare had written comedies such as *As You Like It* and *Twelfth Night* which depended on disguise and mistaken identity but not in such profusion. If, like Johnson, we are looking in *Cymbeline* for truth to life we shall be disappointed and if we are to avoid rejecting it as a failure we must look in it for something different.

A more rewarding way of approaching it is to enquire what *Cymbeline* is about, to discover the kind of questions Shakespeare raises, the topics his characters discuss. He gives us some clues in the opening scene, where two gentlemen are talking about the latest crisis at the court, the marriage of the King's daughter to Posthumus. This is an expository scene in which the audience is fed with the information it needs if it is to understand the plot. But as well as telling us that the heir to the throne has married a commoner, the two gentlemen repeatedly make distinctions between the outward impression which people create and their true, inner nature. Thus, although the courtiers, we are told, give every appearance of sharing the King's anger at this unsuitable match, they are secretly delighted by it:

> Not a courtier
> Although they wear their faces to the bent
> Of the King's looks, hath a heart that is not
> Glad at the thing they scowl at.

A contrast is being drawn between what people are and how they look, as though Shakespeare were already thinking of the disguises which are to be put on later in the play. Whereas the courtiers disguise their true feelings, however, Posthumus, we learn, is a man of integrity whose physical appearance is a true manifestation of his actual character:

> I do not think
> So fair an outward and such stuff within
> Endows a man but he.

This correspondence between the physical and the moral qualities is, incidentally, a feature which Iachimo later recognizes in Imogen:

All of her that is out of door most rich!
If she be furnish'd with a mind so rare,
She is alone th' Arabian bird.

Whereas the court is filled with dissemblers who conceal their feelings, Imogen and Posthumus stand out by virtue of their directness and honesty, and, indeed, Imogen's most striking and likeable quality is her spontaneity, her tendency to speak her mind and act on her impulses. For example, hearing that her banished husband had landed at Milford Haven, she at once expresses a longing to see him and is so filled with emotions that she becomes practically incoherent:

> O for a horse with wings! Hear'st thou Pisanio?
> He is at Milford Haven. Read, and tell me
> How far 'tis thither. If one of mean affairs
> May plod it in a week, why may not I
> Glide thither in a day? Then, true Pisanio –
> Who long'st like me to see thy lord, who long'st –
> O, let me 'bate! – but not like me, yet long'st,
> But in a fainter kind – O, not like me,
> For mine's beyond beyond! – say, and speak thick –
> Love's counsellor should fill the bores of hearing
> To th' smothering of the sense – how far it is
> To this same blessed Milford.

Imogen and Posthumus are thus distinguished by their natural honesty, the correspondence between what they seem and what they are. Their weakness is that they are inclined to trust others as much as they expect others to trust them. Posthumus is taken in by the lies of Iachimo and Imogen is deceived by her husband's letter.

It becomes apparent quite early in the play, however, that the court is a place where no one can be trusted. We see ample evidence of the deceitfulness of the court and the mistrust which it breeds in the scene (Act I Scene v) between the Queen and Cornelius the doctor. She has asked Cornelius to give her a casket of poisons and assures him that she intends to use them only on 'cats and dogs', 'creatures we count not worth the hanging – but none human'. In fact, however, she plans to inflict them on her enemies. The doctor hands over the casket but shortly reveals to us that it contains no poisons but harmless opiates. The Queen's known deceit provokes Cornelius to deceive her. The deceptions in this scene do not end here, however. Shortly after the entrance of Pisanio, the Queen drops the casket apparently by accident but in fact deliberately. As Pisiano picks it up (which is what she intends he should do) she tells him to keep it because it contains a medicine 'which hath the King five times redeem'd from death', but as the scene concludes she expresses the hope that the supposed poison will destroy both him and Imogen. Nothing in this scene is what it appears to be. This is the world in which Imogen, deprived of her husband, must survive and, with good reason, she feels very vulnerable.

The distinctions and similarities between seeming and being are thus made in both the dialogue and action from the very start of the play, and as it develops they begin to accumulate. Cymbeline, who appears to rule Britain, is actually ruled by his wife; the Queen, who appears to be kindly, is in fact malevolent; Cloten has the outward trappings of nobility – he is the Queen's son and, dressed in the garments of Posthumus, he is physically indistinguishable from him – but is actually a fool and a braggart; the two brothers appear to be Welsh peasants but are really princes; and the courtier Belarius is living under the name of Morgan. In the play's most extraordinary episode, the disguised princes strew the bodies of the disguised Imogen and Cloten whom the former mistakes for her husband. Everyone is masquerading as someone else.

An elaborate structure of misunderstanding is thus created out of the dialogue, characters and situations. Moreover the contrast between sophisticated dissembling and simple honesty extends to the locations in which the play is set. Italy is throughout associated with treachery. Not only does Iachimo actually deceive Posthumus but the Italians generally are assumed by the Britons to be habitually devious. Pisanio, for example, is quick to deduce that some 'false Italian – as poisonous-tongu'd as handed – hath prevail'd' on Posthumus's natural trustfulness. Imogen, too, believes that

> Some jay of Italy,
> Whose mother was her painting, hath betray'd him.

The worst thing she can say of him when she is told of his sexual exploits is that he has 'forgot Britain'. Italy is thus portrayed as a place of deception, malice and licentiousness. It does, however, have the appearance of courtesy and civility, and this is created chiefly by the style in which the Italians converse. The sophisticated tone is recognizable in Iachimo's account of Posthumus:

Believe it, sir, I have seen him in Britain. He was then of a crescent note, expected to prove so worthy as since he hath been allowed the name of. But I could then have look'd on him without the help of admiration, though the catalogue of his endowments had been tabled by his side, and I to peruse it by items.

The artificiality of the language and the elaborate construction of the sentences give Iachimo, who is actually cynical and untrustworthy, a veneer of courtliness and grace.

The mannered prose of the Italians is quite different in style from the verse in which Belarius and the two young princes pay their morning homage to the day:

| | |
|---|---|
| *Belarius* | Hail, thou fair heaven |
| | We house i' th' rock, yet use thee not so hardly |
| | As prouder livers do. |
| *Guiderius* | Hail, heaven! |
| *Arviragus* | Hail, heaven! |

Accustomed to a basic, rural life, they have few social graces and their simplicity is revealed in the directness of their speech. The Welsh scenes are, throughout, set up in contrast to the Italian scenes. Whereas Iachimo conceals his treachery by appearing genial and courteous, the two boys, like Imogen, are incapable of hiding their feelings, as their guardian points out:

> This Polydore . . .
> When on my three-foot stool I sit and tell
> The warlike feats I have done, his spirits fly out
> Into my story; say 'Thus mine enemy fell,
> And thus I set my foot on's neck'; even then
> The princely blood flows in his cheek, he sweats,
> Strains his young nerves, and puts himself in posture
> That acts my words. The younger brother, Cadwal,
> Once Arviragus, in as like a figure
> Strikes life into my speech, and shows much more
> His own conceiving.

They spontaneously demonstrate their emotions in their faces.

The freshness, innocence and simplicity of Imogen and her brothers are also conveyed to us by the language used to describe them. *Cymbeline* is full of references to birds and wild flowers which always occur in connection with these three characters. Imogen as she lies asleep seems to Iachimo like 'a fresh lily', and the mole on her breast 'like the crimson drops i' th' bottom of a cowslip'. To her brothers she is as welcome as 'the night to th' owl, and morn to the lark', and the dawn song with which Cloten serenades her with its references to the singing of birds and opening of flowers is appropriate to the naturalness of her character. This accumulation of images gives a special weight to the simple statement made by Arviragus as his foster-father enters bearing Imogen's body:

> The bird is dead
> That we have made so much on.

The wild flowers with which they strew her body are a visual expression of an idea which has already been present in the dialogue.

Whereas the Italian scenes are devoted to sexual intrigue, the Welsh scenes are concerned with the occupations necessary for survival – hunting, self-defence and rural hospitality. Yet, though Belarius is glad to be free from the luxury of the court, the exiled princes complain that they have not enjoyed the benefits of a civilized education. 'We have seen nothing;' they protest, 'We are beastly.' Hence the two locations are placed in opposition to each other and neither is shown to be ideal. The Italians, though shrewd, quick-witted and elegant, are worldly and unscrupulous, and the exiles in Wales, though manly, warm-hearted and genuine, are limited in their experience; they will, as Arviragus says, have no store of memories with which to occupy their old age. When, at the end of the play, they return to take their rightful place at the court, they bring to it a much-needed integrity, but we can also foresee that their new life will be to their advantage. In them the virtues of the court and the country will be balanced and reconciled.

The characters, situations, locations and language of *Cymbeline* are used to create contrasting ideals and ways of life. In other words it is a symbolic play and not the kind of naturalistic drama that Johnson was looking for. The two historical periods in which it is set allow Shakespeare to compare the courtliness and subtlety of the renaissance with the rough simplicity of first-century Britain, and the multiple improbabilities of the plot are a means of depicting various permutations of outward and inward appearance and reality. The closing scene with its extended series of unlikely revelations is improbable not in the way Johnson saw it but in the sense that a miracle is improbable. In other words it should excite in us a sense of wonder and delight. Its dramatic power arises from the sense of release we feel as all the misconceptions built up during the first four acts are steadily cleared away. The earlier part of *Cymbeline* creates a complex number of dramatic ironies which arise from the disguises and dissemblings of which it is made up. All the major characters, as we have seen, are at some time the creators or victims of deception; only the audience has access to the whole truth. Hence we find ourselves in the position of trapped spectators, knowing how the complications of the drama could be unravelled but unable to intervene and settle them. This dramatic irony in which the audience has the knowledge of the play's conflicts but is unable to make use of it, creates a mounting tension in our minds which is released only as the truth is gradually unfolded in the final scene. There is, however, one irony which the audience is not allowed to perceive until the play is almost over, and that is that the apparently unjust and painful misconceptions which constitute the greater part of it are stages in a divine plan. This revelation comes to us with the astonishing and spectacular appearance of Jupiter with his words of reassurance both to Posthumus and ourselves:

> Be not with mortal accidents opprest:
> No care of yours it is; you know 'tis ours.
> Whom best I love I cross; to make my gift,
> The more delay'd, delighted. Be content.

This is Shakespeare's last and boldest portrayal of the difference between seeming and being, for what has hitherto seemed to be a series of accidents is now shown to have been deliberately controlled by supernatural powers. The last word in the play is 'peace'.

It is a peace, however, which is reinforced by associations which are no longer familiar to us but would have been known by at least some of Shakespeare's contemporaries. *Cymbeline* ends at Milford Haven, a place of very special significance in Shakespeare's time, for it was there that Henry Tudor landed at the head of an army which went on to defeat Richard III and thereby bring peace to England and the end of the Wars of the Roses. The descendants of Henry Tudor, moreover, included the monarch who was on the throne when *Cymbeline* was first performed, James I, who was himself an agent of reconciliation, for on his accession he had united the formerly hostile nations of England and Scotland. Milford Haven was therefore connected in the Jacobean mind with peace and harmony of a kind which is brought about in the play itself. It has further associations of this kind. The ruler over the Roman empire at the time of Cymbeline was Augustus Caesar, of whom Caius Lucius is an emissary, and it was in his reign that Christ was born who, by his incarnation and sacrifice, made possible the reconciliation of man with God. Shakespeare would know from Holinshed's *Chronicle* (from which he drew much of his material) that this was a time of universal peace:

For that it pleased almighty God so to dispose the minds of men at that present, not only the Britons, but in manner all other nations were contented to be obedient to the Roman empire . . . The whole world through means of the same Augustus, was now in quiet, without wars or troublesome tumults.

The reconciliations with which Cymbeline ends are miraculous workings out of peace under the influence of divine agents at a place which had entered English mythological history as a source of concord and amity. As the Soothsayer declares,

> The fingers of the pow'rs above do tune
> The harmony of this peace.

# The Winter's Tale

As well as creating a wider range and variety of characters than any other dramatist – from Iago and Falstaff to Rosalind and Lady Macbeth – Shakespeare also portrayed a greater range of experiences. His characters fall in love, fight in battle, plot assassinations, write poetry, govern kingdoms, put on plays, marry, commit murder, get drunk and die. But the experience which preoccupied him more consistently and frequently than any other was the experience of time. There are many proverbs which describe the effects of time, but the two most common of them contradict each other: time is said to consume all things and it is also said to be a great healer. The destructive power of time is the subject of some of Shakespeare's greatest sonnets:

> When I have seen by Time's fell hand defaced
> The rich proud cost of outworn buried age;
> When sometime lofty towers I see downrased,
> And brass eternal slave to mortal rage;
> When I have seen the hungry ocean gain
> Advantage on the kingdom of the shore,
> And the firm soil win of the wat'ry main,
> Increasing store with loss and loss with store;
> When I have seen such interchange of state,
> Or state itself confounded with decay;
> Ruin hath taught me thus to ruminate –
> That Time will come and take my love away.

It is also one of the subjects of the two parts of *Henry IV*, in which, as the Prince ripens towards the power he will inherit with the throne, Falstaff and the King grow old and sicken towards death. The healing effects of time, on the other hand, can be observed in some of Shakespeare's comedies. It is time which, as Viola says, 'untangles the knot' of mistaken identities in *Twelfth Night*, and time which brings together the various pairs of lovers at the end of *As You Like It*, a comedy which begins in 'winter and rough weather' and concludes in 'spring time, the only pretty ring time'.

The play which creates the strongest impression of the movement of time is, however, *The Winter's Tale*, a late work, written in about 1611, just before *The Tempest*. 'The Triumph of Time' was the subtitle of *Pandosto*, the prose romance, or novel, by Robert Greene from which Shakespeare took the outlines of the plot of this play, and into Greene's story he introduced the character of Time himself as a chorus. Time's opening words explain that his influence will be more complex than it has been in the sonnets or the comedies:

> I, that please some, try all, both joy and terror
> Of good and bad, that makes and unfolds error,
> Now take upon me, in the name of Time,
> To use my wings.

In *The Winter's Tale* Time is both creative and destructive: during the sixteen years which the action occupies, Perdita is born, she and Florizel fall in love, and eventually the family and friends are reunited, but during those same years Mamillius dies, Antigonus is killed, Leontes endures a period of solitude and penance and wrinkles appear on the face of Hermione. The play embraces the contrary sensations of joy and terror, portrays both the good of Hermione's fidelity and the bad of Leontes's destructive paranoia, pleases some of the characters but 'tries' (or 'tests') all of them. It is neither a comedy nor a tragedy but a tragi-comedy, not only in the sense that its characters come to the very edge of disaster and are then allowed a reprieve, but also in the sense that its action encompasses both tragic and comic experiences: birth and death, youth and age, sophisticated court and simple country life, rustic dances and judicial trials, bears and pickpockets. It is probably Shakespeare's most inclusive play, the one which holds the most extensive mirror up to nature.

In the opening scenes, the characters are much preoccupied with memories of time past, especially Polixenes, who fondly recalls his childhood friendship with Leontes and the innocence which they once shared but have subsequently lost:

> We were as twinn'd lambs that did frisk i' th' sun
> And did bleat the one at th' other. What we chang'd
> Was innocence for innocence; we knew not
> The doctrine of ill-doing, nor dream'd
> That any did.

His wistful recollections of boyhood, which he compares to the freshness and vitality of spring, suggest that he would have preferred, had it been possible, never to have grown up. A similar nostalgia for pre-sexual innocence is expressed by Leontes, as he recognizes in his son Mamillius his own childhood features, and bitterly contrasts the boy's harmless games with the furtive, loathsome sexual games in which he imagines his wife is indulging with Polixenes:

> Go, play, boy, play; thy mother plays, and I
> Play too; but so disgrac'd a part, whose issue
> Will hiss me to my grave. Contempt and clamour
> Will be my knell. Go, play, boy, play.

Whereas *The Winter's Tale* opens with a recollection of childhood which is associated, through Shakespeare's language, with the season of spring, the increasingly painful events which occupy most of the first section (up to the end of the third act) gradually become associated with winter, particularly when, following Hermione's apparent death, Paulina delivers to Leontes her terrible injunction:

> Do not repent these things, for they are heavier
> Than all thy woes can stir; therefore betake thee
> To nothing but despair. A thousand knees
> Ten thousand years together, naked, fasting,
> Upon a barren mountain, and still winter
> In storm perpetual, could not move the gods
> To look that way thou wert.

Her description of the stormy winter landscape is followed shortly afterwards by an actual storm in the midst of which Antigonus arrives with the new-born Perdita on the remote and barren shore of Bohemia. 'We have landed', says one of the mariners, 'in an ill time;'

> the skies look grimly
> And threaten present blusters.

It is at this point – when Mamilius is already dead, Hermione has apparently died, Leontes has begun his long vigil of repentance, the infant has been exposed to the hazards of a wild, winter country, the ship has been wrecked and Antigonus devoured by the bear – that the play comes closest to tragedy. But what appears to be a tragic ending is in fact the beginning of a new movement away from tragedy. The link between the violent first section of the play and the pastoral second section is the child Perdita, placed on the earth by Antigonus and taken up again by the old shepherd, whose words to his son mark the division between the two sections and indicate what the difference between them will be:

Thou met'st with things dying, I with things new-born.

Although there is a break in the play at this point, after which the action is resumed sixteen years later, Shakespeare creates the impression that the winter during which the previous scenes have taken place is followed immediately by the spring, the season of 'things new born'. Autolycus is its herald:

> When daffodils begin to peer,
>   With heigh! the doxy over the dale,

> Why, then comes in the sweet o' the year,
> For the red blood reigns in the winter's pale.

By the next scene, however, it is clear that the year has advanced into high summer for, throughout the episode of the sheep-shearing feast, Shakespeare creates a rich visual and poetic impression of fruitfulness and plenty. On her first entrance, Perdita, who has now, like the year, come to maturity, seems to usher in the summer season itself, garlanded as she is with flowers:

> Here's flow'rs for you:
> Hot lavender, mints, savory, marjoram;
> The marigold, that goes to bed wi' th' sun,
> And with him rises weeping; these are the flow'rs
> Of middle summer, and I think they are given
> To men of middle age.

In their feast the rural folk celebrate and give thanks for their fellowship one with another and for the blessings of nature.

Although there is what Leontes calls a 'wide gap of time' between the first and second sections, Shakespeare associates the process of division and re-union within the family with the cycle of the seasons during a single year. By this means, the process in which the characters are engaged – from their initial, painful separation to their final, joyful reconciliation – is made to resemble the natural, seasonal process of destruction and recreation, death and resurrection. The seasonal references also connect the older characters, especially Leontes and Polixenes, with winter, and the younger characters, Florizel (whose name is derived from the Latin word meaning 'flower' or 'blossom') and Perdita, with spring. Indeed, on her return to Sicilia, Perdita is said to be as welcome 'as is the spring to th' earth'. The implication is that the difference between the generations parallels the difference between the seasons; man and nature are alike in that the new stock grows from the roots of the old, and the violence committed by the older generation is overcome by the innocence and optimism of the young. By connecting his characters with the natural landscape, Shakespeare also gives to the play the features of one of the myths evolved in antiquity as a way of accounting for the cycle of the seasons. One such myth was that of Proserpina (actually mentioned in Act IV Scene iv line 116), who was compelled to spend half the year confined to the infernal regions of Hades but on whose annual return to earth in the spring nature itself burst into life in sympathy with her arrival. *The Winter's Tale* can be seen as Shakespeare's version of such a myth in which the land of Sicilia suffers a period of darkness, sterility and mourning as a result of Leontes's violence but is brought to life again by Perdita's return to her father's winter court.

As well as being a play about the passage and effects of time, *The Winter's*

*Tale* is also, therefore, a play about nature, the repeated seasonal processes of which are analogous to the separation, reunion and revival of Leontes and his family. It is also a play which arouses in the minds of the audience a strong sense of nature of a different kind: the natural, instinctive affections which bind together husband and wife, parents and children, friend and friend, master and servant, man and the land where he is born. Throughout his work, Shakespeare shows a deep awareness of the bonds which hold together communities, especially the intimate communities of family and household. These bonds are often broken at the beginning of the tragedies: Lear banishes his daughter Cordelia and is, in turn, cast out by her sisters; Macbeth murders his kinsman and his guest, Duncan; and Hamlet sees in his mother's remarriage a betrayal of loyalty to his father. Moreover, most of his comedies end with the formation or re-establishment of links of this kind, as the lovers assemble for the ritual of marriage or, in *As You Like It*, the Duke and his courtiers prepare to return home. *The Winter's Tale* begins with the breaking of the bonds which unite the family and, for this reason, its first section resembles the tragedies, but it ends with the re-establishment of these links in a way which resembles the endings of the comedies.

By attempting to murder his childhood friend, banishing his new-born daughter and falsely accusing his wife of adultery, Leontes behaves in a way which we recognize as violently 'unnatural'. The bonds which he has severed are described explicitly by Hermione in the speech she delivers in her defence, and, in defining them, she explains how necessary they are to give meaning and support to life:

> To me can life be no commodity.
> The crown and comfort of my life, your favour,
> I do give lost, for I do feel it gone,
> But know not how it went; my second joy
> And first fruits of my body, from his presence
> I am barr'd, like one infectious; my third comfort,
> Starr'd most unluckily, is from my breast –
> The innocent milk in its most innocent mouth –
> Hal'd out to murder; myself on every post
> Proclaim'd a strumpet; with immodest hatred
> The child-bed privilege denied, which 'longs
> To women of all fashion; lastly, hurried
> Here to this place, i' th' open air, before
> I have got strength of limit. Now, my liege,
> Tell me what blessings I have here alive
> That I should fear to die.

Her words, while providing a summary of the action up to this point, express in feelingly personal terms how essential are the relationships of which she speaks, and with what monstrous inhumanity her husband has destroyed them. It is only when he himself believes that he has lost her irrecoverably that he, in turn, discovers how necessary she was to him as the object of his love.

Whereas the first section of *The Winter's Tale* portrays the painful fragmentation of a family, the second section shows us a community united in the celebration of its companionship. The interdependence of the rural folk of Bohemia is expressed by the communal occupations of singing, dancing and feasting in which they participate. Their genial sense of hospitality is also conveyed in the old shepherd's recollections of the time when his wife was mistress of the feast:

> When my old wife liv'd, upon
> This day she was both pantler, butler, cook;
> Both dame and servant; welcom'd all; serv'd all;
> Would sing her song and dance her turn; now here
> At upper end o' th' table, now i' th' middle;
> On his shoulder, and his; her face o' fire
> With labour, and the thing she took to quench it
> She would to each one sip.

The sheep-shearing festival is like a rural scene painted by Breughel. It expresses a spontaneous delight in the companionship which exists between neighbour and neighbour, old and young, hostess and guests, the labourers and the soil on which they depend and whose fruitfulness depends on them. But, like Breughel's rustics, Shakespeare's country people are not idealized or sentimentalized. For all their good humour, they are coarse, slow-witted and easily deceived. Their simplicity allows Autolycus to cheat and profit from them and, as he does so, we recognize their limitations.

The gradual reassembly in the last act of the domestic group we glimpsed very briefly at the beginning of the first act is also brought about by the inherent, natural needs of the characters. The instigator of the return to Sicilia is Camillo, who longs to

> Purchase the sight again of dear Sicilia
> And that unhappy king, my master, whom
> I so much thirst to see.

But it is also the irresistible love of Florizel for Perdita which drives them, together, from his father's wrath and, under Camillo's guidance, steers them back to Leontes's court. As the love of Leontes for the supposedly dead Hermione makes him confine himself to his long period of mourning and remorse, so the love of Florizel for Perdita impels him to defy his father, risk the loss of his succession to the crown and take flight to Sicilia:

> Not for Bohemia, nor all the pomp that may
> Be thereat glean'd, for all the sun sees or

> The close earth wombs, or the profound seas hides
> In unknown fathoms, will I break my oath
> To this my fair belov'd.

It is not mere chance which brings family and friends together but the desire to satisfy natural and irresistible needs, and it is the apparently miraculous fulfilment of those needs which makes the final moments of the play – the reunion of Hermione with her daughter and husband – so deeply moving.

The resurrection of Hermione is the most radical change which Shakespeare made to Robert Greene's story. In *Pandosto* the queen dies of grief and never revives. To Shakespeare's first audiences, some of whom may have known Greene's story (for it was a popular work and had been reprinted many times), the statue scene must have been astonishing. To modern audiences unfamiliar with *Pandosto* it is still highly dramatic, largely because of the care with which Shakespeare prepares the way for it. Our last sight of Leontes as he begins his long vigil is of a man deeply bereaved and when, sixteen years later, he reappears, he is still totally possessed by feelings of guilt and loss:

> Whilst I remember
> Her and her virtues, I cannot forget
> My blemishes in them, and so still think of
> The wrong I did myself; which was so much
> That heirless it hath made my kingdom, and
> Destroy'd the sweet'st companion that e'er man
> Bred his hopes out of.

In Leontes we observe a man who thirsts for the reconciliation which neither he nor we can yet hope for. Moreover, in order not to diminish the dramatic power of the final scene, Shakespeare allows the revelation of Perdita's identity and the reunion of Leontes with Polixenes to take place off stage and it is in the aftermath of the excited account, by the three courtiers, of their meeting that we come to the climactic episode. Even then the moment of reconciliation is delayed and, when Paulina draws back the curtain to reveal the statue, Leontes responds with an astonished silence. The sense of awe and expectation increases as Paulina calls for music and the statue begins to breathe human life:

> Music, awake her; strike.
> 'Tis time; be stone no more; approach;
> Strike all that look upon with marvel. Come;
> I'll fill your grave up. Stir; nay, come away.
> Bequeath to death your numbness, for from him
> Dear life redeems you.

The moment derives its power from the care with which Shakespeare has gradually led us up to it and holds both the characters and audience in prolonged suspense before the apparent miracle occurs. He arouses our expectations, sustains them, fulfils them and then surpasses them.

Yet in the final lines of the play, the dramatist makes us as much aware of what has been lost as of what has been restored. The dead Mamilius will never return, Paulina resolves to mourn for her 'mate, that's never to be found again', and the signs of age on Hermione's face are evidence of the wasted years of what could have been love and companionship. Time, which pleases some, tries all.

# The Tempest

There is a note in the account books of the Master of the Revels, the official responsible for providing entertainment for the monarch, that *The Tempest* was presented on Hallowmas Night (1 November) 1611 before James I at Whitehall. It was probably written earlier in that year, and when it was first performed it appealed to the taste and interests of its audiences. King James, an enthusiastic and discriminating patron of the arts, had a particular fondness for the kind of drama known as the masque, and he commissioned many of Shakespeare's contemporaries, including Fletcher, Chapman, Dekker, Ford and Ben Jonson, to compose them for his entertainment. The masque, an early form of opera, was distinguished by its elaborate and spectacular scenic effects, its combination of music, song and dance with spoken dialogue, and the inclusion of mythological and allegorical figures among its characters. Shakespeare, significantly, was the only major dramatist of his time who did not compose any of these extravagant courtly spectacles. He preferred, apparently, to work entirely for the popular theatre where his plays were seen not simply by the upper classes but by a cross-section of the whole community. Nevertheless he was much influenced by this fashionable dramatic form and incorporated into his later plays its characteristic features. These are particularly noticeable in *The Tempest* with its striking visual and musical effects, such as the opening storm, the banquet brought in by 'several strange Shapes' which suddenly vanishes with, according to the stage direction, 'a quaint device', the songs of Ariel, the descent of the goddesses, Iris, Ceres and Juno, from above the stage, and the 'graceful dance' of the nymphs and reapers. Shakespeare offered to the patrons of his own theatre a glimpse of the kind of spectacle normally available only to the aristocracy.

*The Tempest* also reflects the fascination of Shakespeare's contemporaries with the discovery of hitherto unknown lands and peoples. The first pioneering voyages of discovery, such as those of Columbus to South America and Magellan by the western route to the Pacific, had already taken place a century or more earlier, but expeditions into unexplored seas and continents continued: in 1580 Drake became the first Englishman to sail round the world, and four years before *The Tempest* was performed, the first English settlement (called Jamestown after the reigning monarch) was established in Virginia. The early explorers of the American continents, impressed by the fertility of the soil, the unfamiliar customs of the native inhabitants, their seemingly innocent nakedness and their common ownership of property, wondered whether they had by chance stumbled upon a survival of the Golden Age formerly described by the poets of classical antiquity. The French philosopher Montaigne, hearing of the apparently idyllic way of life enjoyed by the natives of South America, compared their customs with those of his European contemporaries and found the former far superior:

It is a nation ... that hath no kinds of traffike, no knowledge of Letters, no intelligence of numbers, no name of magistrate, nor of politicke superioritie; no use of service, of riches or of povertie; no contracts, no successions, no partitions, no occupation but idle; no respect of kindred, but common, no apparell but naturall, no manuring of lands, no use of wine, corne or mettle. The very words that import lying, falsehood, treason, dissimulations, covetousnes, envie, detraction, and pardon, were never heard of amongst them.

Montaigne's essays had been translated into English by John Florio in 1604 and Shakespeare created out of this passage the speech of Gonzalo when he first arrives on Prospero's island (Act II Scene i lines 137–62).

As portrayed by Shakespeare, however, Prospero's little colony is not the utopia imagined by Gonzalo. It has its 'magistrate', or governor, in Prospero himself, 'letters' are known in his attempt to educate Caliban, and, since the community depends on the labours of Caliban and Ariel for its survival, there is 'use of service'. 'Treason' is plotted within moments of Gonzalo's description of his ideal commonwealth, for Antonio and Sebastian attempt to assassinate their companion Alonso, King of Naples, and, later, Caliban conspires with the two servants to supplant Prospero. In *The Tempest* Shakespeare not only quotes extensively from Montaigne's essay but provides an argument against it: the Golden Age can be no more than a dream because men themselves are unwilling, or unable, to make it become real. The play depicts Prospero's struggle to create, out of corrupt and rebellious human material, as close an approximation to a well-ordered society as it will allow. His enterprise is foreshadowed in the opening scene, where the master of the ship attempts to command the crew and passengers sufficiently to bring his vessel to safety. It is a vivid and apt metaphor for the efforts of the ruler to control his unwilling subjects.

The cast of characters in *The Tempest* seems an oddly miscellaneous one: a deposed duke, a savage and deformed slave, an airy spirit, a drunken butler, the crew of a ship and three classical deities. Shakespeare appears to have selected these otherwise unrelated characters in order to depict within a single play practically all the basic human relationships: those between a ruler and his subjects, fathers and their children, masters and servants, lover and beloved. Within Prospero himself, moreover, we glimpse intermittently the struggle, or internal tempest, between the humane impulse towards mercy and the instinctive appetite for revenge, the Ariel and the Caliban of which his own – and our – nature consists. The characters are thus arranged in a series of parallels. As the ruler is to his subjects, so is the father to his children, the master to his servants. It is, perhaps, for this reason that some critics have concluded that Prospero is a representation of Shakespeare himself, for the relationship of an author to his characters is analogous to that of a ruler to his dependants, whether in a nation or a household. The theory that Prospero represents Shakespeare is further supported by the fact that *The Tempest* is the last play for which he was wholly responsible. His one later play, *Henry VIII*, was probably written in collaboration with John Fletcher. Prospero's epilogue, his farewell to his art, has therefore been seen as Shakespeare's own valediction to the theatre. There are a number of strong arguments against this idea. In the first place, the play makes perfectly good sense without it. Secondly it does not make *The Tempest* more intelligible; on the contrary, it obscures the fact that Prospero is portrayed with a good deal of critical detachment; he is by no means an ideal figure. Moreover it is hard to imagine that an author as creatively prolific as Shakespeare deliberately embarked on what he had resolved would be his final work.

As the play opens, Prospero has been given a unique opportunity to remedy the wrongs he suffered twelve years earlier, to regain his dukedom, to ensure that it passes to Miranda, his rightful heir, and to establish peace between Milan and Naples by her marriage to Prince Ferdinand. His chance to return to power arises from a combination of circumstances: the skill he has acquired in the supernatural arts, the chance arrival within the circle of his power of the boat containing all his enemies, and the occurrence of a conjunction of the stars which is favourable to his project. As he explains to Miranda at the end of his narrative,

> By accident most strange, bountiful Fortune,
> Now my dear lady, hath mine enemies
> Brought to this shore; and by my prescience
> I find my zenith doth depend upon
> A most auspicious star, whose influence
> If now I court not, but omit, my fortunes
> Will ever after droop.

In other words, should his project fail, he will be given no second chance. It must, moreover, be carried out with some haste. The play begins at midday and Prospero's regular, anxious enquiries about the time imply that after six o'clock the stars will no longer be in his favour. Hence the play acquires a certain dramatic suspense from our knowledge that the plan must be completed promptly and that it may not actually succeed.

Shakespeare organized the various plots of *The Tempest*, like the characters, in a series of parallels, each one consisting of some form of conspiracy or rebellion. As Antonio has deposed his brother Prospero in Milan twelve years earlier, so he now tries to persuade Sebastian to assassinate his brother Alonso and to seize the kingdom of Naples. Sebastian himself points out the similarity: 'Thy case, dear friend,' he assures Antonio, 'Shall be my precedent.' These two political conspiracies are comically paralleled in Caliban's plot to murder Prospero and make Stephano, the drunken butler, lord of the island. It is characteristic of the corrupt nature of the characters depicted in this play that, on their first arrival in apparently virgin territory, the instinct of two of them is to carry out a political assassination, and that, before he can recover his own dukedom, Prospero must first stop the, presumably unforeseen, conspiracy against Alonso. This repeated pattern of rebellion creates the impression of a perilously unstable social structure which, by implication, extends beyond the limits of the play. *The Tempest* is not simply a play about Prospero's attempt to regain his dukedom, but a representation of the perennial struggle to keep anarchy at bay. It is an imaginary tale about real problems.

It is within Prospero's capacity simply to wipe out his opponents, an act of revenge which he chooses to forgo in favour of bringing them voluntarily to repentance and submission to his will. His intentions are clearly set out in Ariel's warning to Antonio, Sebastian and Alonso:

> But remember –
> For that's my business to you – that you three
> From Milan did supplant good Prospero;
> Exposed unto the sea, which hath requit it,
> Him, and his innocent child; for which foul deed
> The pow'rs, delaying, not forgetting, have
> Incens'd the seas and shores, yea, all the creatures,
> Against your peace. Thee of thy son, Alonso,
> They have bereft; and do pronounce by me
> Ling'ring perdition, worse than any death
> Can be at once, shall step by step attend
> You and your ways; whose wraths to guard you from –
> Which here, in this most desolate isle, else falls
> Upon your heads – is nothing but heart's sorrow,
> And clear life ensuing.

But although Prospero can place his enemies in circumstances conducive to 'heart's sorrow' – by exposing them to the storm and terrifying them with his magic shows – he cannot force them to repent. His supernatural art enables him to control them physically but their minds are immune to his influence.

The powers even of this exceptionally gifted ruler are limited and, in the end, his project is only a partial success.

His deposition seems to have been the most radically disturbing experience of Prospero's life. The profound effect which it has had on him appears in the disjointed, impassioned way in which he describes it to Miranda and in his repeated, and needless, commands to her to pay attention. It was a crisis, moreover, which cost him more than a dukedom. He is the last of a series of Shakespearean heroes – which includes Hamlet, Troilus, Lear, Othello and Leontes – who undergo a real or seeming betrayal of trust and, as a consequence, lose their faith in human nature. Prospero's disillusionment with mankind in general appears not only in the contempt with which he treats those who have actually betrayed him – Antonio, Alonso and Caliban – but also in his obsessive suspicions of Ferdinand, whom he insistently and repeatedly warns against pre-marital sexual intercourse:

> If thou dost break her virgin-knot before
> All sanctimonious ceremonies may
> With full and holy rite be minist'red,
> No sweet aspersion shall the heavens let fall
> To make this contract grow; but barren hate,
> Sour ey'd disdain, and discord, shall bestrew
> The union of your bed with weeds so loathly
> That you shall hate it both.

Since Ferdinand appears to be a model of propriety, this threat tells us more about Prospero's embittered state of mind than about Ferdinand's sexual proclivities. The experience which has given him wisdom has also soured him. Whereas Miranda, in her optimistic ignorance of human nature, greets the new arrivals on the island with delight, Prospero's knowledge of man's ingratitude has left him disenchanted:

> *Miranda*                     O wonder!
> How many goodly creatures are there here!
> How beauteous mankind is! O brave new world
> That has such people in't!
> *Prospero*                    'Tis new to thee.

His tired, wistful comment chillingly reveals the lasting effect which personal betrayal has had on him.

There are signs that, as a consequence of his disillusionment, he is strongly tempted to use his superhuman powers simply to destroy his enemies in a bloody act of vengeance. And even when, encouraged by the compassionate Ariel, he decides to take the 'rarer action' of mercy, it is obvious that he can forgive Antonio only by a determined effort of will. His gesture of reconciliation is totally devoid of warmth:

For you, most wicked sir, whom to call brother
Would even infect my mouth, I do forgive
Thy rankest fault – all of them; and require
My dukedom of thee, which perforce I know
Thou must restore.

The rebellious human material with which Prospero is compelled to work includes himself and this, too, fills the play with suspense. It could easily have ended not in reconciliation but in slaughter.

Considering the limitations of his power and the unwillingness of his subjects to obey him, Prospero's return to power is no mean achievement. Ferdinand and Miranda obligingly fall in love at first sight, Alonso's conscience is awakened and even the pathetically trusting Caliban, discovering the folly of his new masters, resolves to be wise in future. To his brother's hard-won gesture of forgiveness, however, Antonio makes no response; his silence testifies to his inhumanity and the impenetrable mystery of his malevolence. And, though he gains his dukedom, Prospero at the same time loses those who have supported him in his years of exile, Ariel, who is given his promised freedom, and Miranda, who in finding a husband must necessarily desert her father. As Shakespeare had long since recognized, every gain necessitates a corresponding loss in the imperfect world which we inhabit. Although, with its masque-like style and exotic setting, The Tempest is a play of its time, its essential subject, man's struggle to create an ordered society and the cost which this entails, is timeless.

# KING HENRY THE EIGHTH

In 1623, seven years after Shakespeare's death, John Heminge and Henry Condell, two members of the King's Men, the theatrical company for which he had written and with whom he had himself acted, assembled and published the first collected edition of his plays, the so-called First Folio. The thirty-six plays gathered together in their edition, together with *Pericles* which they did not include, are generally agreed to constitute Shakespeare's complete dramatic works. One of the plays published in the First Folio was *Henry VIII*.

Although during the eighteenth century an occasional scholar or editor commented that the style of certain passages seemed untypical of Shakespeare, *Henry VIII* was, for over two hundred years, assumed to be wholly the work of the great dramatist. In 1850, however, a scholar named James Spedding published an essay, 'Who Wrote Shakespeare's *Henry VIII*?', in which he expressed his conviction that the dialogue had been composed in two quite different and distinct styles, the one full of the vividly complex metaphorical writing characteristic of Shakespeare, the other plainer, less imaginative, and, to use Spedding's own words, 'diffuse and languid'. This latter style he identified as typical of Shakespeare's successor as the principal dramatist to the King's Men, John Fletcher, with whom Shakespeare may have collaborated in the writing of another play, *The Two Noble Kinsmen*, at about the same time. *Henry VIII*, Spedding concluded, was not composed wholly by Shakespeare but had been written by the two dramatists in collaboration.

Following the publication of Spedding's essay, the authorship of *Henry VIII* has been the subject of a scholarly debate. Those who believe that it is wholly Shakespeare's work have written of it enthusiastically as a well-constructed, profound and subtle expression of his genius; those who have regarded it as a work of collaboration have complained of its loose construction, unevenness of style and shallowness or inconsistency of characterization. The scholars who think that Fletcher did have a hand in it, though they have not agreed precisely which or how many scenes were written by him, nevertheless believe that the two playwrights worked together very closely and that scenes written entirely by one alternate with scenes written entirely by the other. Their arguments in favour of joint authorship rest exclusively on their own subjective impressions of the style and, since no other evidence has been, or is likely to be, discovered, the problem will almost certainly never be solved. The strongest evidence in favour of Shakespeare's sole authorship is provided by the two people most likely to know the truth, the dramatist's former intimate colleagues, Heminge and Condell, who presumably included *Henry VIII* in the First Folio in the belief that it was entirely his. For convenience I shall, throughout the rest of this introduction, refer to the author of the play as 'Shakespeare'.

The two basic ingredients of a history play, the dramatic and the historical, are potentially in conflict with each other. A play, like any other work of art, should ideally be shapely, well organized and satisfyingly constructed. It should, as Aristotle said of tragedy, have a beginning, a middle and an end. History, on the other hand, is shapeless. Kings and queens, military and political leaders, rise to power, succeed or fail and are defeated or die in a manner which exhibits no consistent, discernible pattern, and, though the life of an individual has a beginning, a middle and an end, the life of a nation neither starts nor finishes. In *Henry VIII* Shakespeare managed to fulfil his function both as a historian, recording the random succession of events of which he had read in the great history book of his time, the *Chronicles* of Holinshed, and as a dramatist, selecting and arranging these events so that they fell into an orderly, satisfying pattern. The play has at the same time the unity and shapeliness of drama and something of the uncomplicated loose-endedness of historical reality.

One way in which he achieves this double effect is by creating the impression that, although his play has a beginning, a middle and an end, nevertheless it consists of only one portion of a continuous historical process which has begun long before the start of the first scene and will continue after the last scene is over. He does so by making his characters recall past events and look forward to events which will occur in the future. The play starts in the aftermath of a spectacular diplomatic occasion, the meeting between Henry VIII and Francis I of France in 1520, a ceremonial encounter known as the Field of the Cloth of Gold with which the hostilities between the two countries was formally brought to an end. The festivities which accompanied this meeting lasted for about two weeks during which the nobility of both countries, extravagantly clothed and jewelled, were lavishly entertained with banquets, dances and military and dramatic spectacles. The ostentatious splendour of the occasion is described by an eyewitness, the Duke of Norfolk, in the conversation with which the play opens:

> To-day the French,
> All clinquant, all in gold, like heathen gods,

Shone down the English; and to-morrow they
Made Britain India: every man that stood
Show'd like a mine.

The audience receives the impression that they have been thrust immediately into the middle of a historical process which is already in motion.
The description of the meeting between the two kings (which turns out to be
less important for the development of the plot than its prominent position at
the opening leads us to expect) introduces a discussion of the man who
arranged it, the Lord Chancellor and Archbishop of York, Cardinal Wolsey.
Wolsey, a man of humble origins, is, we learn, already the most powerful
politician and one of the richest men in the country, is presuming to run the
affairs of state independently of the King and, by his ruthless arrogance and
accumulation of private wealth, has created enemies.

As the opening scene recalls the past, so the final scene predicts the future.
The newly born princess, Elizabeth, is carried onto the stage from her
baptism and Cranmer, the Archbishop of Canterbury, foretells that both she
and her successor, James I (who was actually on the throne at the time when
the play was first acted), will become models of wisdom and goodness to
their subjects who, under their government, will prosper and live in peace:

Peace, plenty, love, truth, terror,
That were the servants to this chosen infant,
Shall then be his, and like a vine grow to him;
Wherever the bright sun of heaven shall shine,
His honour and the greatness of his name
Shall be, and make new nations; he shall flourish
And like a mountain cedar reach his branches
To all the plains about him; our children's children
Shall see this and bless heaven.

Yet, although Cranmer's prophecy is calmly optimistic, the dramatic tableau
with which *Henry VIII* concludes conveys less reassuring implications which
would not be lost on Shakespeare's first audiences. Cranmer, who has
replaced Wolsey as the King's favourite by the end of the play, later fell from
power, like his predecessor, and during the reign of Mary Tudor was
burned at the stake. Moreover, as Katharine, Henry's first queen, was
divorced and discarded, so Anne, his second wife and the mother of
Elizabeth, was cast off and sent to the execution block. These facts were common knowledge to the playgoers at the Globe Theatre, who could not fail to
recognize that, although the play might conclude hopefully, history itself
continued to be an unpredictable and unending series of triumphs and
defeats.

Shakespeare also conveys the impression of the continuing movement of
history by making first Buckingham, then the Queen, then Wolsey and

finally Cranmer the focus of our attention. The repeated pattern of their falls from or ascents to power helps to give the play its dramatic shape but also conveys the implication that, as each of these major characters has undergone an ascent and a decline, so, in the future, other statesmen will enjoy a brief period of supremacy – what Richard II calls 'a breath, a little scene, to monarchize, be fear'd, and kill with looks' – before they, in turn, are overtaken by their rivals. Buckingham, the Lord High Constable and a descendant of Edward III, is executed for allegedly aspiring to the throne; Queen Katharine, the daughter of the King of Spain, finds herself a victim of Wolsey's enmity and Henry's troubled conscience, is discarded and dies in retirement; Wolsey, his avarice and duplicity exposed by the enemies he has himself created, is suddenly thrust from power and dies in obscurity, and although Cranmer is in the ascendant at the close of the play, the firmly established pattern of power and decline makes us feel little confidence that he will remain permanently in favour. Wolsey's embittered complaint at the moment of his downfall has an application to the fates of all these characters:

> O, how wretched
> Is that poor man that hangs on princes' favours!
> There is betwixt that smile we would aspire to,
> That sweet aspect of princes, and their ruin
> More pangs and fears than wars or women have.

Within the continuing movement of history portrayed in *Henry VIII*, the personal tragedies of Buckingham, Katharine and Wolsey are contained. The audience is invited, in the words of the Prologue, to observe 'How soon this mightiness meets misery'.

Most of Shakespeare's other historical plays are constructed in a similar way. In *Richard II* the decline and death of the King are accompanied by the rise to power of Bolingbroke, and in the two parts of *Henry IV*, while Prince Hal matures steadily towards his accession to the throne, Falstaff grows visibly old and is discarded, and the King sickens and dies. Similarly in *Julius Caesar*, Rome is first dominated by Caesar himself, then, briefly, by his murderers Cassius and Brutus, who in turn are outwitted and defeated by Mark Antony, and as that play concludes we are given the first hints of the ultimate supremacy of Octavius, as yet a subsidiary character in the drama. In all these historical plays Shakespeare enables us to watch events from two conflicting points of view, that of the men of power themselves who devote themselves to the fulfilment of their ambitions and attempt to control history in accordance with their own desires, and that of the all-seeing dramatist who is able to observe their careers in a much broader historical context which makes their aspirations and achievements seem short-lived, precarious and trivial. 'If you consider the infinite extent of eternity,' wrote the philosopher Boethius, with whose writings Shakespeare was probably familiar, 'what satisfaction can you have about the power of your name to endure?'

In their moments of defeat or imminent death, Buckingham, Katharine and Wolsey are induced to examine their lives in this wider context, to recognize the pettiness of worldly success and to prepare themselves for the eternal life on which they are about to embark. As the ascents and falls of the major characters provide the play's basic dramatic pattern and shape, so their speeches of self-examination provide its moments of greatest emotional and moral intensity. Although their characters and situations are very different – Katharine is wholly innocent, Buckingham's guilt or innocence are left uncertain, and Wolsey is patently self-indulgent and corrupt – their states of mind in defeat are not dissimilar. In the process of losing their power and possessions they achieve a more secure and satisfying inner calm and stability.

Stripped of his titles, Buckingham nevertheless sees himself as richer than his 'base accusers that never knew what truth meant', and, though condemned to death, as he protests, unjustly, he yet believes that 'Heaven has an end in all.' The Queen, though she asserts her innocence, and sees herself as the victim of Wolsey's enmity, also puts her trust in God:

> Heaven is above all yet; there sits a Judge
> That no king can corrupt.

This disenchantment with the devious ways of the world and consequent trust in the providence of God is expressed even more eloquently by Wolsey, who, in defeat, undergoes a swift and radical transformation of character. The man who aspired to become Pope counsels his servant Cromwell to 'fling away ambition' as profitless, recognizes that 'corruption wins not more than honesty' and, in the very moment of his crisis, confesses that he has never been 'so truly happy':

> I know myself now, and I feel within me
> A peace above all earthly dignities,
> A still and quiet conscience. The King has cur'd me.

The process whereby Wolsey finds fulfilment in disgrace is later reported by Griffith:

> His overthrow heap'd happiness upon him;
> For then, and not till then, he felt himself,
> And found the blessedness of being little.
> And, to add greater honours to his age
> Than man could give him, he died fearing God.

In the moments of tragic introspection these characters are forced to undergo, material and political success appear worthless in comparison with personal integrity, faith in God's, rather than their own, will, and the tranquillity of mind which accompanies such virtues.

Shakespeare makes this distinction between worldly power and inner peace of mind not simply by means of the plot but by interspersing scenes of public ceremony with scenes of private, intimate conversation. Katharine makes a powerful public appearance in the council chamber defying Wolsey, but is later portrayed in retirement with her servant Griffith; Anne, having been depicted as a private person confiding in the old lady, is next seen processing in state to her coronation, and Wolsey, after his appearance as Chancellor and judge, is left in defeat to reveal his private thoughts to Cromwell. In all these secluded, intimate episodes, public affairs are looked at with detachment, from a distance. Anne's attitude to power before her sudden advancement is similar to that of Katharine and Wolsey in decline:

> I swear, 'tis better to be lowly born,
> And range with humble livers in content,
> Than to be perk'd up in a glist'ring grief
> And wear a golden sorrow.

The various aristocrats and gentlemen who gossip excitedly about the splendour of official ceremonies such as the coronation and the baptism are enraptured by these exterior shows, but the public figures themselves, in their intimate, confessional moments, reveal the anxieties which such displays conceal.

The most striking dramatic feature of *Henry VIII* is, however, its many scenes of elaborate public ceremony, both displayed and reported: the description of the Field of the Cloth of Gold and of Anne's coronation, and the spectacles of Wolsey's banquet, Katharine's trial and Anne's coronation procession. The stage directions for these scenes in the Folio text are unusually detailed, and both these and an account of what must have been one of the earliest performances of the play indicate that it was lavishly produced. In a letter written in July 1613, Sir Henry Wotton reports that a new play has just been acted 'representing some principal pieces of the Reign of *Henry 8*, which was set forth with many extraordinary circumstances of Pomp and Majesty ... the Knights of the Order, with their Georges and Garter, the Guards with their embroidered Coats and the like'. Yet at their moments of deepest insight, the major characters recognize the unimportance of worldly goods and the precariousness of that temporal power which ceremony symbolizes: 'Vain pomp and glory of this world, I hate ye,' cries Wolsey in defeat. The displays of pageantry characteristic of *Henry VIII*, though they may entertain the audience, are not included for that purpose alone but are a means of conveying the play's central idea: they are shown in order to be seen through. *Henry VIII* is a play about the glamour of power and its ultimate triviality.

The one character who remains secure through all the political crises and shifts of power is the King. Critics hostile to the play have complained that he is an indistinct, tentatively sketched character and they try to account for Shakespeare's apparent uncertainty about the King by suggesting that the dramatist was compelled for political reasons to conceal the faults of the father of Queen Elizabeth and the inaugurator of English protestantism. It is true that, in comparison with the fiercely righteous Katharine and the lordly, self-assured Wolsey, Henry makes a less forceful dramatic impression. Moreover, since he undergoes no drastic crisis, his emotions are less fully exposed. Nevertheless his is a disturbing presence. He is impulsive, vigorous, affectionate towards the wife he feels bound in conscience to cast off, loyal and warm-hearted towards his counsellors Wolsey and Cranmer as long as they appear trustworthy, but sudden and decisive in his condemnation of treachery once it has been exposed. Shakespeare gives the impression that Henry is a man of action, an extrovert, irritable and testy when the ecclesiastics prolong the divorce proceedings, and embarrassed when circumstances compel him to reveal in public his moral scruples about his marriage to Katharine. Like many apparent extroverts he keeps his intimate feelings hidden, which is why his sudden bursts of irritation or affection are so unpredictable. During the course of the play, however, Henry grows in independence and shrewdness. He makes his first appearance, as the stage direction tells us, 'leaning on the Cardinal's shoulder' and is totally taken in by Wolsey's flattery and apparent care for the state; but by the end of the play he sees through the accusations made by Cranmer's enemies to the Archbishop's essential goodness, and he singlehandedly undertakes to protect him. It is the King's presence which gives continuity to *Henry VIII* and we can also see in this youthful, assertive, quick-tempered monarch the man who was to degenerate into a tyrant.

Those critics who believe that Shakespeare wrote the whole of *Henry VIII* support their argument by pointing out its resemblances to his other late plays. In all of them there is an emphasis on the virtues of the younger generation – Florizel and Perdita in *The Winter's Tale*, Ferdinand and Miranda in *The Tempest*, the infant Elizabeth in *Henry VIII* – under whose future influence a stability may be created which the old have failed to achieve, and, arising out of this process, a belief by the characters that divine providence works steadily for good through the vicissitudes of history. In this final play, even if he was no more than its co-author, Shakespeare was writing on subjects which we know had preoccupied him towards the end of his professional life. At the same time its construction harks back to his very first work. Like the three parts of *Henry VI*, it is made up of the ascents to power of great men and their falls into death and insignificance. Shakespeare's vision of the unending continuum of history and the consequent relative insignificance of individual people appears to have stayed with him throughout his life. Yet paradoxically it is largely to Shakespeare that such men – Richard of Gloucester, Henry V, Wolsey and the rest – owe their immortality.